Published by Universe Publishing // A division of Rizzoli International Publications, Inc. // 300 Park Avenue South // New York, New York 10010 // www.rizzoliusa.com // © 2006 David Renard // All rights reserved. No part of this publication may be reproduced, stored in a retrieval system, or transmitted in any form or by any means, electronic, mechanical, photocopying, recording, or otherwise, without prior consent of the publisher. // 2006 2007 2008 2009 / 10 9 8 7 6 5 4 3 2 1 // Printed in China // ISBN 10: 0 - 7893 - 1497 - 5 // ISBN 13: 978 - 0 - 7893 - 1497 - 0 // Distributed by Random House // Library of Congress Catalog Control Number: 2006924068. // Every attempt has been made by the author to obtain all appropriate permissions. // Designed by Frost Design (www.frostdesign.com.au).

THE LAST MAGAZINE

By David Renard

A mon amour Jessica

The author would like to thank
Kaya Sorhaindo (www.themetaproject.com)
for his help with concept development;
John Hearn for his ideation and Last Stand;
Andrea Thompson and Taka Hiro Imamura
for their photography; Angelo Cirimele,
Jan-Willem Dikkers, Nick Hampshire, Steven
Heller, Jan Van Mol, Rankin, and Bob Sacks for
placing their thoughts and experiences
on paper; Charles Miers, Martynka Wawrzyniak,
and Leah Whisler from Rizzoli; Vince Frost
for his design; Kristin M. Jones for her editing;
Jordan Hruska and Timothée Letouzé for their
helpful research; everyone at Total Circulation
Services, Ink on A, Global News, and Union
Square Magazine Shop for letting us take
pictures and for supporting the stylepress; Ant
Farm (www.antfarmphotography.com) for
the use of their studio; and, most of all, the
magazines, whether they are in this book or
not, no longer exist, are publishing today,
or have yet to put out their first issue. Without
them none of this would be possible.

CONTENTS

010 Biography
014 The Last Magazine (in Print)
    David Renard
018 Quotes
022 The Business of Content
    Bob Sacks
030 The E-Paper Catalyst
    Nick Hampshire
038 Alternative Publishing
    in the Twentieth Century
    Steven Heller
046 Early Days of *Dazed*
    Rankin
050 More on the Stylepress
    Angelo Cirimele
054 Unique PHYSICALITY
104 Exceptional DESIGN
172 Unorthodox CONTENT
206 The *Issue* Journey
    Jan-Willem Dikkers
242 By and for COMMUNITY
260 Beyond Printed Matter
    Jan Van Mol
282 Stylepress Index

BIOGRAPHY

David Renard

David Renard co-created Stare, a publishing and advertising agency, more than seven years ago, producing magazines that included *Stare* and *Critic Eye*. This led to the creation of MU Inc/Netcirculation, the largest nationwide distribution network for high-end boutique fashion, art, photography, and design periodicals. He also consults with more established publishers on strategic planning, circulation, and marketing. From 1994 to 1998, he worked at Gartner Group, the foremost provider of research and analysis on the global IT industry, first advising executives and board directors of Fortune 500 companies regarding the impact of technological innovations on the financial industry, then spearheading a new European subsidiary that developed research-driven decision support tools.

Angelo Cirimele

Angelo Cirimele lives and works in Paris. Passionate about the interaction between new and traditional media, he collaborated on various independent titles before launching *Magazine* in 1999, a meta-magazine that observes and analyzes the trendy international editorial scene. He also currently co-edits, with Publicis Style Press, an annual guide to one hundred cool magazines and coordinates the fashion supplement of the *Courrier International*. Cirimele teaches regularly at the Ecole Cantonale d'Art de Lausanne, the postgraduate program of the Palais de Tokyo, and the Ecole des Beaux Arts de Rennes.

Jan-Willem Dikkers

A creative director, publisher, and photographer based in Paris, Jan-Willem Dikkers began his career assisting the art directors at Shahid and Company and DKNY in New York. After becoming creative director of Armani Exchange at age twenty-three, he ran eight seasons of their advertising campaigns. Two years later he started his boutique advertising agency, which services clients in the fashion and publishing industries, and shortly thereafter began publishing *Issue* magazine. In 1999 Dikkers worked with AR Media, New York, on the rebranding of Estée Lauder and the creation of AR Media's publishing division, through which he produced *Versace* magazine and launched *Influence* magazine as editor in chief.

Nick Hampshire

A publisher, writer, entrepreneur, and author of over twenty books on information technology, Nick Hampshire is widely acknowledged to be one of the leading authorities in digital publishing. Having spent many years as a publisher, he has a profound understanding of the needs of book and magazine publishers, content creators, and readers. As a technologist he was a pioneer of personal computing in the United Kingdom, and for the last quarter century he has consistently worked at the leading edge of information technology. Hampshire is currently technology director of AFAICS Research.

Steven Heller

Steven Heller is art director of the *New York Times Book Review* and cochair of the School of Visual Arts MFA Designer as Author program. He has written, edited, or co-edited over ninety books on design and popular culture, including *Merz to Emigré and Beyond: Avant-Garde Magazine Design of the Twentieth Century* (Phaidon Books) and *Cover Story: The Art of American Magazine Covers 1900–1950* (Chronicle Books).

Rankin

A photographer, publisher, and most recently a film director, Rankin brings a mischievous wit to everything he does. His intimate portraits, distinctive fashion and commercial work, and groundbreaking art projects have marked him as one of the world's leading image-makers. Rankin started *Dazed & Confused* magazine with Jefferson Hack in 1991, overseeing its development as creative director. His new publishing endeavors, the fashion bi-annuals *Another Magazine* and *Another Man*, reflect a changing view of his work and the world it occupies. His short film *Perfect* premiered at the Los Angeles Film Festival and was screened internationally to great acclaim. *The Lives of the Saints* is his first feature film.

Bob Sacks

Having been involved with printing/publishing since 1970, Bob Sacks is a veteran of the industry. He has held positions in major media companies and startups that have included publisher, editor, freelance writer, director of manufacturing and distribution, senior sales manager, circulation director, chief of operations, pressman, and cameraman, in companies such as McCall's, Time Inc., New York Times Magazine Group, International Paper, Ziff-Davis, CMP, and Bill Communications (VNU). Today, his Precision Media Group conducts private consulting programs and publishes "Heard on the Web: Media Intelligence," a daily e-newsletter that delivers pertinent industry news to a diverse, worldwide publishing community of over 10,750 media industry leaders. Launched in 1993, it is the longest-running e-newsletter in the world.

Jan Van Mol

Jan Van Mol started his own advertising agency in Brussels when he was still a student. Nine years ago he sold the agency to start Ad!dict Creative Lab, a unique laboratory with an unmatched pool of four thousand international creatives from thirty-two disciplines. These lab members conduct research in order to develop new branding tools that help bring innovation to corporations—including Diesel, Nike, Toyota, BMW, and Sara Lee—nonprofit organizations, and local and national governments. Van Mol also publishes the acclaimed *Ad!dict* magazine, which presents the collaborations of over two hundred different lab members within each issue.

The Last Magazine (in Print)

Magazines, as we know them, are dying. Ink and paper, the materials that have defined magazines for over 250 years, are dissolving gradually into digital bits and bytes. This evolution will have profound implications for how publications are conceived, sold, and consumed. Newsstands, crowded with titles, conceal the industry's inexorable decline, which is signaled by shrinking revenue, consumer usage, and consumer spending, especially in today's youth culture. Indeed, the market for printed periodicals will decrease by 15 percent through 2016 in North America and Europe. Within twenty-five years a mere 10 percent of the paper-based magazine industry will remain, sustained by connoisseurs, aficionados, and aging Luddites. As mass-market publishers, by far the largest and most vulnerable segment of the industry, relinquish the traditional printed medium for a more responsive, digital one, they will leave in their wake a much smaller market led by the thriving high-end specialty titles. ▮▮▮▮▮▮▮▮ The next decade will see intensifying pressures on publishers. First, consumers have developed a growing appetite for media-rich entertainment, news, analysis, and opinion delivered the instant they are relevant. As Bob Sacks, director of Precision Media Group, writes, this "is a handicap for any printed magazine that suffers from old age the minute it leaves the printer's loading dock" (p. 22). Second, advertising agencies and their clients are growing accustomed to high standards of accountability—demanding the same specific and timely data on the quantity and quality of viewers/readers that is now delivered by Internet Web sites. Advertising in a periodical today, which generally contributes between 30 percent (in Europe) and more than 60 percent (in the United States) of a magazine's revenue, requires a leap of faith from advertisers because of the absence of detailed sales and consumption information. ▮▮▮▮▮▮ At the same time, the cost of distribution is soaring, especially in North America and Europe, not only because of the recent spike in gas prices but also because of major inefficiencies at the publisher, distributor, and wholesaler levels. The average percentage of copies sold worldwide has declined to 40 percent (and to below 35 percent in the United States) due to an industry-wide laxness that leads most to overcompensate and print copies that are, in effect, destined to be shredded. Finally, environmental pressures, until recently manifest only in rising paper prices caused by shrinking supply and declining consumption, will flare, as "green" alternatives become economically viable and socially desirable. The combined stresses of immediacy, accountability, distribution, and ecology will ultimately rouse mass-market magazines to action and force them to shelve the "print" moniker for a more modern substitute: e-paper. ▮▮▮▮▮▮ Mass-market publishers are very slowly reacting to these pressures and tepidly coming to terms with the reality that this industry does not need to be delineated by print. In the words of Philippe Guelton, EVP-COO of Hachette Filipacchi US, "The bigger difficulty for us is to truly understand and accept and implement the idea that we are not defined by paper or by a distribution form" (p. 18). It is increasingly important for mass-market publishers to realize that their competitive differentiators must be liquid content that can be delivered on any medium and reciprocated customer relationships that go beyond the one-sided delivery of information. ▮▮▮▮▮ Imagine all the benefits of paper with the breadth of possibilities offered by the Internet. Tablet computers, PDAs, third-generation mobile phones, and e-books have each been touted as the "killer" application, set to replace the printed word. All have failed thus far because the inveterate book or magazine reader still seeks a physical experience: rolling up a title, making handwritten notes on an article, and flipping the pages. Catering to these tactile relationships is one key to consumer adoption. Another is delivering media-rich content that meets and extends the definition and sharpness of ink on paper. A third is providing clear business/professional and social benefits to individuals who want to be connected to the immediacy of the Internet and

by David Renard

The market for printed periodicals will decrease by 15 percent through 2016 in North America and Europe. Within twenty-five years a mere 10 percent of the paper-based magazine industry will remain, sustained by connoisseurs, aficionados, and aging Luddites.

sift through large amounts of data without wasting paper. E-paper, on the other hand, meets and exceeds these expectations. It is portable, flexible (unlike a computer screen), updatable, searchable, and as easy to read and use as a printed sheet of paper—with many more media options. According to Nick Hampshire, technology director of AFAICS Research, by 2020 this technology's worldwide market will be worth at least $20 billion (p. 30). ■■■■■■ Over the next few years, mass-market titles will follow the lead of newspapers, academic journals, business-to-business magazines, and newsweeklies and move to stanch their hemorrhaging circulation and revenues by more aggressively embracing digital delivery. Only then will publishers start to reap the benefits of these increasingly pervasive technologies and keep up with the usage patterns of younger generations not dependent on the same regular diet of printed matter. Paper-based periodicals that do persevere in North America and Europe will do so on a much smaller scale as the *stylepress*: physically and aesthetically engaging, vibrant creative chroniclers of trends. **These will be the last printed magazines.** ■■■■■■ Since at least the mid-1990s, this new wave of independent, high-end magazines, fusing elements of the ephemeral periodical and the perennial book, has arisen with explosive force. Two principal factors have enabled this development. On one hand, the cost of creating these publications has been declining, thanks to affordable and accessible design software and a developed communications infrastructure essential for sharing and collaborating. On the other, would-be publishers have been energized by the growing acceptance of these titles as a respectable medium in which to showcase artistic ideas and experiment with concepts. Their targets are typically narrowly defined communities of interconnected individuals who share a similar aesthetic outlook. According to Steven Heller, author of *Merz to Émigré and Beyond: Avant-Garde Magazine Design of the Twentieth Century*, this is not a new occurrence: "Contexts may differ and themes vary but the overwhelming desire among indie mavens has been to assemble critical masses of unconventional material—and this dates back to the invention of the steam printing press in the early nineteenth century" (p. 38). ■■■■■■ The stylepress have at their source the presentation of creativity led by the editor's (publisher's/aggregator's/creative director's) vision. To quote Jan Van Mol, publisher of *Ad!dict* magazine, "It's the canvas of the magazine artist." (p. 260). Jan-Willem Dikkers, publisher of *Issue* magazine, agrees: "Such magazines are not produced; they are lived." (p. 206). This is such an incredible strength that they transcend the boundaries of traditional publications in fundamental ways: through their physicality (format, materials, and packaging), unusual design, provocative content, and dedication to particular communities. ■■■■■■ The stylepress are devised throughout the world by individuals or small groups for slightly larger groups. Their creators are motivated by the desire to express themselves and contribute to the innovative spirit of those communities. Rankin, copublisher of *Dazed & Confused* and *Another Magazine* says of his first project "As well as being driven by pure ambition, we saw it as a way of causing mischief" (p. 46). These publications are relatively uncompromised by the demands of advertising and the circulation realities of the magazine market and are very often unconcerned with their own continuity and periodicity. Many of these titles publish only one or two issues, preserving the option of "putting another one out" at a later, unspecified time. But, because they represent an attractive (through the desire to emulate one's peers or just publish a personal manifesto) and seemingly trendy showcase, new titles are burgeoning throughout the market. And this trend shows no sign of turning back, as individuals continue to see these magazines as a symbol of status and adherence to a particular social "tribe." Although "the general public is mostly unaware of them, reserving these small jewels for the connoisseurs . . ." (Angelo Cirimele, publisher of *Magazine*, p. 50), today's worldwide market for the stylepress hovers around $13 million and is projected to grow to more than $500 million over the next twenty-five years. ■■■■■■ The 150 magazines from over twenty countries you will see in the following pages are a celebration of the stylepress. For some, it will be a visual anthology showing how they break and exceed the generally accepted practices of traditional periodicals in at least one, if not all, of the areas of physicality, design, content, and community. For others, it will be a visual road sign announcing what lies ahead, and maybe, for the most astute, a key to holding on to print a little longer. ■■■■■■ **For more, please go to www.magfuture.com.**

The stylepress: physically and aesthetically engaging, vibrant creative chroniclers of trends. These will be the last printed magazines.

"I still believe in the magazine industry. What we do, our core competency, is trusted editing skills. Whether we do it on paper or not remains to be seen, but in an age of too much information, isn't our core competency worth more, not less?"

Anne Moore, chairwoman, Time Inc. // Quoted in Nat Ives, "Time Inc.'s Ann Moore: Core Competency Is Editing: Magazine Giant's Chairwoman Talks About Future After Re-Org," *AdAge.com*, December 16, 2005 <http://www.adage.com/news.cms?newsId=47196>.

"Working in print, pure and simple, is the early Twenty-first Century equivalent of running a record company specialising in vinyl."

Andrew Gowers, former editor, *Financial Times* // Quoted in Stephen Brook, "Gowers: No Future in Print," *Mediaguardian.co.uk*, November 9, 2005 <http://media.guardian.co.uk/presspublishing/story/0,7495,1638499,00.html>.

"I spend four-fifths of my time worrying about technology."

Richard Charkin, president, The Publishers' Association, UK (chief executive of Macmillan Publishers, Ltd.) // Quoted in Robert Mccrum, "The Future of the Printed Page," *The Observer*, January 24, 2006 <http://www.taipeitimes.com/News/editorials/archives/2006/01/24/2003290526>.

"What the market needs is 'a reading device the size of a paperback with a good screen and long battery life that can download book, newspaper, and magazine pages.'"

Jacob Weisberg, editor, *Slate.com* // Quoted in Robert Mccrum, "The Future of the Printed Page," *The Observer*, January 24, 2006 <http://www.taipeitimes.com/News/editorials/archives/2006/01/24/2003290526>.

"Screens, screens, and screens. We believe that consumers will engage with content primarily through these screens. They will customize all content to the screen they elect to engage with, and they will engage in it when and where they want to. . . . Like it or not, you are now just another group of content providers. And to stay in the game, you have to deliver content that is malleable."

Renetta McCann, CEO, The Americas Starcom MediaVest Group // Renetta McCann, "How Magazines Can Leverage Their Unique Relationship with the Consumer," speech given at the World Magazine Congress of the International Federation of the Periodical Press (FIPP), May 23, 2005, New York <http://www.magazine.org/press_room/speeches/12152.cfm>.

"Scarcely a day goes by without some claim that new technologies are fast writing newsprint's obituary."

K. Rupert Murdoch, chairman and CEO, News Corporation, speaking to the American Society of Newspaper Editors on April 13, 2005 // K. Rupert Murdoch, speech to the American Society of Newspaper Editors, April 13, 2005 <http://www.newscorp.com/news/news_247.html>.

"Magazines don't need to be equated with print. It's a content-driven model now. It's not about distribution."

John Battelle, founder and former publisher of *The Industry Standard* and cofounding editor of *Wired* // Quoted in Mike Shields, "Batelle: Mags Must Adapt to Web," *Mediaweek*, December 12, 2005 <http://www.mediaweek.com/mw/search/article_display.jsp?vnu_content_id=1001657523>.

"Advertisers and readers will always support glossies, right? No, they won't. We're not yet seeing vast revenue declines at top-shelf magazines like we are at newspapers simply because the flush high-end glossies still have a lock on ad dollars from the curiously old-fashioned fashion world. . . ."

Simon Dumenco, "The Media Guy," weekly commentator on *AdAge.com* // Simon Dumenco, "We're Sorry Ms. Wintour, but You'll Have to Walk: Media Guy Predicts the End of the Town Car Era," *AdAge.com*, January 30, 2006 <http://www.adage.com/news.cms?newsId=47661>.

"At Hachette, we've announced that we'll offer all of our consumer magazines in digital format at the end of first-quarter 2006. Digital editions offer the opportunity to add rich media to our editorial and our advertising pages, among other advantages. . . . And in the future, digital technology will enable us to provide advertisers with faster distribution and audience measurement and reporting. . . . And we all know it is much more efficient and profitable for advertising agencies to deploy budgets in electronic media than in magazines."

Jack Kliger, president and CEO, Hachette Filipacchi U.S., Inc., and chairman, Magazine Publishers of America // Jack Kliger, "Breakfast with a Leader" speech to the Magazine Publishers of America, December 7, 2005 <http://www.magazine.org/Press_Room/speeches/14463.cfm>.

"The bigger difficulty for us is to truly understand and accept and implement the idea that we are not defined by paper or by a distribution form. We are as magazines defined by content, editors, and a relationship with marketers."

Philippe Guelton, EVP-COO, Hachette Filipacchi U.S., Inc. // Quoted in Nat Ives, "Hachette Adds Executive to Oversee Web Biz," *AdAge.com*, January 10, 2006 <http://www.adage.com/news.cms?newsID=47404>.

"Bill Gates says that in technology things that are supposed to happen in less than five years usually take longer than expected, while things that are supposed to happen in more than 10 years usually come sooner than expected."

Michael Kinsley, founding editor, *Slate.com* // Michael Kinsley, "Extra Extra! The Future of Newspapers," *Slate.com*, January 7, 2006 <http://www.slate.com/id/2133847>.

"Jim Spanfeller, president-CEO of Forbes.com, responding to an audience question about when Forbes.com will surpass the print edition in terms of revenue, said, 'probably in about 18 to 20 months.' Forbes.com is run as a separate company within Forbes Inc."

Mary Griffin and Ellis Booker, *BtoBonline.com* // Mary Griffin and Ellis Booker, "As Digital Dollars Grow, B-to-B Publishers Debate Impact of Blogs," *btobonline.com*, May 3, 2005 <http://www.btobonline.com/article.cms?articleId=24198>.

"Burda has spent the past few years zealously pushing his media company into everything digital, even insisting that he will never open a printing plant again. . . . 'Printing will not go away, but I do not plan to open a single new printing plant,' Burda said. 'We now concentrate on using social software to build closer relations with the communities of readers around our magazines.'"

Thomas Crampton, *International Herald Tribune*, speaking about Hubert Burda of Hubert Burda Media, publisher of *Focus* // Thomas Crampton, "Burda Looks Beyond Printing," *International Herald Tribune*, November 13, 2005 <http://www.iht.com/articles/2005/11/13/business/burda14.php>.

"Magazines are magazines because that's what the technology, printing, and distribution demanded. Now technology allows any means of publishing, broadcasting, and conversing; now printing is a cost center; now controlling distribution does not bring the advantages it once did. So we need to stop thinking of media brands as tied to their medium. . . The definition of a magazine story should not be that it's printed in a magazine."

Jeff Jarvis, creator of *Entertainment Weekly*, former president of *Advance.net*, and writer of *BuzzMachine blog* // Quoted in Mark Glaser, "Future of Magazines: Net Could Empower Readers," *USC Annenberg Online Journalism Review*, May 24, 2005 <http://www.ojr.org/ojr/stories/050524glaser/>.

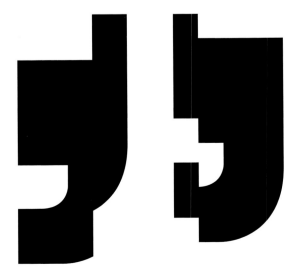

" . . . content will be more important than its container. . . . The franchise is the content itself."

Tom Curley, president and CEO, The Associated Press // Tom Curley, keynote address, Online News Association Conference, November 12, 2004 <http://journalist.org/2004conference/archives/000079.php>.

"We would like to believe that Internet-versus-print is analogous to TV-versus-radio in the fifties: the new doesn't necessarily wipe out the old. But I think paper media today are more like sailing ships around 1860—still dominant but enjoying their last hurrah. I think it's late in the magazine era."

Kurt Andersen, cofounder of *Spy* and *New York* columnist // Kurt Andersen, "The Good Old Boy of Time Inc.," *New York*, January 23, 2006 <http://newyorkmetro.com/nymetro/news/columns/imperialcity/15550/>.

The Business of Content

3

by Bob Sacks

The printed page and the printing press are no more or less than tools. They are tools that perform a very specific function: the distribution of information. In reality it is the distribution of information that matters, not the tools used to deliver it.

I've heard it said that the future is already here but it is just not widely distributed. I think that is a thought worth pondering. As advanced as we seem today, more technology and superscience are around the corner than we can possibly imagine. Amazing advancements are everywhere and in every industry. Publishing is no exception, and one can make the case that it is even a leader in this progress. In the space of one generation, we have gone from analog printing to the rocket science of electronic paper in a digital age. But make no mistake—what is happening now is not science fiction; it is science fact. ■■■■■■ In the 1970s magazines were still setting type using hot lead. In the early 1980s large-run magazines were still printing using letterpress. (An interesting side note: Just twenty-five years ago the magazine industry was using the same technology—letterpress—that Gutenberg invented five hundred years ago.) In the 1990s we learned to make digital plates, which resulted in speeds and accuracy never before thought possible. Now in the twenty-first century we have streamlined and adapted into an entirely new phase of the publishing/printing industry. We are exploring new and more effective ways of distributing information. ■■■■■■ The first and most important thing to understand in this new digital universe is the seismic shift from distributing analog printed products to a much broader-based system of qualified information distribution. Once you understand that, you arrive at what I call "El-CID," or Electronically Coordinated Information Distribution. It will be El-CID that will empower publishers and printers to perform at their best and create business models that are based on the multipath universe of information distribution. El-CID is our ability to deliver information to multiple platforms in an instant and on a global basis. That is what the new, successful magazine business paradigm must be if we intend to survive in the media industry. The future of publishing is the ability to access any and all the information there is, all the time, quickly and reliably. ■■■■■■ In the coming years, the magazine industry will be at the mercy of a public that faces ever more media choices. As the options continue to multiply, the task of capturing readers' attention will be tougher than ever. New information delivery methods, combined with the potential for customization, promise to shake up the playing field for the industry's established players. ■■■■■■ Today the magazine industry is in a state of flux, but I believe that huge opportunities and an era of great publishing expansion will follow this cycle of change. It is happening already, but it hasn't reached that economic watershed moment when you turn around and say, "Wow! Where the heck did that come from?" The industry has come a very long way, over hundreds of years, to arrive at this crossroad. Mixed signals are everywhere. Who are we, and where are we going? ■■■■■■ Currently, in the United States, over 6,000 consumer magazines are in print. Last year alone over 1,100 new titles were released. That works out to three new magazines a day, every day of the week. That sure sounds encouraging. And recent Publishers Information Bureau (PIB) reports suggest that magazine advertising is in a growth mode. But surely we need to exercise some caution and understand that rate card-reported revenues can be misleading. The number of actual ad pages is a far more accurate barometer of the industry's health than the reported revenue. The actual ad page count shows a modest but positive growth in ad pages in the last year. ■■■■■■ Let's look at one more statistic and see if we can draw some conclusions. Based on data analyzed by the Audit Bureau of Circulations (ABC), U.S. magazine sales grew very nicely from 245 million copies in 1970 to 366 million in 1990. Then from 1990 to 2006 the actual growth of magazines stopped dead. We still only sell 366 million copies a year. So it seems that, no matter how many new magazines we launch, the total number of copies sold has not changed for nearly sixteen years. Is it possible that we have run out of magazine readers, and that publishers are just stealing them from each other? ■■■■■■ Here is one way to look at these developments. The printed page and the printing press are no more or less than tools. They are tools that perform a very specific function: the distribution of information. In reality it is the distribution of information that matters, not the tools used to deliver it. All technologies and tools are eventually replaced or at least superseded by newer and more efficient technology. ■■■■■■ Our readjustment from print to electrons took five hundred years of development and redeployment, but we are on the threshold of a better tool. El-CID is what the next successful publishing paradigm must be if we intend to survive in the information distribution industry. We must no longer consider ourselves as just print publishers, journalists, and media professionals. We are information distributors. ■■■■■■■■ We are now at a fork in the road where the consumers can take information that has been designed and programmed for them or can design and program the media for themselves. What we are left with is what I call "MeMedia." In the very near future we will move from mass media to micro-MeMedia, from mass marketing to permission-based marketing and publishing. In short, our emphasis is going to be on the business of selling content, and the creation of that content through intelligent reporting, news gathering, editing, packaging, and design, regardless of the magazine's delivery method. In the end, the ultimate goal is to create timely, yet timeless, addictive information that answers the simple basic question: what's in it for me? ■■■■■■■ Generations have now grown up believing the credo that information should be free. They see no reason to pay for news. Instead, they access a newspaper Web site or surf Google News, where they select from literally thousands of information sources. They receive Really Simple Syndication (RSS) feeds on their PDAs or visit bloggers whose views mesh with their own. In short, they customize their news-gathering experience in a way no single printed paper or publication could ever do. ■■■■■■■ In a recent survey, the Online Publishers Association found that eighteen- to thirty-four-year-olds are far more apt to use their free time to log on to the Internet than engage in other activities: surf the Internet—46 percent; watch TV—35 percent; read a book—7 percent; listen to radio—3 percent; read a newspaper or magazine—3 percent. Add to these statistics that America's youth are very savvy multitaskers and that they pack eight and a half hours of media exposure into six and a half hours of each day. ■■■■■■■■ To be successful today, publishers must understand the seismic shift we have gone through from distributing printed products to a much broader-based system of qualified information distribution. We now have the ability to deliver information to multiple platforms in an instant and on a global basis. The most successful printers and publishers will create business models based on a multipath universe of content distribution. This means we must no longer consider ourselves as just publishers, printers, journalists, and media professionals, but information distributors. That is what the new successful business paradigm must be if we intend to survive in the publishing industry. The future of publishing is enabling access to any and all the information there is, all the time, quickly and reliably. ■■■■■■■ One of the many new developments in information delivery is the digital magazine. And what is a digital magazine? It is usually an exact PDF reproduction of the printed product but reproduced in digital format on the screen of your choice. Digital magazines should not be confused with Internet HTML pages. They are better, much better. Digital magazines can deliver the same personal, intimate, page-turning experience as a printed magazine. So reading a digital magazine is as rewarding an experience as reading a traditional magazine or newspaper. Here is the core of this brilliant design: it has a beginning, middle, and end, just like its older brother, the printed magazine. It has

The future of publishing is enabling access to any and all the information there is, all the time, quickly and reliably.

design and art; it has an editorial voice and an identity not easily reproduced by an ordinary, isolated HTML page. ■■■■■■■ An HTML page stands alone as a single page among billions of single-storied, solo Internet pages. There is usually a home page and a list of articles. You find the article or link you like and off you go to some page stored who knows where on the Ethernet. And that is that. You may be directed back to the home page or not, but there is no continuity, no real identity, no style, no familiar page-turning experience. No real beginning, no middle, and surely no satisfying end. ■■■■■■■ A digital magazine is different, very different. It has all the style, charm, and identity of a traditional magazine, and you can turn pages from the cover all the way to the end; you can jump to the middle and back. But digital magazines deliver much more than their printed brothers. They can deliver audio, video, and dynamic, rich media action to any page. Digital magazines are analog magazines on steroids. Headlines or body art can attract attention with creative flair, movement, and eye-catching emphasis. Unlike traditional media, a digital magazine can be constantly updated before the download, which is a handicap for any printed magazine that suffers from old age the minute it leaves the printer's loading dock. It can also have dynamic links to anywhere on the Internet. An ad page can direct the interested consumer to more specific and detailed information on the home page of the advertiser. The editorial pages can direct the reader to more charts, videos, and editorial content than was originally contained in the printed product. ■■■■■■■ Digital magazines cost less to manufacture and distribute than physical magazines. Without the expense of paper, ink, and printing, manufacturing costs are miniscule. Distribution costs are only a fraction of the freight and USPS charges for today's printed products. These advantages, coupled with the compelling interactive experience offered by these magazines, make delving into the digital age most appealing. ■■■■■■■ The future is never here and the present is never the end of the trail. The magazine business will thrive and grow, but not as we have known it in the past. In the next few years the combination of a national WiFi network and the introduction of a workable e-paper solution will gain traction and be combined with the developing digital magazine. When that happens, it will be a new golden age for the magazine business. We will deliver the tried-and-true magazine experience with blazing speed and completely fresh, updated information. Minute to minute and second to second, the possibilities are endless.

The E-Paper Catalyst

by Nick Hampshire

This is a vision of a new device and a new technology. The new device is the e-reader. The new technology is a thin, bendable display, with a high-quality screen that not only looks as good as the printed page, but, like print, can be viewed in any ambient light condition and from any angle. This new technology is e-paper.

Imagine . . . ▮▮▮▮▮ It is 2012. You come down for breakfast, take your e-reader off its docking stand next to the PC, sit down to eat your favorite cereal, drink a cup of coffee, and read the morning's business news. ▮▮▮▮▮ The e-reader is A4 in size and as thin and light as a copy of Newsweek. You can easily grasp it in one hand and read text that is displayed as clearly and as crisply as on a printed page. You can hold it in one hand and eat your breakfast with the other. ▮▮▮▮▮ In its docking stand, which is connected to your PC, the e-reader has been automatically downloaded with copies of the morning newspaper and a couple of magazines to which you subscribe. These have arrived via the PC's broadband connection. They are now stored in the e-reader's internal memory, together with documents you copied into it at work the previous day and a couple of books you are reading. ▮▮▮▮▮ You shove the e-reader into your briefcase. It bends easily to accommodate the other contents, and you know it will not be damaged if you drop it or sit on it, unlike your laptop PC. ▮▮▮▮▮ You have a business trip to make and a plane to catch. At the airport you decide to buy something extra to read on the plane. You stop at the newsstand kiosk and select a couple of magazines and a book. While you pay with your credit card, the magazines and books are automatically downloaded onto the e-reader in your case using the e-reader's wireless link. ▮▮▮▮▮ On the plane you read a magazine, moving from page to page by pressing the page-turn buttons on the side of the reader. The pages are easily readable even when the plane banks and bright sunshine floods onto the reader through the window. You bookmark a couple of articles and use the highlighter to mark some interesting sections in one of them . . . ▮▮▮▮▮ **. . . E-Paper** ▮▮▮▮▮ This is a vision of a new device and a new technology. The new device is the e-reader. The new technology is a thin, bendable display, with a high-quality screen that not only looks as good as the printed page, but, like print, can be viewed in any ambient light condition and from any angle. This new technology is e-paper. ▮▮▮▮▮ The conventional glass-based LCD display technology currently found in laptop PCs, PDAs, and mobile phones has many limitations: The displays are heavy, rigid, fragile, and use a lot of battery power. In addition, backlit LCD displays are almost invisible in bright light, and if viewed for a long time can cause eyestrain. E-paper overcomes most of these limitations. ▮▮▮▮▮ E-paper is, however, not a single technology; it is a family of different leading-edge technologies that are being developed by companies around the world. This family shares the common features of being lightweight, rugged, bendable, low power, and readable in ambient light, as well as having a high-resolution and high-contrast display. ▮▮▮▮▮ All these different types of e-paper involve the combination of two such technologies: the frontplane, which is the visual part of the display (in other words, the electronic ink), and the backplane, which controls what is displayed (the electronic paper). ▮▮▮▮▮ There are many developing frontplane technologies, including electrophoretic, bichromal, electrowetting, flexible phase dispersion LCD, and electrochromic. And backplane technologies, including organic electronic and flexible poly-silicon. ▮▮▮▮▮ These technologies are being developed by companies around the world, such as Hewlett-Packard, IBM, Sony, Hitachi, Philips, Xerox, Samsung, Siemens, and many more. These companies have over the last few years spent several hundred million dollars on e-paper R&D. The race is now on to convert this investment into commercial products that can capitalize on what most analysts agree will by 2020 be at least a $20 billion worldwide market for e-paper displays. ▮▮▮▮▮ Of these developing technologies, the current leaders and the ones most likely to be found in the first generation of e-reader devices, such as the one owned by our user in 2012, will be a combination of an electrophoretic frontplane and an organic electronic backplane. This

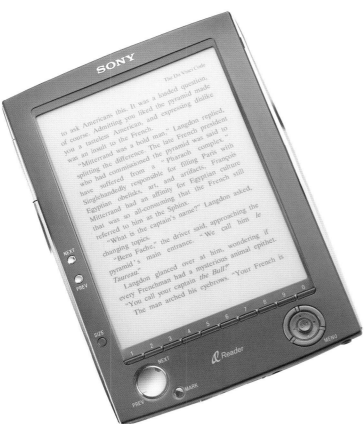

combination will be used in commercial displays from 2007 onward and is ideal for e-publication reader devices. Two companies, Philips Polymer Vision of the Netherlands and Plastic Logic of the United Kingdom, have already demonstrated prototypes of such displays. Other display technologies will take longer to develop commercially and will probably not be seen until after 2010. ▆▆▆▆

Underlying Technology ▆▆▆▆▆▆ To understand what makes e-paper—the combination of an electrophoretic frontplane with an organic electronic backplane—special, we need to examine each of these technologies more closely. ▆▆▆▆▆▆ Organic electronics is a technique for building circuits from polymers (i.e., plastics that have very special electrical properties). The technique involves intricately layering different polymers, each with distinct electrical characteristics, to form an electronic circuit. ▆▆▆▆▆ This circuit is the backplane of an e-paper display. It is, in fact, a large matrix of minute electronic switches that can be turned off and on to control the state of a single picture point within the display. A monochrome sheet of e-paper using an electrophoretic frontplane will have around 40,000 such "switches" per square inch of display surface. ▆▆▆▆ Flexible display pioneers Philips Polymer Vision and Plastic Logic have developed the technology for making such backplane circuits using special soluble versions of these polymers. This means that the circuitry can be fabricated at room temperature, on a flexible plastic substrate or "printing" surface, using conventional screen-printing and ink-jet technologies. ▆▆▆▆▆ Flexible organic electronic backplanes are, therefore, fully functional electronic circuits that are printed onto sheets of plastic using special plastic inks, in a process that is both cheap and fast. This process allows the backplanes, and therefore the sheets of e-paper that will be made using them, to be produced in a wide range of different sizes—currently anything up to A3, and in the future, much larger. ▆▆▆▆▆ The electrophoretic frontplane is also flexible and made of plastic. Its big advantage is that it uses reflected light in the same way as a sheet of printed paper, as opposed to generating light like a TV or a backlit LCD. A typical example is the technology developed by Massachusetts-based e-paper pioneer E-Ink. ▆▆▆▆▆ In an E-Ink frontplane extremely small black-and-white pigment particles are given opposite electrical charges, then suspended in a clear fluid and encapsulated in microcapsules. Each tiny spherical microcapsule is smaller than the diameter of a human hair. These microcapsules are then mixed with a clear flexible plastic to form a thin sheet that is just one microcapsule thick. This is the frontplane. ▆▆▆▆▆ When an electric field is applied across an area of this thin sheet of frontplane material, the pigment particles within the microcapsules move in opposite directions, turning one side of the capsules in the area exposed to the electric field white, the other black. Reversing the polarity of the field makes the particles move in the opposite direction, and the white becomes black and the black becomes white. ▆▆▆▆▆ The high contrast of electrophoretic e-paper displays is due to the fact that what we see is light being absorbed or reflected by pigment particles, in exactly the same way that light is absorbed or reflected by the black ink or white paper of a printed page. This accounts for the

high contrast ratio of such displays, at least 10:1, which is about the same as newsprint, as opposed to the contrast ratio of an LCD display, which is only about 5:1.

This also means that, like printed paper, electrophoretic e-paper can be read under virtually any ambient light conditions. Whereas conventional computer displays are washed out in bright light, an electrophoretic e-paper display becomes easier to read. Furthermore, an electrophoretic e-paper display does not produce the eyestrain that is so common with even short-term use of a computer display. Another distinctive feature of e-paper display is its high resolution, with over twice as many pixels per inch as a conventional computer display. This high resolution gives electrophoretic e-paper a sharpness and print quality that is close to that of printed paper. This quality will improve even more as e-paper resolution increases from a maximum of 200 pixels per inch today to more than 400 within a couple of years.

Electrophoretic e-paper displays also exhibit what is known as bistability. This means that when an electric field has been used to move the particles of ink within a microcapsule, those particles stay in their new position, without any further need for the electric field. Until, of course, they are moved again by being exposed to a field of reversed polarity. The great advantage of bistability is that it reduces the amount of power needed by a display to less than one hundredth of that required by an equivalent LCD display. This means that an e-paper display–based e-publication reader can work for weeks on a single battery charge, as opposed to hours for an LCD version. This in turn makes e-paper–based readers lighter and easier to use. The manufacturing of e-paper displays using these technologies simply involves bonding a sheet of frontplane electrophoretic film onto a plastic backplane with its organic electronic circuitry. The resulting display is bendable, or even rollable, and possesses all the properties of the backplane and frontplane technologies.

Color Displays Of course, the nature of electrophoretic e-paper technology means that it is particularly well suited to monochrome displays. Color versions have already been demonstrated, however.

Although these early versions of color e-paper displays have a lower resolution than the monochrome, their color image quality is comparable to color printing on uncoated paper stock and they maintain the sharpness of text that is such a feature of the monochrome versions.

The color image is created by placing a screen made from an array of minute colored transparent windows, four for each pixel, in front of the microcapsule sheet. Light reflecting off the white pigment particles passes

through each of the four color filters to create the appearance of a colored pixel. ▮▮▮▮▮▮ The pixel color that our eye sees is determined by both the combination of colors from the four filters and the brightness of the light coming through each. ▮▮▮ At the moment such displays are capable of showing 4,096 different colors at a screen resolution of between 80 and 120 pixels per inch. But we can expect to see both resolution and color range improve over the next few years. ▮▮▮▮▮▮ The four colors used to create a color e-paper display are red, green, blue, and black/white. This is quite different from computer displays and televisions, which use three colors: red, green, and blue. The choice of a RGBW color system for e-paper gives a much sharper image for displaying text than the three-color RGB used on most conventional digital displays. ▮▮▮▮▮ To get color e-paper with an image quality comparable to that of glossy magazines, however, we will probably have to wait for the development of another frontplane technology, for which there are two main contenders, flexible LCD and electrowetting. Both technologies are currently still in the lab demonstration stage, but we may well see them in commercial products by 2012. ▮▮▮▮▮ **What to Expect** ▮▮▮▮▮ In the long term, most likely by 2020, the e-paper technologies being developed today will give us paper-thin full-color flexible displays that will rival the print quality of paper. Such displays will have all the necessary electronics integrated into the display, with reader units having several pages bound together much like a current book or magazine, with the binding housing the power supply, data storage, and communications circuitry. ▮▮▮▮▮ A reader of this sort will have all the look and feel of a printed-paper publication, but at the touch of a button the user will be able to change it instantly to any one of hundreds of different publications stored on its internal memory. A stylus-type pen will enable the user to mark or copy any contents to a built-in notebook instantly for later downloading to a PC. ▮▮▮▮▮ Although it is very important that e-paper display–based readers look and feel like printed-paper publications, the fundamental difference between a digital reader and a printed paper document will be the reason why most people will quickly switch from paper to e-paper when it comes to reading books, magazines, newspapers, and even office documents. ▮▮▮▮▮ Advertisements in magazines and newspapers will be interactive—make a mark on an advertisement with the stylus and your details will be sent to the advertiser's Internet server and a copy of a catalog or brochure will be remotely loaded onto your reader for later perusal. Your newspapers and magazines will be delivered automatically

Cross-Section of Electronic-Ink Microcapsules

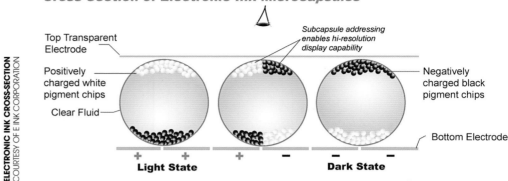

ELECTRONIC INK CROSS-SECTION
COURTESY OF E INK CORPORATION

Top Transparent Electrode

Subcapsule addressing enables hi-resolution display capability

Positively charged white pigment chips

Clear Fluid

Negatively charged black pigment chips

Bottom Electrode

Light State **Dark State**

to your reader each morning. No need for the newsboy. ■■■■■■■ But perhaps most significant, the interactive and multimedia display capability of e-paper publications will be their most appealing feature. The fact that a news story in a magazine can have an attached video or audio clip. Or the ability to electronically search through a pile of digital magazines for the article you saw last month on sailing holidays in the Virgin Islands. ■■■■■■■ One thing is certain: The development of e-paper displays will give rise to a new generation of e-publication readers—monochrome in 2007 and color in 2008—that are portable and easy to use. Some e-reader displays will roll up into a small portable device that will slip into a pocket, while others will be just bendable so that they will fit into a briefcase. Some will also include wireless communications capability that will allow linkage to the Internet. Or e-paper may just converge with mp3 players, next-generation mobile phones, and other communication/entertainment tools. But, above all, what these e-paper–based readers will all give us is an alternative to printed paper. ■■■■■■■ Such devices are already coming onto the market: In early 2006 Sony introduced the "Reader," a paperback-book-size monochrome e-paper display. This $349.99 unit can store up to eighty books and is small enough and light enough to be easily carried in a bag or pocket. A similar device, named "Iliad," is being marketed by iRex, a company associated with Philips, and announcements of e-paper display–based readers are expected in 2006 from Toshiba, Panasonic, Sharp, and a number of Korean and Chinese manufacturers.

■■■■■■■ Such readers have already proved to be very popular in China and Japan. In China they will be issued to all 165 million Chinese students over the next few years, with textbooks being provided in digital format. In Japan it is already quite a common sight to see commuters on the Shinkansen reading a book or magazine from an e-reader device. ■■■■■■■ The prices of such devices are starting to drop. One Chinese company is planning to sell an e-paper display–based reader for under $200. Analysts who have studied the development of this market expect the price to fall even further. A recent report by AFAICS Research forecasts that basic monochrome e-paper reader devices will sell for under $100 in about 2010. ■■■■■ The development of e-paper display–based readers gives us an alternative that will offer readers, authors, designers, and publishers the same quality of visual reading experience that printed paper offers, with publications having the same page size, layout, and typography as the paper editions. But at the same time it will offer us all the other advantages of document storage, electronic delivery, keyword searching, and content manipulation that have so far only been available to computer users. ■■■■■ E-paper technology will change the world of publishing, and without a doubt within a few decades we will look back on paper-based publications, as we now look back on parchment scrolls, and say, "How quaint."

TECHNOLOGY AND PRODUCT CONCEPT DEMONSTRATION
COURTESY OF PLASTIC LOGIC

But, above all, what these e-paper-based readers will all give us is an alternative to printed paper.

Lexicon

Ambient light: Normal everyday lighting conditions in which one would expect to be able to read a printed book, magazine, or newspaper.

LCD (Liquid Crystal Display): The type of display technology used in laptop computers and increasingly used in flat-screen monitors and TVs.

PDA (Personal Digital Assistant): A handheld device with a small screen that is used to store and display a digital diary, a digital contacts book, etc. The functionality of this category of device is currently being absorbed into the new generation of smart cell phones.

Electrophoretic: Display technology where microscopic particles of pigment suspended in a liquid are attracted to an electric charge, in much the same way that a small piece of paper is attracted to a plastic pen that has been rubbed on a jersey. Attracted by an electric charge, these particles of pigment change the color of the display to the pigment color and reverse the electric charge, and the display color reverts to that of the liquid in which the pigment particles are suspended.

Bichromal: A display technology where minute plastic beads, painted in one color on one side and another color on the other side are made to rotate electrically so that one color or the other faces the viewer (hence bichromal, the Greek for two-color).

Electrowetting: A display technology where ink droplets are placed in very small cups. Normally the ink droplet will spread across the entire bottom of the cup, obliterating the white bottom and displaying the ink color; however, if a voltage is applied the ink droplet retracts, much like a bead of water in a Teflon pan, exposing the white area below. A matrix of these microscopic cups forms the display.

Flexible phase dispersion LCD: A display manufacturing technique where small droplets of liquid crystal are held in a thin plastic film. As with any conventional LCD display, the application of an electric charge across this film will change its transparency, allowing light to be transmitted from a backlight source.

Electrochromic: A display technology that uses a thin layer of special chemicals that changes color when an electric current passes through it.

Organic electronic: Certain types of organic chemicals—those primarily consisting of carbon, oxygen, and hydrogen atoms—are capable of acting as conductors of electricity, much like metals, or acting as semiconductors in the same manner as an element like silicon. By using advanced printing techniques, it is possible to build circuits with these organic electronic chemicals, circuits that function in the same way as those conventionally constructed from metal conductors and semiconductors. The advantage of organic electronics is that the circuits can be fabricated more cheaply and easily than their metal counterparts, and they can be fabricated on flexible plastic substrates. These advantages mean that organic electronic devices are more lightweight and cheaper than their conventional counterparts as well as being both flexible and rugged, all features that are vital in the creation of practical e-paper displays.

Flexible poly-silicon: An advanced technique of creating flexible circuitry on either a thin steel or plastic substrate that uses conventional silicon technology. This technique has the advantage of providing a flexible, rugged circuit suitable for use in e-paper displays while at the same time retaining the use of a well-understood electronic technology.

A3 and A4 (sizes in in/cm): Standard paper sizes—A4 is 210 mm x 297 mm (8.31 x 11.69 inches). A3 is twice this size—297 mm x 420 mm (11.69 x 16.54 inches).

RGBW: This is an e-paper display color encoding technique that uses a quadruplet of color dots to define each colored image point. The quadruplet of colors are red, green, blue, and white/black. This differs from the conventional CMYK color coding used in the print world, which also uses a quadruplet of color dots but with the colors cyan, magenta, yellow, and black/white. The main reason for this difference is that the RGBW coding is very close to the RGB coding that is standard on most digital displays and will thus facilitate the easy movement of content from other digital media to e-paper displays without need for software conversion.

5

Alternative Publishing in the Twentieth Century

by Steven Heller

New indies are nudging into the realms once dominated by the for-profit magazines that wallpaper news shops. These are not merely eclectic but, like indies from the past, they are alternatives to mainstream culture, art, fashion, lifestyle, and popular culture magazines; and they are not published merely to cater to focused demographics or marketing whims but because their publishers, editors, designers, photographers, and artists are compelled to satisfy their own desires and inspire others.

The early twentieth century was littered with magazines and gazettes created as soapboxes for misfits and mavericks who foisted radical and controversial ideas on fellow travelers and innocents alike. Despite the technical difficulty and expense involved in printing and publishing magazines, an irresistible—almost uncontrollably obsessive—urge drew artists of all kinds to the printed page. Indeed, anyone who espoused a cause or ideology was likely to launch a small magazine. For those who belonged to an avant-garde faction, publishing was a veritable requisite. ■ In dank, smoke-filled rooms Futurist, Dadaist, and Surrealist art provocateurs wrote dissonant poetry, composed asymmetric layouts, and pasted together expressive collages, which they published in crudely produced publications that extended the artists' reputation and resonance. Each movement, in its own way, proffered the Modernist notion of art as a total experience that should not be detached from day-to-day life, politics, or technology. So as Europe careened headlong into the modern epoch—and the devastation of a world war—romantic and elitist notions of bourgeois artistic propriety were obliterated. Artists, writers, designers, and typographers routinely advanced ideas that attacked accepted mores, but without the agency of mass-produced publications their respective rants and manifestoes might never have reached their intended audiences. These art and culture periodicals (or "zines," as they are called today) were weapons of cultural warfare. ■ Of course, magazines were not exclusively a medium for incendiary movements. During the late nineteenth and early twentieth centuries the publication and distribution of mainstream periodicals reached a zenith. Increased literacy and consumerism created a need for all kinds of publishing venues. In the absence of electronic media, magazines were the mass media of the era. Yet the alternative culture periodicals did more than simply inform and entertain the public; they provoked action (and reaction)—disruptive and sometimes violent, progressive, and even regressive responses for and against shocking ideas and ideals. Type and image on paper triggered such incredible passions that in some nations laws were enacted to restrict that which roused and incited. ■ But avant-gardists flagrantly ignored these laws and refused to appeal to mass taste. Indeed, the avant-garde's job was to make sure that bad transcended good and the unholy subverted the sanctified. The zine catapulted unprecedented and unpopular ideas into the larger cultural discourse. In Italy, Germany, Switzerland, and France avant-garde periodicals such as *Futurismo, Noi, Dada, Merz,* and *La Revolution Surréaliste* were designed to rally the faithful while offending the compliant. When radical ideas escaped from underground hideaways into the public domain, they often rattled propriety and toppled standards. ■ Graphic *design* became the code of revolt. Words were the building blocks of meaning, but graphic design (typography, layout, image) more than just framed ideas—it telegraphed intent. Radical ideas had to appear vanguard to be vanguard. The sensory impact eccentric type composition made on the reader marked the end of conventionality. The design of most Dada publications during the early 1920s, for example, both intentionally and intuitively disrupted professional design standards. Dadaists redirected traditional reading patterns, from left to right and up and down, to all around a page. They cobbled graphic styles from mainstream printing sources and wedded them to Futurist and Cubist pictorial theories of disruption and fragmentation. Standard typefaces were not just mere letterforms composed in neatly regimented columns; they were used as textures applied (or painted) on a tabula rasa. Rejecting the sanctimonious separation of high and low art, Dada employed vernacular visuals, like show-card lettering and common newspaper advertisements, as one part of the art/anti-art aesthetic. Aesthetic quality was not a high ideal; rather, Dada was intent on revealing through its messy printed manifestations that no remnant of the sanctified past, not even neutral or transparent typefaces, would be tolerated in their new world order. ■ Various radical ideas introduced through

MERZ

DADA

The history of independent magazines is replete with stories of egotistical editors and designers who have sought their own publishing nirvana.

Futurist, Dada, and Surrealist magazines were, however, eventually adopted by the mainstream. The New Typography (codified by Jan Tschichold in 1925), a synthesis of these avant-garde movements as well as approaches introduced through Russian Constructivism and Dutch de Stijl, provided new standards for quotidian advertising and publication design. Its leading practitioners, who thought of themselves as avant-garde, sought to alter conventional attitudes toward design yet remain viable (and employable) in the commercial realm. Even Kurt Schwitters's personal Dada zine, the nonsensically titled *Merz*, was at various times transformed from an experimental outlet for avant-gardisms into a sample book of progressive graphic design, where he exhibited ways of applying The New Typography to commercial advertisements. ▪▪▪▪▪▪ That avant-garde movements influenced commerce may be disappointing to purists or anticapitalists but was nonetheless axiomatic. The lifespan of an avant-garde depended on how long it continued to offend, but once entrepreneurs saw the profitability of offensiveness in the marketplace radical ideas were invariably consumed (and doubtless neutered) by the very culture they once affronted. After the initial shock of Surrealism wore off, it quickly became a favored advertising and marketing style, because it enabled commercial artists to imaginatively manipulate all kinds of forms, inject mystery into commercial images, and remain accessible to a broad consumer audience. Surrealism tapped into the public's fascination for dreamlike allure. ▪▪▪▪▪▪ Plus ça change . . . is a pretty good way to describe the history of independent publishing. Futurist, Dadaist, Surrealist, and other early Modernist periodicals fell out of favor by the 1930s but were the forefathers of later independent zines. In fact, the most obvious progeny was the underground press of the late 1960s. Undergrounds inherited the spirit if not the visual language of their predecessors and share many of the basic traits, including raucous amateurish design and typography. In truth, however, most contributors to *The East Village Other, Chicago Seed, Oracle,* or *Los Angeles Free Press* had no idea that Futurist and Dada magazines even existed, let alone copied their styles. But they did have common motivations, like the need to express dissenting voices and create visual languages that embodied those voices. ▪▪▪▪▪▪ The underground press, which lasted roughly from 1964 (when the *LA Free Press* was founded) through 1973 (after which a few papers lingered for another few years until they either demised or evolved into community weeklies), was a loosely knit confederation of over six hundred small, medium, and large circulation periodicals, most independently published in the United States but also including noteworthy papers in Canada, Holland, and England. The primary reader was between fifteen and thirty years old, but most were college-age males, and these periodicals addressed the political, social, and cultural zeitgeist—notably sex, drugs, and rock 'n' roll. ▪▪▪▪▪▪ When these predominantly tabloid newspapers first began publishing, offset printing was inexpensive and cold-type composition systems had become more accessible. Combined with a need among young people to distance themselves from the stodgy, bourgeois magazines of their parents' day—*Life, Look,* and *The Saturday Evening Post*—this made periodical publishing the perfect outlet for attacking the establishment. The underground took two distinct paths: One was cultural or hippie, the other politically radical. At times they intersected, but mostly the latter hoped to change American values through revolution and the former wanted to ignore America altogether. These points of view were easy to spot from their respective editorial content. Hippie papers, such as the psychedelic *San Francisco Oracle,*

were rooted in the language of drugs, which took on symbolic importance—always in the forefront of each story, image, and layout (often so layered with cacophonous visuals that only someone on drugs could parse and decipher it). On the political side, *The Los Angeles Free Press* and *Berkeley Barb* routinely covered the Vietnam War, civil rights protests, police brutality, and other social issues. Under the new-left banner political undergrounds represented communists, Marxists, socialists, anarchists, Black Panthers, pacifists, and feminists. The political papers adhered to no-nonsense design strategies while the hippie tricksters used any graphic means possible. ■■■■■■■■ All undergrounds looked unprofessional, but the degree to which they were depended on who was involved at any given time. Some articles were well written and adroitly edited, though many were not. Some artists and photographers were skilled, though most were amateurish. Some of the contributors had serious aspirations as reporters, commentators, or artists, yet the majority were gadflies. Jeff Shero, editor of New York's *RAT*, summed up this mercurial nature of the underground in 1968 when he wrote: "We make up for sloppy writing by verve and passion." But the goal, if not always realized, was to effectively cover the zeitgeist through the lens of youth culture. Underground editors believed that mainstream press was swallowing whole the Madison Avenue hype that allowed the media to distort reality. In contrast, the undergrounds routinely used the personal pronoun (anathema to objective journalism) to report on stories of police brutality, CIA recruitment on college campuses, and draft board inequities among races. Eventually, this unsanctioned approach rubbed off on the mainstream, and is prevalent on weblogs today. ■■■■■■■■ By the early 1970s the underground press movement was dead. In its wake, however, a kindred publishing genre of Do-It-Yourself (D.I.Y.) zines emerged—literally thousands of small, independent, handmade, photocopied publications produced to satisfy the passions of individuals reaching out to like-minded souls. They filled various needs: Some were obsessive, such as one for collectors of Pez candy dispensers; others celebratory, such as the many that were directed at *Star Trek* aficionados; and many were kinky, such as one for fetishists of bald-headed women called *The Razor's Edge*. Photocopy technology enabled inexpensive production, so most were resolutely amateurish, yet not all zines were totally unknown. A few novice publishers began niche periodicals that addressed emerging new subcultures and, being first, they garnered sizeable audiences. The most popular of these zines both covered and defined punk, the cultural movement that poster designer Art Chantry called "a late 20th century aesthetic, political, social and philosophical revolution against status quo positions of reigning norms, a reactionary movement defined by nihilism, anarchy and a quasi-religious devotion to the concept of 'D.I.Y. as the solution to all problems on all levels—private as well as public.'" ■■■■■■■■ Under the punk umbrella D.I.Y. ran from the totally artless, such as *Sniffin Glue*, which was produced with Magic Marker–scrawled lettering, photocopied, and stapled together to raw but professional-looking tabloids, including *Slash*, *Search and Destroy*, and *The Rocker*. Punk zines represented the "Anybody can do it!" school of art and design. Torn-paper edges and misspelled typewriter typography were the visual equivalent of loud out-of-tune punk music or vomit-stained thriftstore duds. Eventually, punk became a full-bodied commercial style, but before that the magazine that gave the movement its

0
4
1

PUNK

name, *Punk*, entered uncharted territory when it premiered in New York in 1976. *Punk*'s cofounder and designer, John Holmstrom, said the magazine used the word "punk," which denoted petty thugs and jailhouse paramours, to distinguish its music from syrupy pseudo-psychedelic hippie pop of the post–Sergeant Pepper era. ▆▆▆▆▆ Because he couldn't afford professional typesetting, Holmstrom hand-lettered the entire contents of *Punk*, from its logo to captions, in a comic-book style. Although he proudly called it "crummy-looking," *Punk* did not sacrifice legibility for style, and used "a lot of straight lines in layouts" to make the lettering "look orderly." One issue featuring Holmstrom's own crosshatched, comic drawing of Lou Reed as Frankenstein on the cover established the magazine's bawdy, in-your-face illustration style, a cross between comic books and old English engravings. The overall design format was as stiff as the brittle white newsprint on which it was printed, yet it retained visual energy that recalled Futurism and Dada. ▆▆▆▆▆ Strands of Futurist DNA were present in many of the D.I.Y. periodicals, notably the San Francisco–based *Search and Destroy: New Wave Cultural Research* (it eventually evolved into *RE:Search*), edited by V. Vale from 1977 to 1979, which reveled in total disregard for design tenets. Its pages, composed with an IBM Selectric typewriter, looked similar to broadsheets posted on lampposts raving about government conspiracies. But at the

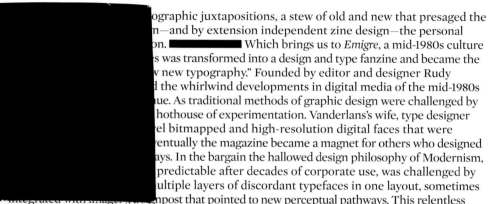

...ographic juxtapositions, a stew of old and new that presaged the ...n—and by extension independent zine design—the personal ...on. ▌ Which brings us to *Emigre*, a mid-1980s culture ...s was transformed into a design and type fanzine and became the ...w new typography." Founded by editor and designer Rudy ...d the whirlwind developments in digital media of the mid-1980s ...ue. As traditional methods of graphic design were challenged by ... hothouse of experimentation. Vanderlans's wife, type designer ...el bitmapped and high-resolution digital faces that were ...entually the magazine became a magnet for others who designed ...ays. In the bargain the hallowed design philosophy of Modernism, ... predictable after decades of corporate use, was challenged by ...ultiple layers of discordant typefaces in one layout, sometimes ...integrated with imagery, a signpost that pointed to new perceptual pathways. This relentless discordance was somewhat akin to the typography of the late 1890s Victorian era and also echoed Futurist and Dada experiments. ▌ *Emigre* was entirely built on the revolutionary Macintosh and was put through its paces to see how far it would alter design language. It showcased leading proponents and exponents of new digital typography, and Vanderlans's editorial policy was to feature typography that the established magazines overlooked by design or ignorance. More than a *Salon des Réfusés*, it was an outreach to those who refused to follow convention. With this as his self-imposed mandate, Vanderlans did not exercise conventional editorial control over his content but rather published rambling interviews and allowed guest editors from hothouse art schools to produce entire issues. *Emigre* encouraged a reevaluation of old methods and aesthetics in the light of a new technological era, and it became a wellspring of progress that provided templates for mimicry. ▌ In design

FETISH

The Magazine of the Material World

Fall 1980

Contexts may differ and themes vary but the overwhelming desire among indie mavens has been to assemble critical masses of unconventional material—and this dates back to the invention of the steam printing press in the early nineteenth century.

WET

OBSESSION

Jul/Aug 1978 $1.50

The history of independent magazines is replete with stories of egotistical editors and designers who have sought their own publishing nirvana. Contexts may differ and themes vary but the overwhelming desire among indie mavens has been to assemble critical masses of unconventional material—and this dates back to the invention of the steam printing press in the early nineteenth century. A sage once said that power belonged to those who owned their own printing press, and independent publishers learned that borrowing or renting a printing press (or copying machine) was just like owning one. Many key indie magazines were launched by those intent on exerting influence on public taste and opinion, and a few were started as personal logs or records by popular authors such as O. Henry (his magazine was the original *Rolling Stone*) and artists like Thomas Nast (Mrs. Grundy). What accounts for this irrepressible passion to publish? Printed publications are tactile and, therefore, authoritative. Holding a freshly printed and tightly bound article while whiffing the scent of its paper and ink and caressing its dull or shiny, smooth pages cannot be equaled. Intimacy is the key. Turning pages is the quintessence of interactivity. It may not allow the reader to click on related links that branch into netherworlds of information, but rather it focuses attention on the word and image at hand (and in hand). During the 1950s and 1960s the legendary art director Alexey Brodovitch described the magazine as a cinematic event where the reader experienced content at self-controlled pace. His mantra, "Astonish Me!," commanded designers to make the magazine a transforming activity—and that legacy continues.

EMIGRE

Since the advent of the personal computer, pundits have routinely forecast the death of print, but such prognostication reveals the limits of crystal ball gazing. Even as mass-market periodicals migrate to the Web, the urge for some to publish on paper has not diminished. The evidence is obvious. New indies are nudging into the realms once dominated by the for-profit magazines that wallpaper news shops. These are not merely eclectic but, like indies from the past, they are alternatives to mainstream culture, art, fashion, lifestyle, and popular culture magazines; and they are not published merely to cater to focused demographics or marketing whims but because their publishers, editors, designers, photographers, and artists are compelled to satisfy their own desires and inspire others.

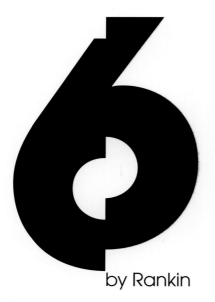

Early Days of *Dazed*

"We wanted to call the magazine 'Did you ever get the feeling you are being cheated?' But it didn't really work on the masthead." —Rankin ■■■■■■ Back in the very, very early days of *Dazed & Confused* magazine, it wasn't even a magazine. We produced it as a folded poster to begin with. Apart from that it was the most economical format we could think of, we liked the idea of keeping it with no cover as such, to represent and create an open forum in which people could come together. Jefferson (Hack) and Ian (Taylor, the magazine's cofounder and first art director) were on a bit of a Led Zeppelin tip at the time, and the track "Dazed & Confused" summed up how we were feeling about everything. Magazines didn't have a clear voice at that time. We thought a lot of writers were becoming too self-important, so we wanted the magazine to be as unmediated as possible. ■■■■■■ We launched in the early 1990s, during a creative explosion in London in terms of photography and writing. It was the height of Ecstasy culture, and there were lots of crossovers between different creative communities. So much was going on in our own backyard, but few magazines were reflecting that. We felt right at the heart of what was happening through the club night we were promoting, but the things that we were into and the buzz we felt weren't being talked about in media culture; that's why we felt we needed to have a go at making a magazine that was relevant to us and the people we knew. The club ran for about a year and a half, and then we got bored with it. At the time we were producing *Dazed* every three months or so—whenever we could, really. ■■■■■■ What set us apart, I think, were Jefferson's and my eye for spotting talent, Jefferson's understanding of culture and what is relevant, my very honest approach to portraiture, and Ian's—and then Matt Roach's—design. We have always had a brilliant fashion team, led first by Katie Grand, then Katy England. We made an impact straight away in terms of how magazines could be run. Shoestring budgets, everyone working for the love of it—it sounds romantic and idealistic now even to us, but it was a great feeling devising radical editorial concepts. And pioneering new avenues of sponsorship (the inverted "alternative front cover," for instance) and novel methods of distribution helped us to establish a firm foothold. ■■■■■■ As well as being driven by pure ambition, we saw it as a way of causing mischief, or, as Bono put it when we were working on the Jubilee 2000 project, "the right kind of mischief"—being a thorn in the side of the establishment and the status quo. The beauty of the magazine in its infancy was that we all worked on it for nothing. There was no money. We all recognized that the magazine was a platform for new ventures, a way of regaining control of our lives. We shared a passion for photography, journalism, design, and emerging youth culture. We wanted to express the thoughts and desires of our generation. Obviously, we were inspired by magazines like *I.D.*, *The Face*, and *Interview* in their heyday, but we were frustrated by their failure to acknowledge what was under their noses. ■■■■■■ We had no money and no experience—just a single telephone line and a single shared computer. But what we lacked in support and resources we

by Rankin

We launched in the early 1990s, during a creative explosion in London in terms of photography and writing. It was the height of Ecstasy culture, and there were lots of crossovers between different creative communities. So much was going on in our own backyard, but few magazines were reflecting that.

The beauty of the magazine in its infancy was that we all worked on it for nothing. There was no money. We all recognized that the magazine was a platform for new ventures, a way of regaining control of our lives.

made up for with a shared vision. We were beginning our journey as publishers; Jefferson was starting off as a writer and editor, and I was beginning my career as a photographer. It was a symbiotic relationship, one that both of us thought probably wouldn't last much longer than a couple of years. We were young, naïve, and having as much fun as possible, but we were also dedicated to making *Dazed & Confused* the best magazine it could be. We were ambitious, arrogant, and idealistic about the content and the way we were putting it out as a magazine. We didn't know if we had enough good ideas to keep it consistently interesting for people or if Jeff and I and the people around us would change. As we learned on the job, we became more confident to up the ante, and determined to work harder and faster and take more risks to make it work. We were very DIY, very punk, or as Jeff puts it, "very cowboy." He means our pioneering spirit, I think. ▮▮▮▮ We sometimes say how lucky we've been to have the opportunity to do what we've done, but then I think about it and, really, there was very little luck involved. We worked extremely hard to invent fresh ways of telling a story and capturing an image, and to be blunt about finding new ways to get the money to put it all in print. We had great ideas and were very good at getting them realized. Our only truly unmitigated disasters both happened when we handed over control to people who wanted to make TV documentaries, but we were young and obnoxious and arrogant and felt we needed exposure. The reality soon hit home, though—it was as if we'd been invaded. I still shudder with embarrassment to think of them. ▮▮▮▮▮ Looking back at old issues, I love that we did get it so right so much of the time. I'm thinking of the careers of some of our contributors, like Nick Knight, Alexander McQueen, and Jake and Dinos Chapman—they all skyrocketed. We broke the style magazine mold with our art and literature coverage. Some of our more social and political themed issues, though, really stand out the most for all of us. And our madcap off-the-page ventures—a week-long live magazine in an old tramshed, Renegade TV, our television "hijack," was us taking a Situationist stab at programming a very *Dazed* line-up of talent. When we asked Channel 4 for a weekend of airtime, a night, then five hours? It ended up being more like two hours. Some of it was great and some of it was not so great, but we had total control. There was no one saying no—we liked that. It laid the foundations for the beginning of a new direction for my interests, in film and television.

More on the Stylepress

"If you want to make a magazine, there are two solutions: Either you create the product the market expects, or you make the magazine that you believe needs to be made, for you and you only." This is how a shrewd friend answered when I told him about a magazine idea, and it still seems valid today as a way to evaluate an editorial project. ▬▬▬ The stylepress answers an imperious need to publish something (fanzine, magazine, journal, etc.), and it remains very dependent on the creator's whims, at a graphic, photographic, and content level. It is therefore generally the result of an individual initiative, independent from the market's rules. As such, we mostly find in it "overinvested" categories compared to the potential readership: illustration, graphic design, or the fashion/art pair. This inadequacy with respect to the market has also produced something else: the de facto creation of a distribution network that runs parallel to traditional magazine newsstands. One finds today, in most large cities, concept stores—museums or boutiques that develop a space for these kinds of publications. ▬▬▬ Actually, it is difficult to arrive at a definition, as the stylepress seems mostly to take pleasure in toying with the rules; but let us try to sketch a radical portrait. The stylepress has an elastic conception of periodicity; it rarely employs professional journalists; it knows the best creative directors (the envy of mainstream magazines and advertising agencies); it unearths young photographers who will in some cases become rich and famous; it is always one innovation ahead, whether it be on the subject matter, angles, rhythms, physicality (book, loose sheets, jacket, format, etc.); and it is only found in a few chosen places, therefore it is "trendy." ▬▬▬ If we were philosophers, we would seek to dismantle the cause-and-effect mechanism, and we would question the reasons for the appearance of these magazines. I will not expound on the accessibility and portability of computer ware (hard and soft), nor the digitalization of photographs and the disappearance of film at the printers. I believe that the true cause lies elsewhere: In the first place, mass-market periodicals are unsatisfactory, too often functioning like a communications relay for the political and economic or industrial authority. This inevitably leads to individual initiatives. But most of all, the know-how inherent in the making of a magazine needs a "showcase." A creative director must be able to show his or her more creative work, develop a laboratory space, and solicit future clients with a more creative and artistic approach rather than mere job execution. The same applies to authors, photographers, and editors. Consequently, all this beau monde plays and is paid with something other than money. ▬▬▬ Let us be clear: The best magazines, the most daring, and the most inventive are built by creative directors and editors who often draw nothing but esteem—and some side contracts. These magazines, which are often expensive, sell few copies but do so in high-end stores throughout the world. Their financial equilibrium generally relies on the support of a few luxury (Dior Homme, Hermès), denim (Levi's, Diesel), or sport (Adidas, Nike, Puma) brands. To the beat of world economic enthusiasms or tensions, these magazines develop or disappear. During the last few years, we have certainly lost many, but this movement does not break down, because we always need to see new photographers, new creators, and new prototypes. And, as with many things, the general public is mostly unaware of them, reserving these small jewels for the connoisseurs.

by Angelo Cirimele

Mass-market periodicals are unsatisfactory, too often functioning like a communications relay for the political and economic or industrial authority. This inevitably leads to individual initiatives.

"If you want to make a magazine, there are two solutions: Either you create the product the market expects, or you make the magazine that you believe needs to be made, for you and you only."

PHYSICALITY

The architecturally enclosed *VOLUME* and *PetitGlam*; the wooden gun-shot wounded *nice magazine*; the spray-painted *WERK*; the gargantuan *kilimanjaro* and *V*; the Lilliputian *LA CiNCA i.A.* and *commons & sense*; the *De Avontuur Bevat* card; the book-like *MADE* and *ROSEBUD*; the hand-stacked boxes of *ASIAN PUNK BOY* and *NORTH DRIVE PRESS*; the uncut and uncovered bulk of *MINED* and *MARK*; the bubble-wrapped *GUM*; the portfolio of *JE T'AIME TANT*; the *IS NOT* wild poster. / / These periodical objects, and they are magazines, physically test the boundaries established by the traditional printed press. They invest in the third dimension, too often ignored by the mass-market that is a simple function of advertising page count. The stylepress, whether flagrantly, as in the titles above, or as a class, typically make a statement with their chosen size, paper texture and quality, printing process, and packaging.

Why does the magazine experience have to be confined to "flipping" through pages?

N°

AUGUST 2001. #1. $ € 5 BEF 385 CHF 19.80

166

118   **64**

12
Desiree Heiss gives her interpretation of
the Winter 2001-2002 collections
from the first generation of Belgian designers.
Photography by Bettina Komenda

28
by Suzy Menkes

32
A decade of Dirk Van Saene's collections, remixed for today.
Photography by Ronald Stoops

44
by Alix Browne

48
A personal view of artist Chris Brodahl
on the Winter 2001-2002 collections.
Photography by Raymond Jacquemyns

62
by Angelique Westerhof

64
On 5 huge posters Inge Grognard gives
her personal vision on contemporary make-up.
Photography by Ronald Stoops

74
An homage to Hannelore Knuts, featuring
the Winter 2001-2002 collection of Junya Watanabe.
Photography by Jean-Pierre Khazem

84
Five favourite fashion moments, chosen by Dirk Van Saene,
illustrated by Madeleine Wermenbol

92
Flemish interior revisited. Photography by Bert Houbrechts and Kurt De Wit

102
by Takeji Hirakawa

104
Chris Brodahl 'breathes' the latest Haute Couture collections
in her own environment. Photography by Dirk Van Saene

118
Highlights of a new generation of designers.
Styling by Haidee Findlay Levin, photography by Anushka Blommers & Niels Schumm

130
by Peter De Potter

134
Bernhard Willhelm's collection drawn by Emmanuelle Mafille

146
by Elisabeth Paillié

148
Add or deduct! Photography by Bert Houbrechts and Kurt de Wit

160
by Angelique Westerhof. Photography by Elisabeth Broekaert

166
Revolution! Walter Van Beirendonck's Winter 2001-2002 collection.
Photography by Elisabeth Broekaert

A
ISSUE 1 /NETHERLANDS/9x11.6 in (229x295 mm)
A DIFFERENT PERSONALITY CREATES EVERY ISSUE CHANGING
THE FORMAT, DESIGN, AND CONTENT.

CRITIC EYE
ISSUE 1/ UNITED STATES/ 12.3x16 in (312x406 mm)
"EVERYONE HAS AN OPINION, WHETHER TEXTUAL OR VISUAL"

CRITIC

First Issue US$3

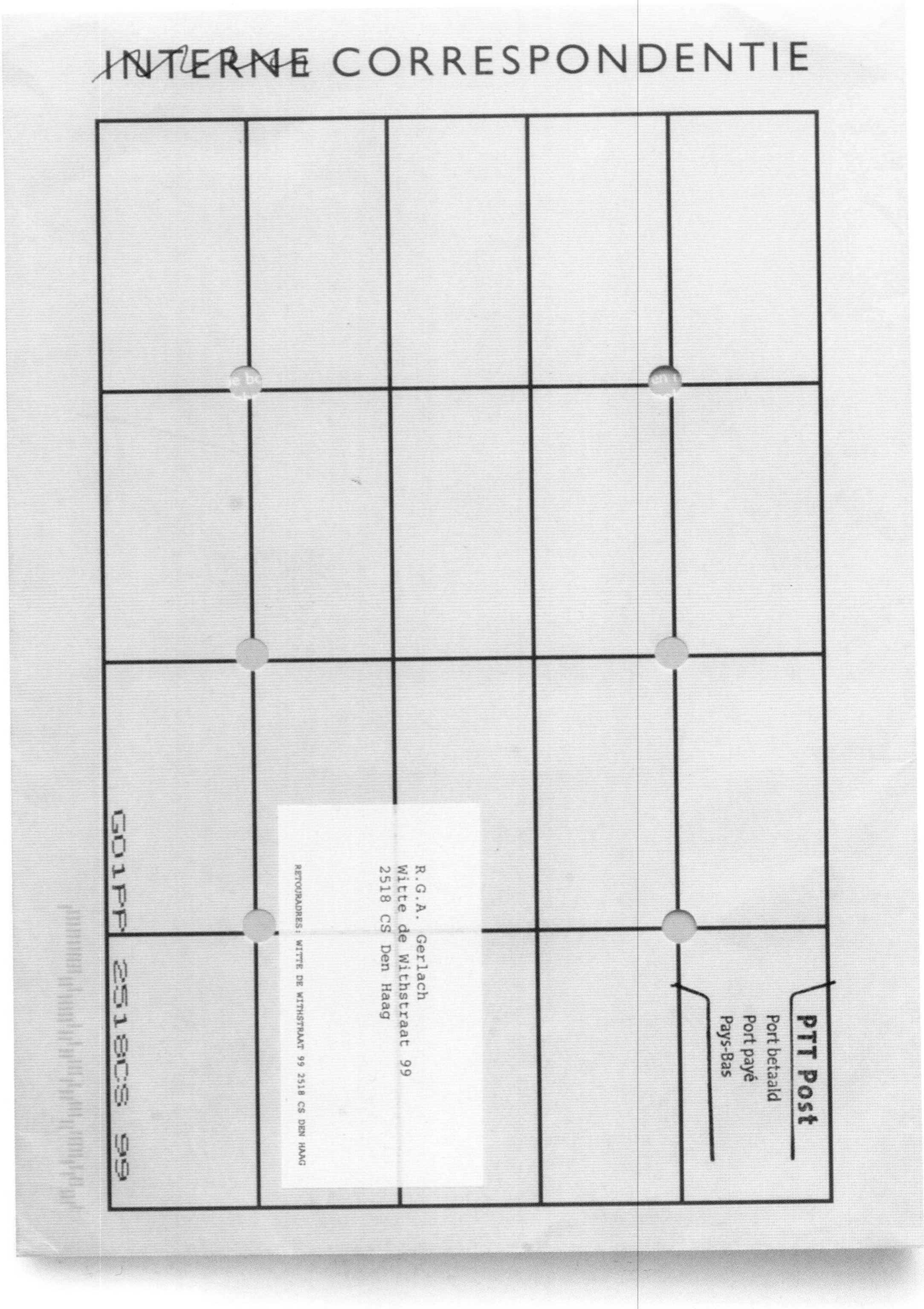

~~INTERNE~~ CORRESPONDENTIE

G01PP 2518CS 99

R.G.A. Gerlach
Witte de Withstraat 99
2518 CS Den Haag

RETOURADRES: WITTE DE WITHSTRAAT 99 2518 CS DEN HAAG

PTT Post
Port betaald
Port payé
Pays-Bas

INTERNE CORRESPONDENTIE

PTT Post
Port betaald
Port payé
Pays-Bas

R.G.A. Gerlach
Witte de Withstraat 99
2518 CS Den Haag

RETOURADRES: WITTE DE WITHSTRAAT 99 2518 CS DEN HAAG

G01PP 2518CS 99

DE AVONTUUR BEVAT
IN BIBLIOTHEEKBOEKEN ACHTERGELATEN BLADWIJZERS

Het fototijdschrift verschijnt vanaf 16 oktober eens in de twee weken. Dit is het eerste nummer, er volgen nog tien, in totaal komen er dus elf nummers uit. De nummers zijn niet los verkrijgbaar; het tijdschrift is alleen voor abonnees. Abonnees worden kan door het insturen van de antwoordkaart, maar ook per e-mail of telefoon. Het abonnement kost € 16,50 en gaat pas in wanneer het abonnementsgeld is ontvangen op gironummer 6126610 ten name van gebr genk, den haag. Draai niet wanneer u ook de volgende afleveringen van de avontuur bevat wilt ontvangen, want dan kan het tweede nummer volgens plan op 16 oktober verschijnen.

met dank aan de openbare bibliotheek den haag, stroom hcbk en de xx multiple galerie

ANTWOORDKAART

ja, ik word abonnee

naam

adres

postcode

woonplaats

☐ stuur mij een bewijs van betaling

GEBR. GENK. UITGEVERS
WITTE DE WITHSTRAAT 99
2518 CS DEN HAAG (NL)

EXES

PHOTOGRAPHERS IN EXCELSUS

Helmut NEWTON Guy ARONDELLE VERA Bob BARNERT Luis SANCHIS
Ihl WENDEL Gustaf SCHOKKENS Thiemo SANDER
Malte PARIS Guy BOURDIN

EXES
ISSUE 1/ITALY/11.8x15.75 in (300x400 mm)
LARGE FORMAT HANDCRAFTED FASHION
PHOTOGRAPHY MAGAZINE WITH MULTIPLE COVER
LAYERS AND PHOTO SENSITIVE INK

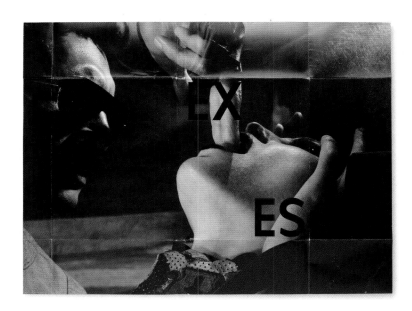

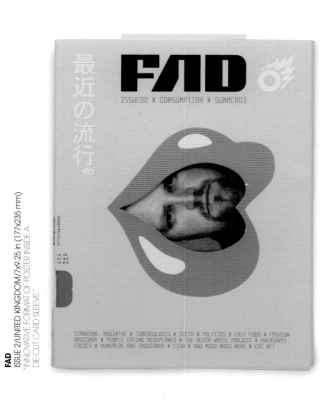

FAD
ISSUE 2/UNITED KINGDOM/7x9.25 in (177x235 mm)
"INNOVATIVE FORMAT OF POSTER INSIDE A
DIE-CUT CARD SLEEVE"

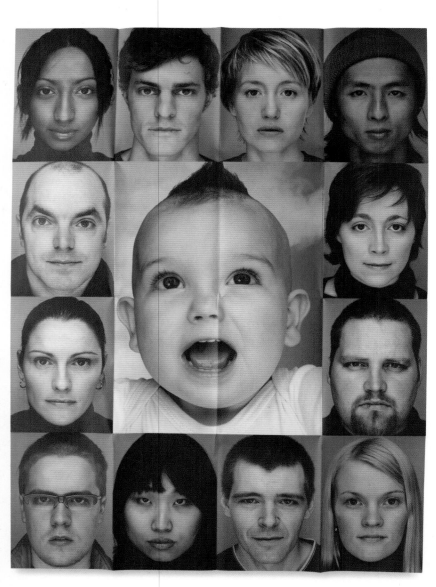

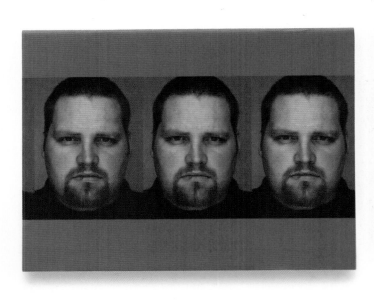

FT

PURE FASHION

FAIRY TALE
ISSUE 6/FRANCE/9×13 in (230×330 mm)
"A CONTEMPORARY FASHION, ART
AND PHOTOGRAPHY MAGAZINE"

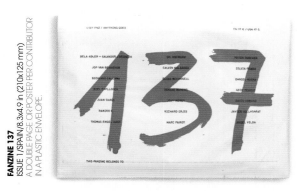

FANZINE 137
ISSUE 1 / SPAIN / 8.3x4.9 in (210x125 mm)
A DOUBLE PAGE OR POSTER PER CONTRIBUTOR
IN A PLASTIC ENVELOPE.

0
6
8

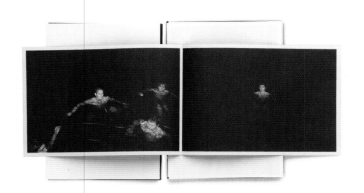

JACK SPADE
WARREN STREET
NEW YORK

FIDGET
THIS IS NUMBER
0073
IN A LIMITED
EDITION
JACK SPADE
ZIPPER BAG

ALEXANDER DE CADENET/FENDI
YASMIN LE BON/MARTIN MARGIELA
SOPH./LOUIS VUITTON/HERMES
REM KOOLHAAS/SKATEBOARDERS
COMME DES GARÇONS/TRUSSARDI
JONATHAN AITKEN/GIVENCHY/ORFI
INDIA FASHION/NEPAL CULTURE
SHIBUYA/HELMUT LANG/JAGUAR
PANOPTIC/WK INTERACT/SKINT
BURBERRY/PEOPLE KISSING

1XJACK SPADE BAG/1XFIDGET/1XWK INTERACT
POSTER/1XSOPH. STICKER $8

FIDGET
ISSUE 2/UNITED STATES/9x11.75 in (230x299 mm)
NEW YORK MAGAZINE SOLD IN A CANVAS-TYPE
BAG. ONE OF THE CONTAINER CHANGES
UNDERGONE WITH EACH ISSUE.

0
7
0

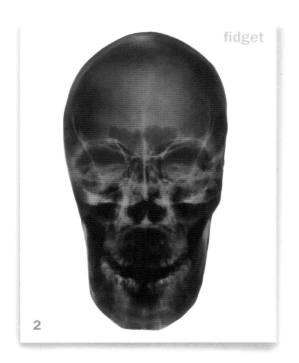

fidget

2

nuf said
Girls in Shibuya. Photography by Reggie Casagrande

Final Home
Photography by Jennifer Tzar

GUM
ISSUE 1 / UNITED STATES / 5x7 in (129x180 mm)
"INCLUDES A BOOK, A COMIC BOOK, POP CARDS,
A SHEET OF STICKERS, AND A SLAB OF OLD-SCHOOL GUM.
ALL MYLAR-WRAPPED FOR YOUR PROTECTION!"

HÉLÈNE

3,60 euros

JOURNAL DU PRINTEMPS 2003
PARAIT CHAQUE SAISON

Numéro 1

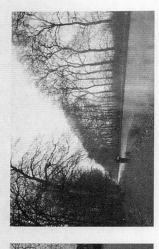

NEVERS, LE CANAL LATÉRAL À LA LOIRE, LA SECTION ENTRE "LA JONCTION" ET "LE PEUPLIER SEUL". C'EST LÀ, ENTRE UNE DOUBLE ALLÉE D'ARBRES, QUE LE 1ER MAI 1993 PIERRE BÉRÉGOVOY S'EST SUICIDÉ. (LILA HELLER, DÉCEMBRE 2002)

EDITORIAL. C'est le printemps et on s'en étonne presque. Dans une période de telle régression, on pourrait imaginer que la nature fasse machine arrière, que les arbres restent nus, éternellement dans l'hiver. Mais ils sont déjà verts, bientôt en fleurs. Malgré ceux qui s'évertuent à nous faire croire qu'il n'y a plus d'autre chemin. Malà nous enlever tout espoir de changement, à coups de lois, de sondages et d'expertises. Là où l'électorat se confond avec le lectorat.

A Rio de Janeiro où nous sommes allés pour ce numéro, c'est l'automne et un peuple espère. Avec lui, ceux qui pensent qu'une autre politique est possible. Au Brésil, en 1968, pendant qu'ici nous faisions une révolution, la dictature sévissait, laissant à certains l'exil comme seule solution. Aujourd'hui, dans une France désespérante, sans autre projet que celui de réprimer, allons-nous laisser faire et donner raison au ministre de l'intérieur, qui pense qu'en laissant les artistes libres comme le vent, il est aussi libre d'organiser sa politique criminelle. Allons-nous aussi donner raison à ce prisonnier de la centrale d'Arles qui écrit sur internet "Mais qui aujourd'hui se préoccupe des conditions de vie et de mort de quelques misérables ?" Car enfin, le dernier combat n'a pas eu lieu. Et il ne prendra sûrement pas la forme d'une manifestation, devenue simple surface de bonne conscience. Depuis quand la lutte se fait sans sacrifice, sans heurt et sans joie ?_ Elein Fleiss

INTERNATIONAL, *Simuler la guerre et la faire en même temps* par Tiphaine Samoyault, p. 2. **EUROPE**, *Géopolitique fictions* par Alain Lacroix, p. 3. **CHRONIQUE**, *Journal-Roman ?* par Dominique Gonzalez-Foerster, p. 2. **15 MINI-TEXTES**, p. 4. **STRATÉGIE**, *Prolégomènes à une guerre* par Jordi Vidal, p. 6. **CHRONIQUE**, *Révolution* par Marylène Negro, p. 6. **ÉTATS-UNIS**, *J'ai changé de pays si vite* par Cora Maghnaoui, p. 7. **CHRONIQUE**, *Biarritz* par Gérard Duguet-Grasser, p. 8. **TÉMOIGNAGE**, *Right?* par Laurent Brondel, p. 9. **SPECTACLE**, *Pourquoi j'aime le cirque* par Arnaud Viviant, p. 8. **TERRITOIRES OCCUPÉS**, *Entretien avec Herman Asselberghs* par Manon de Boer, p. 10. **CHINE**, *Avant de noyer le dragon* par Ruben Dao, p. 11. **8 PHOTOGRAPHIES**, p. 12. **ENQUÊTE**, *Des artistes et la politique*, p. 14. **RÉCIT**, *Être enceinte* par Nakako Hayashi, p. 15.

MESSAGE, *Adieu* par Michel Butel, p. 15. **CHRONIQUE**, *Lettre de Miami* par Bruce Benderson, p. 16. **SEXE**, *Rencontre rose* par Emmanuelle Mafille, p. 16. **FRANCE**, *Le bar de la plage* par Claude Lévêque, p. 25. **SOCIÉTÉ**, *Voile...* par Eve Couturier, p. 26. **CHRONIQUE**, *Zhong Shui Jiao* par Gil Gonzalez-Foerster, p. 26. **CUISINE**, *Les spaghetti de minuit* par Gérard Duguet-Grasser, p. 27. **CAPITALISME**, *Entretien avec Norbert Trenkle du groupe Krisis* par Olivier Zahm, p. 27. **LITTÉRATURE**, *Proust et le rat* par Nick Tosches, p. 30. **ÉTATS-UNIS**, *Viva Las Vegas* par Jeff Rian, p. 31. **8 PAGES SPÉCIAL RIO DE JANEIRO**, p. 17. Textes par Elein Fleiss, Dora Herzog, Olivier Zahm. Entretiens : Eryk Rocha par Federico Nicolao, Ferreira Gullar par Lila Heller.

SHAPESHIFTER
RESIN DOGS
KORA

24TH april

THE PALACE

Over 1

TICK
ON SA

Phone: Ticke
Online: www.tie
Polyester Records

LEEJEANS.C

Hardware Corporation, Loaded Entertainment.
KillRockstar and inthemix.com.au present...

DIGITAL
FESTIVAL

SLAM	**KAI TRACID**
SCRATCH PERVERTS	**THE HACKER**
NU NRG	**DAVID CARRETTA**
JAMES CURD	**ANNE SAVAGE**
FREEFORM FIVE	**PROTEUS**
GREENSKEEPERS	

Plus Melbourne's finest
over 5 arenas

**AY
APR**

ANDS

LOVE

Is Not Magazine

PREFACE **LOVE IS**

Under
ware

LOOP

Letters

SIBLING INCEST: P
who gives a fuck?

Eat (me) *Out.*

The Lawyer

So, here's the deal:

WHEN GOOD PLANS
Turn Ugly

 W

CADS!
WOMANISERS!
LOVERATS!

*Fredrik
Finds a
Dead Body*

 T

Newalbum 'Two Shoes' instore April 17

IS NOT
ISSUE 1 / AUSTRALIA / 78.75x59 in (2000x1500 mm)
'APPROACH IT FROM ANY ANGLE; LEAN IN FOR A CLOSER LOOK; EMBARK ON A
TREASURE HUNT TO FIND A STORY THAT ENDS IN ANOTHER LOCATION'

JE T'AIME TANT
ISSUE 1/FRANCE/11.65x8.45 in (296x215 mm)

"A COLLECTION OF IMAGES THAT TAKES THE FORM
OF A LITTLE EXPOSITION, WHICH EVERYONE CAN REARRANGE
TO MAKE THEIR OWN."

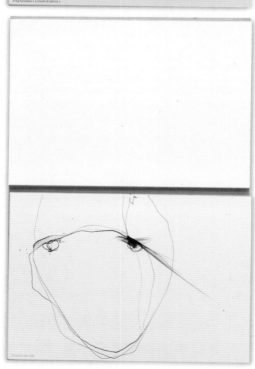

JE T'AIME TANT

photographs & illustrations - n°1 - 2005 december

AUTHORS

Xavier BOI

Jenny BROWN

Marion FERNANDEZ

Fuji FURUSAWA

Michael HOLLAND

Roberta LP

Katsuto MAKO

Laura OAKDEN

Catherine POLI

Benoît VIAL

WWW.JETAIMETANT.COM

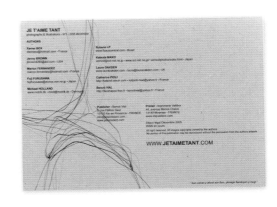

K48
ISSUE 1 / UNITED STATES / 4.85x5.75 in (123x146 mm)
"A KURATORIAL-KOLLABORATIVE TIME CAPSULE OF ART, MUSIC,
FASHION, HEROES, AND GRAPHIC RADDNESS
LOOSELY FOCUSED AROUND AN IDEA."

Kilimanjaro
ISSUE 1 / UNITED KINGDOM / 18.90x26.55 in (480x675 mm)
AN OVERSIZE "PRINTED SPACE DEDICATED TO VISUAL
CULTURE AND EDITORIAL EXPERIMENTATION."

LA CINCA i.A.
ISSUE 1/NETHERLANDS/4.55x6.50 in (116x165 mm)
VERY SMALL MAGAZINE ART PROJECT

IT looks good on YOU

RICHARD KIDD

MAKIN' MISTAKES ALL OVER THE PLACE

Trading Here for

Ghos

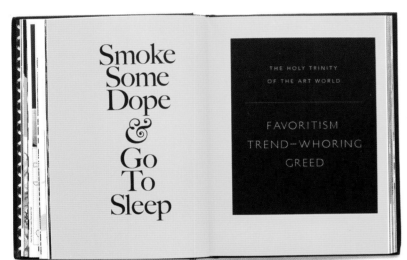

Smoke Some Dope & Go To Sleep

THE HOLY TRINITY OF THE ART WORLD

FAVORITISM
TREND-WHORING
GREED

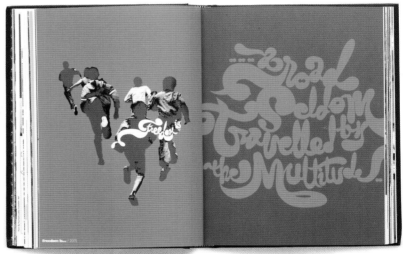

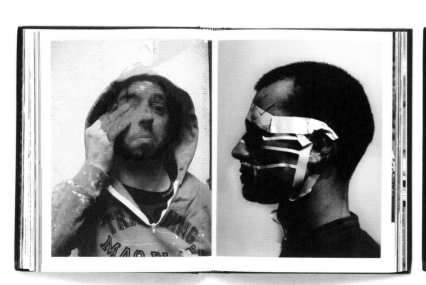

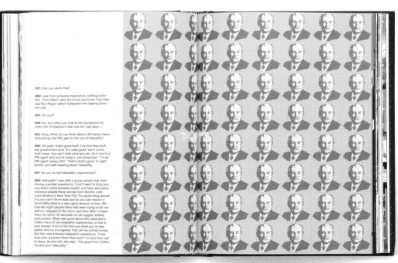

MARK
ISSUE 3 / AUSTRALIA / 8.25×11 in (210×280 mm)
STENCIL-WRAPPED PULP MAGAZINE

MCSWEENEY'S
ISSUE 16/UNITED STATES/8.95x5.9 in (227x150 mm)
"A JOURNAL CREATED BY NERVOUS PEOPLE
IN RELATIVE OBSCURITY"

nice magazine
ISSUE 1/UNITED KINGDOM/9x11.75 in (229x298 mm)
"A DISRUPTIVE MEDIA FORM THAT PLAYS WITH ART, FASHION, AND PROPAGANDA"
A WOODEN MAGAZINE WITH SPENT SHOTGUN CASING.

NORTH DRIVE PRESS
ISSUE 2/UNITED STATES/9.25x13.2 in (235x335 mm)
"UNCONVENTIONAL ARTISTS' PERIODICAL INCLUDING MULTIPLES, INTERVIEWS,
AND TEXTS BY ARTISTS AND WRITERS"

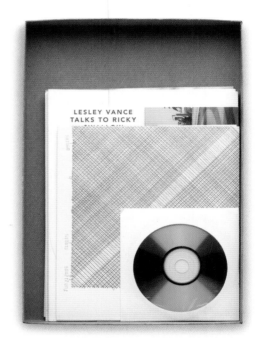

PetitGlam
ISSUE 4/JAPAN/7x5 in (180x130 mm)
SMALL BUNDLE OF EQUALLY SMALL ARTIST BOOKS
IN A PLASTIC SLEEVE

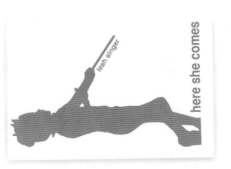

Das ist der Text für ein Buchcover. Vorerst steht hier noch ein beliebiger und nichtssagender Text. Ein Text der in der richtigen grafischen Aufbereitung ausschliesslich dazu dient, den Titel dieses Buches aussagekräftig zu machen. Selbstverständlich ist die hier abgebildete Zeichenkette nur dazu geeignet, einen allgemeinen visuellen Eindruck zu vermitteln. Der tatsächliche Inhalt ist in diesem Moment noch völlig nebensächlich. Der Betrachter soll den Text ja gar nicht lesen um nicht von der äusseren Form abgelenkt zu werden. Dieser Text wird in dieser Form natürlich nie in Druck gehen. Später wird er allerdings sehr ausführlich über das Thema und die Inhalte dieses Buches informieren. Vorerst kommt ihm jedoch nur eine reine Platzhalterfunktion zu, obgleich Schriftart, Schriftgrösse, Zeilenabstand und Laufweite bereits einen verbindlichen Eindruck über das Erscheinungsbild vermitteln sollen. Nur so kann das Cover unter rein formalen Gesichtspunkten objektiv beurteilt werden. Dies ist insbesondere bei einem Designbuch von großer Bedeutung, da hier der Gestaltung des Titels eine wichtige Rolle bei der Kaufentscheidung zukommt. This text is for the cover of a book. At the moment, it is just random meaningless text. It is text that serves to emphasize the title of this publication by being placed in its formal graphical context. Of course the chain of symbols depicted here is only employed to convey a visual impression. The actual contents are totally irrelevant at the moment. The reader isn't even supposed to read the text to insure that it doesn't distract him from the form. Of course this text will never go into print in this version. However, later it will offer very detailed information on the subject and on the contents of the book, though at the moment it is only a placeholder. However, the type of font, font size, spacing and kerning give us a reliable impression of what the books' look and feel will be like. This is the only way the cover can be judged on a purely formal level. The design of the cover is of decisive importance when deciding to buy a book, especially in the case of a design publication.

ROSEBUD
ISSUE 3 / AUSTRIA / 6.7 x 9.65 in (170x245 mm)
"OPERATED WITH THE DESIRE TO EXPLORE AND EXHAUST
THE POSSIBILITIES AND POTENTIALS THAT PAPER AND 2-D STRUCTURE
HAVE TO OFFER"

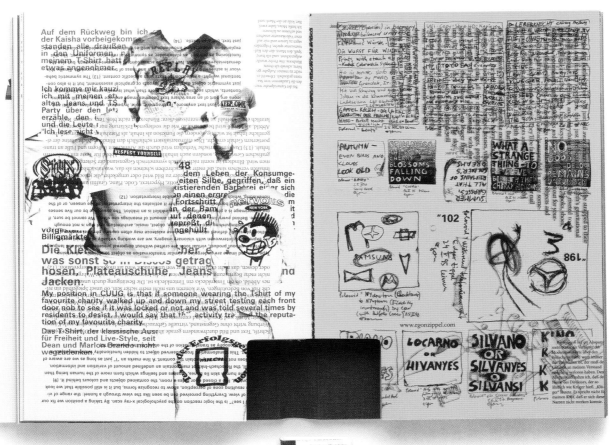

My position in CUUG is that if someone wearing the T-shirt of my favourite charity walked up and down my street testing each front door nob to see if it was locked or not and was told several times by residents to desist, I would say that this activity tarnished the reputation of my favourite charity.

Images of the Moment

An instant photo, ready in just a few seconds. Egon Zippel only needs a pen where others require a cumbersome camera. He takes notes with quick sketches, each labeled with the date and location, these drawings record ideas, characteristics and ideas for pictures. He molds what his senses take in into his stern Polaroid format, creating his personal artistic universe. He has already penned thousands of these images that describe fleeting, irretrievable moments. On there own terms, these pictures have been starting points for other pieces and as a collection, they speak volumes.

NEVER FORGET THAT THE HUMAN RACE WITH TECHNOLOGY IS JUST LIKE AN ALCOHOLIC WITH A BARREL OF WINE

Polaroid & "THE UNABOMBER MANIFESTO" (Chapter 203) NYC 4I98 Egon

---

Das Panzerhaus

Hugo Feinbartel

Ich kann wirklich willkommen aufreden sein! Erst letzte Woche gewann ich den Grand Prix von Monaco und erhielt den Nobelpreis für angewandtes Glücklichsein. Ich besitze eine Zwanzig-Meter-Yacht und mehrere Häuser und Penthousewohnungen und alles andere was ich mir nur vorstellen kann. Ich habe den sex meines Lebens, bin ausgeglichen und kreativ und verreise wohin ich will.

The tank-house

Hugo Feinbartel

I can be completely content! Only last week I won the Grand Prix of Monaco and received the Nobel-prize for applied happiness. I own a 65-feet yacht, quite a few houses and penthouses and everything I can imagine. I have the sex of my life, am balanced and creative and travel where ever I want to.

"113

SHERBERT MAGAZINE
NUMBER 5
THE CHILDHOOD ISSUE

THIS PACK CONTAINS:
- 1 magazine
- 1 coloring book
- 1 CD
- 3 pixy stixs

722 | 800

SHERBERT
ISSUE 1 / UNITED STATES / 7 x 8.5 in (178 x 216 mm)
"BASED ON A LOOSE THEME AND FEATURES EMERGING TALENT IN
THE FIELDS OF ILLUSTRATION, PHOTOGRAPHY, DESIGN, LITERATURE."

stereo
ISSUE 1 /NETHERLANDS/6.3x10.65 in (160x270 mm)
THE TITLE 'REFERS TO THE INTERDISCIPLINARY
NATURE' OF THE PUBLICATION.

Un Paquet de Schismes
ISSUE 1/FRANCE/7x9 in (178x230 mm)
ARTIST BOX, FEATURING INDEPENDENT PROJECTS.
"TERRAIN D'ÉCHANGE."

099

V
ISSUE 1/UNITED STATES/8.45x12 in (215x305 mm)
"IMAGINE A WALL OF FORTY-FOUR TELEVISIONS,
EACH TURNED TO A DIFFERENT STATION."

V MAGAZINE

SEPT/OCT 1999

1

V MAGAZINE

PREMIERE ISSUE

SEPT/OCT 1999

1

VOLUME
ISSUE 1/NETHERLANDS/8.25x11.75 in (209x298 mm)
GOES BEYOND JUST ARCHITECTURE, "PROVOKING DEBATE,
AND OFFERING SITUATIONS, SCENARIOS, SOLUTIONS,
AND TRAJECTORIES."

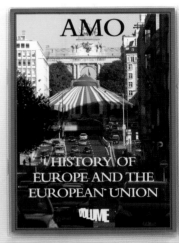

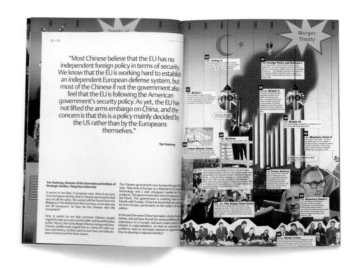

WERK
ISSUE 12/SINGAPORE/8.85x12.45 in (225x317 mm)
"COVERS SPRAY-PAINTED WITH FLUORESCENT PAINT"
A "CREATIVE COLLECTIVE EFFORT"

Tank Razi Razak
top: tricot
COMME des GARÇONS
Hendrix badge, hat &
sunglasses: model's own

DE$IGN

1553

032c

1ST ISSUE "PROFESSIONALISM", BERLIN WINTER 2000/2001
€ 4   www.032c.com

032c
ISSUE 1 / GERMANY / 9.45x12.40 in (240x315 mm)
'VISUAL CULTURE MAGAZINE AT THE INTERSECTIONS
OF FASHION, ART AND POLITICS. FINDING THE NEW
IN THE OLD AND THE OLD IN THE NEW'

24 **David Lindemann** creative partner at Fork, Hamburg/Berlin   25

seriously.

Ad!dict
ISSUE 24/BELGIUM/9.61x11.81 in (244x300 mm)
"PLATFORM FOR CREATIVES IN CROSSOVER PROJECTS."

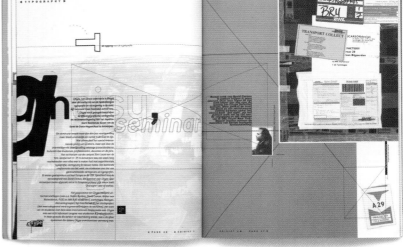

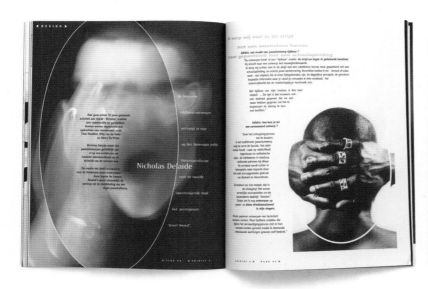

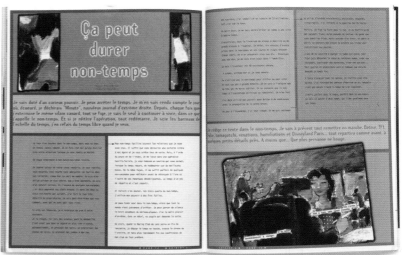

1
0
9

Anathema
ISSUE 1/UNITED STATES/6.02x9.02 in (153x229 mm)
"A SMALL ARTS PUBLICATION DEDICATED TO THE PURSUIT
OF UNACCEPTABLE IDEAS"

PREMIERE ISSUE, BI-ANNUAL AUTUMN/WINTER 2001 US$ 14.99 C$ 15.95

COVER PHOTOGRAPHY BY NICK KNIGHT

ANOTHER MA GAZINE

FOR MEN AND WOMEN

The only international fashion magazine for men & women

First issue featuring: **JUDE LAW, KATE HUDSON, MARIANNE FAITHFULL, HELMUT NEWTON, JAKE CHAPMAN, NICK KNIGHT, KIM GORDON, MARILYN MONROE, TERRY GILLIAM, HARMONY KORINE** and more

The best in new fashion photography & literature for people who want more to read

Brought to you by the publishers of Dazed & Confused

ANOTHER MAGAZINE
ISSUE 1/UNITED KINGDOM/9.84x12.52 in (250x318 mm)
"THE LUXURY FASHION BIANNUAL"

MARIANNE

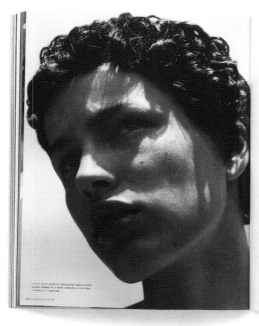

Another Document
Premiere Issue

LETTERS
Readers from another century, and another publication, voice their concerns .... PAGE 2

FEATURE
Malla Factkin ... extend sex symbol and fashion guru, on icon, her old zine and the frantic search for false teeth .... PAGE 3

REFLECTION
Vivienne Miles ... international art dealer, looks within .... PAGE 5

MONOLOGUE
Reverend Paul Bennell ... considers genetic development, rock music and the end of earth as we know it .... PAGE 5

INTERVIEW
Marilles Monroe's aunt and boss, Norman Mailer, calendar pictures and life not without hope .... PAGE 6

FICTION
Hort Kenreve ... if you can't stand noise, why not replace your body with something durable and clean? .... PAGE 8

POSTCARDS
Who are you, where are you? We ask, writers to pop it in the post .... PAGE 11

EXTRACT 1
Virginia Woolf ... reconsiders the very notion of literature and sexuality .... PAGE 12

EXTRACT 2
Humbert Humbert ... Lolita and her scary, Vladimir Nabokov tells us a story .... PAGE 14

REMEMBERANCE
Hubert Selby Jr ... recalls why he started writing .... PAGE 16

DICTIONARY
Gustave Flaubert ... 19th century genius novelist, defines a language .... PAGE 17

PROJECT
Pinny Benner ... London based artist, rewrites scenes from porn film Amsterdam In Wonderland .... PAGE 20

SIX MONTH HORROR SCOPE
Sara Aylett ... explains when the future holds and why you're going to heaven .... PAGE 22

OBITUARY
Harmony Korine

BABY BABY BABY
ISSUE 1/MEXICO/8.66x11.42 in (220x290 mm)
YOUTH CULTURE, ART, AND FASHION MAGAZINE

el tiempo celeste

$40.00 pesos.

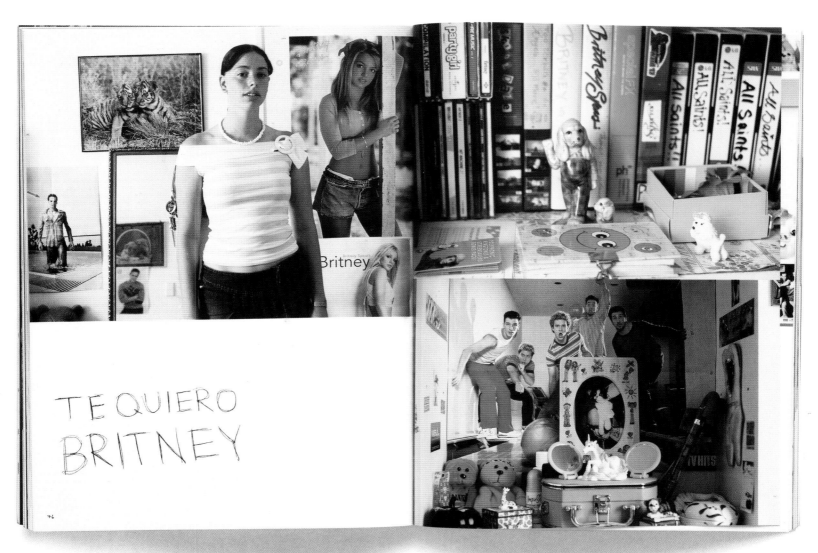

TE QUIERO
BRITNEY

twinkie twins
gemelas twinkie gemelas
twins twins twins
twins twins
twins twins
twins twins twins
twinkle twins
twins twins twins
twins twinkle twins
gemelas twins
twins twins
gemelitas

Fotos : Tony Solis y Adrian Oviedo

BEople

a magazine
about a certain
Belgium

NOV 01 DEC 01 JAN 02

Europe € 9
US $ 8.25
UK £ 5.60
Belgium BEF 363
France FRF 60
Germany DM 18
Spain PTS 1500
Holland NFL 19.83
Switzerland CHF 13.50
Italy L 17 500

01

BEople
ISSUE 1/BELGIUM/9.13x12.01 in (232x305 mm)
"A MAGAZINE ABOUT BELGIAN FASHION,
ART, MUSIC, AND CULTURE".

115

N1berliner

OCTOBER 2002   IT'S AN ATTITUDE

CONSTANT CHANGE STETIGER WANDEL

berliner
ISSUE 1/GERMANY/8.46x12.91 in (215x328 mm)
'A MONOTHEMATIC, TREND AND ART MAGAZINE. OFFERS A
PLATFORM FOR CULTURE, FASHION, POLITICS,
AND URBANITY, WITH A BERLIN ATTITUDE.'

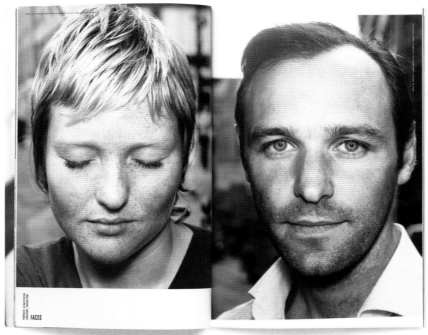

FACES

Drawing on the right side of the Brain

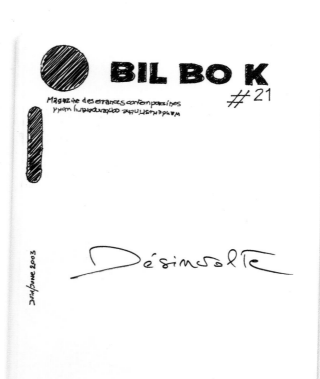

BILBOK
ISSUE 21 / FRANCE / 6.50x9.45 in (165x240 mm)
"WANDERLUST IN THE CONTEMPORARY WORLD"

L'Humaine Comédie

MOROCCO PALACE RESERVEE

THEATRE مسرح

فندق برلين
HOTEL BERLIN

IMPRIMERIE

مطعم هونغ كونغ
RESTAURANT HONGKONG

Achtung

EC 64 Mozart
EuroCity
Wien Westbf -
Linz - Salzburg - München - Stuttgart -
Karlsruhe- Kehl - Strasbourg- Nancy -
Paris (Est)

C'est pour l'imprimeur ↑
qu'il faut écrire! C'est
là qu'on sait qu'un roman
est terminé.

Restaurant YAMATO à Aix-en-
Provence. Sublimes sakés. ↓

D.B. (dans un train entre Turin et Florence)

Je n'aime écrire qu'avec
les pieds nus sur du parquet.

A Cassis, août 2001.
J'essaie d'écrire, mais
avec cette vue?

Fax Weyergans

La désinvolture des années soixante
(Vanessa Redgrave et David Hemmings
dans Blow Up d'Antonioni)

archives Weyergans

Photo : BBK

BULGARIA
ISSUE 2/FINLAND/8.86x10.87 in (225x276 mm)
DESIGN PUBLICATION "THE LATEST IN VISUAL CULTURE"

IVANAH

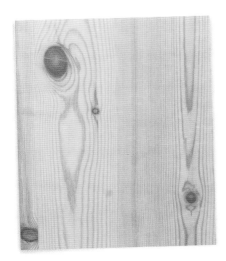

Capricious
by Melanie Bonajo

Capricious
by Michelle Cortez

CAPRICIOUS.
by Justine Kurland

Capricious
by Camille Vivier

CAPRICIOUS
by Ryan McGinley

Capricious
by Vivian Joyner

Capricious
by Miss Liz Wendelbo

capricious.
by Sophie Mörner

CAPRICIOUS
by Louise Enhörning

Capricious
by Hanna Liden

Capricious
by Henrike Stahl

CAPRICIOUS
by Anti Color

CAPRICIOUS
by Ro Agents

Capricious.
by Caitlin Teal Price

ISSN 15733076

9 771573 307001

CAPRICIOUS
ISSUE 1/NETHERLANDS/7.76x10.59 in (197x269 mm)
"SEEKS TO CREATE THE MISSING LINK BETWEEN FASHION
PHOTOGRAPHY AND HIGH ART PHOTOGRAPHY."

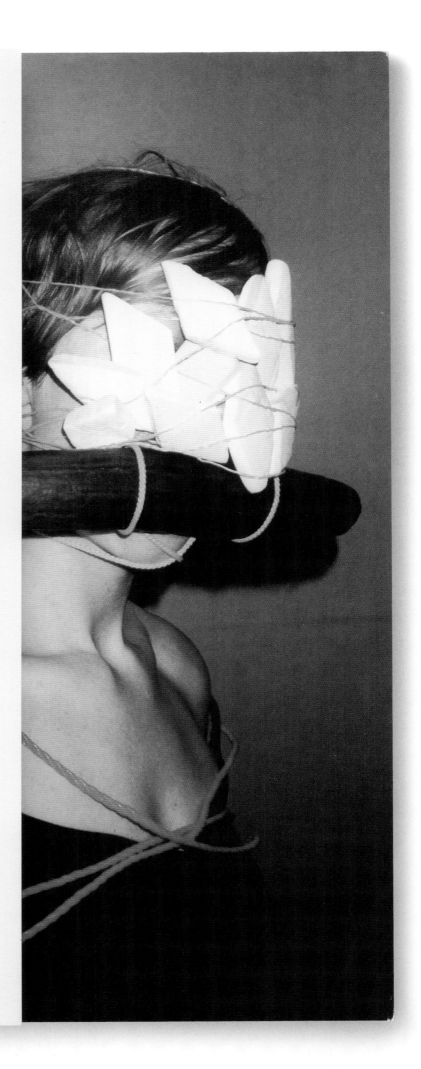

Celeste
ISSUE 15/MEXICO/8.66x11.38 in (220x289 mm)
"DEDICATED TO THE CREATIONS, PERSONALITIES, AND SUBJECTS
THAT OUTLINE THE CONTEMPORARY CULTURE"

clam
ISSUE 4/FRANCE/7.87x10.63 in (200x270 mm)
"TO PROMOTE CREATIVITY, CONCEPTS, AND IDEAS IN FASHION,
ARCHITECTURE, MUSIC, DESIGN, THE ARTS, FREE TIME, TRAVELS,
AND AFRICAN DESIGN . . ."

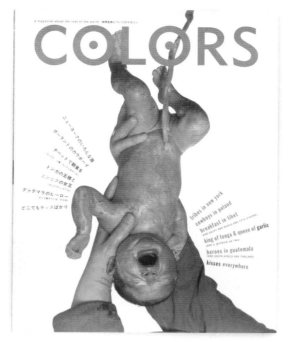

COLORS
ISSUE 1 /ITALY /11.02x13.98 in (280x355 mm)
"THE BENETTON MAGAZINE THAT TALKS
ABOUT THE REST OF THE WORLD"

d(x)i
ISSUE 16/Spain/11.61×16.73 in (295×425 mm)
"A FREE PUBLICATION
THAT OFFERS A COMMITTED VISION TO DESIGN."

d(x)i 16

Pasaporte

¿De qué marca es tu pasaporte?

Hace un par de décadas, cuando uno compraba un producto, lo primero que hacía era fijarse en la etiqueta para averiguar su procedencia de fabricación. Mirar etiqueta > buscar garantía. Operación automática. Y esto era algo se hacía en casi todos los productos fueran coches, zapatos, relojes, juguetes o quién sabe qué. El caso es que más allá de un simple prejuicio. Funcionaba. Así, para ciertas cosas, un "made in USA" no tenía las mismas connotaciones que un "hecho en España", ni mucho menos que un "made in Taiwan" o un "made in Germany".

Hoy es día, poca información puede proporcionarnos el anticuado hipervalorado "made in", puesto que las empresas han sufrido un proceso de "deslocalización", que ha movilizado la producción industrial hacia

países con mano de obra más barata. Y, este fenómeno, está dándose hasta en empresas que producen objetos de lujo (como por ejemplo, las casas de moda).

Ya inmerso en este incomparable marco de la sociedad de consumo, que todo lo extrapola, podría decirse que lo que el signo vigente, desafortunadamente, en el "made in" humano, o sea, el que etiqueta a las personas a través de sus pasaportes, el que las marca y diferencia desde que nacen, haciéndoles pasar libremente por aeropuertos, o como esclavos. Olvidamos, quizás, que el hombre es nómada por naturaleza, que el mundo es de todos, que inmigrante es el ser humano, y que todos tenemos el mismo derecho a buscar una vida mejor.

Equipo d(x)i

DIRECCIÓN EDITORIAL
Amancda Benavent
Silvia Pérez

DIRECCIÓN DE ARTE
Alejandro Escrivá

WEBMASTER
Chelo Soriano

DISTRIBUCIÓN
Imprés Diseño
ten@dxmagazine.com

PUBLICIDAD
Amando Ruiz & Silvia Pérez
Tel. 61 66 64 32 39

ILUSTRACIONES
Werner Sovoby
Javier Altafarla

EDITOR DE MODA

HAN COLABORADO
EN ESTE NÚMERO:
Wilson Guerrero, Alejandro Avila,
Mª José Flores, Pilar Guarnantxia,
Joan Bergarín, David Papagión,
Sergio Ambas, Carmelo Rugo,
Juan Montes, Luis Sender, Eva
Berrocales, Miguel Tilo, François
Calero, Claudia Barrilla, Pablo
Bezemenov, Juan Urrea, Trimona,
Fernando Domínguez, Isaac
Vitor, Pere Martí, Montse Castella,
Mariadi Lecuona, Enrique Galdoz
Alexandri Dessell, Damiani Armant,
Fidel Alcázar, Fermin Ruíz
Monell & Jack Usina y Victor Ginart

OFICINA REDACCIÓN
C/ Pintor Gisbert 11, 7
46006 Valencia, ESPAÑA.
Teléfono 929772008
e-mail: dxi@dxmagazine.com

Nº 16 / Diciembre 04, Marzo 05 // Publicación gratuita.
Portada: Montse Agüe 124. Diseño realizado en base a...

D.L. 48679-2000
ISSN 1577-3178

Tipografía "Talla" diseñada por Pablo Ruiz, para este número de d(x)i

BIJAYA, 7 años
Katmandú, Nepal

Cuando su padre murió, Bijaya sólo tenía cinco años, y su madre se vio incapaz de mantenerle. Lo envió al orfanato estatal de Katmandú, donde pasaba los días cantando y meditando. Allí es por primera vez una televisión. A los seis años lo adoptó Anna, funcionaria de la Generalitat de Catalunya, una quien voló a Barcelona. Le gusta el fútbol, es del Barça como su abuelo y los amigos del cole, su jugador preferido es Rivaldo. Bijaya no quiere ser diferente.

Fotografía: Juan Urrea

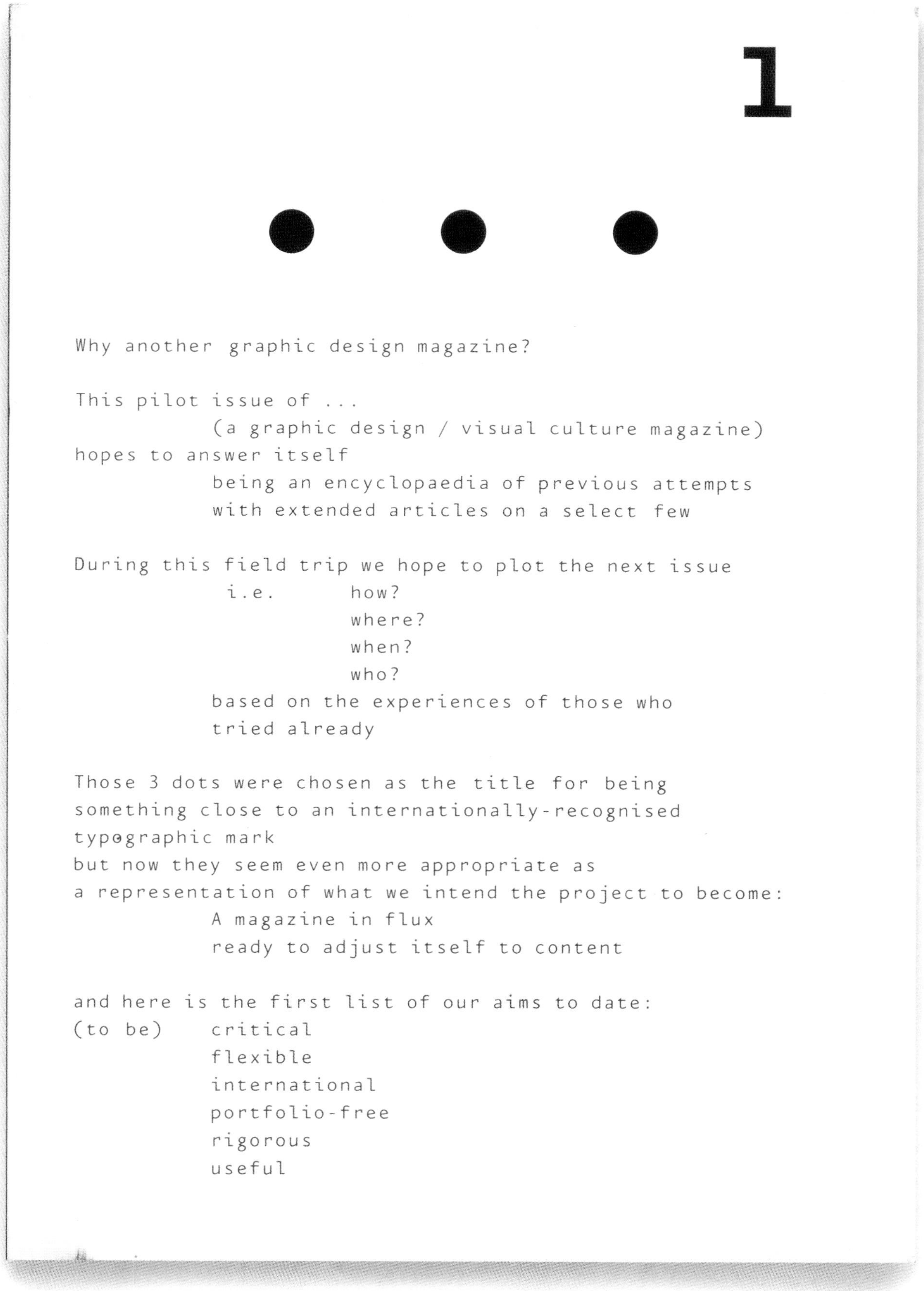

1

● ● ●

Why another graphic design magazine?

This pilot issue of ...
            (a graphic design / visual culture magazine)
hopes to answer itself
            being an encyclopaedia of previous attempts
            with extended articles on a select few

During this field trip we hope to plot the next issue
            i.e.   how?
                     where?
                     when?
                     who?
            based on the experiences of those who
            tried already

Those 3 dots were chosen as the title for being
something close to an internationally-recognised
typographic mark
but now they seem even more appropriate as
a representation of what we intend the project to become:
            A magazine in flux
            ready to adjust itself to content

and here is the first list of our aims to date:
(to be)   critical
            flexible
            international
            portfolio-free
            rigorous
            useful

dot dot dot
ISSUE 1/NETHERLANDS/6.46x9.21 in (164x234 mm)
"HAS IMMATURED INTO A JOCUSERIOUS FANZINE-JOURNAL-ORPHANAGE
BASED ON TRUE STORIES DEEPLY CONCERNED
WITH ART-DESIGN-MUSIC-LANGUAGE-LITERATURE-ARCHITECTURE"

N°12
Printemps/Eté 04
5 euros

Photographie
Valérie Archeno

Publications
Six / Comme des Garçons
Artistes
Permanent Food
A
Romeo Castellucci
Hermès

Editions
7L
Florence Loewy
Colette

Plan
Monica Bonvicini
Lucien Hervé
Ghislain Mollet-Viéville

Mode
Bruno Pieters
Mako Yamazaki
Christophe Lebourg

ENCENS
ISSUE 12/FRANCE/8.66x12.60 in (220x320 mm)
"ARTICULATES SOME POINTS OF VIEW WHERE CREATION
REACHES ITS MOST UNIQUE LEVEL, REINVENTING ITS
FUNDAMENTAL PRINCIPLES FOR EACH ISSUE."

EXIT

EXIT
ISSUE 1 / UNITED KINGDOM / 9.65x12.60 in (245x320 mm)
FASHION MAGAZINE WITH A BLOCK MONOCHROME COVER
ON EVERY ISSUE

Issue One Autumn/Winter 2000 £10

9 771472 003004

FAB
ISSUE NA / ITALY / 7.83x10.63 in (199x270 mm)
"CONCEIVED TO EXPLORE THE FASCINATING INTERACTION
BETWEEN IMAGES AND TEXT"

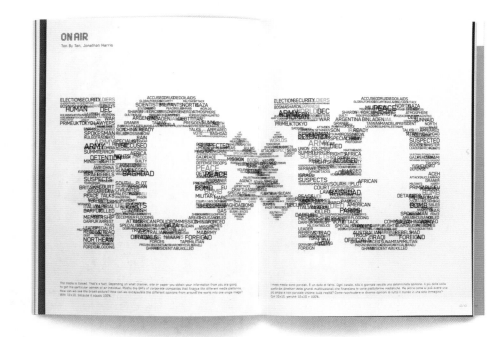

here and there
ISSUE 1/JAPAN/8.27x11.65 in (210x296 mm)
'A VISION OF THE AUTHOR'

here   and   there

nakako hayashi

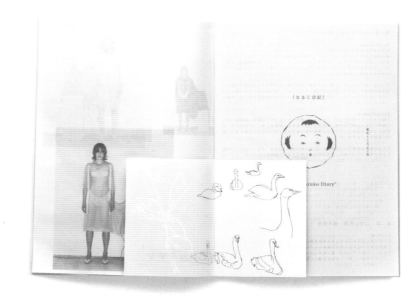

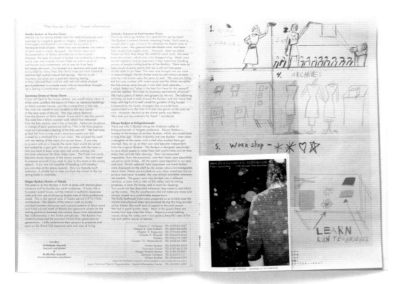

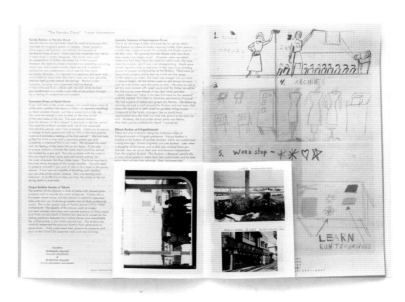

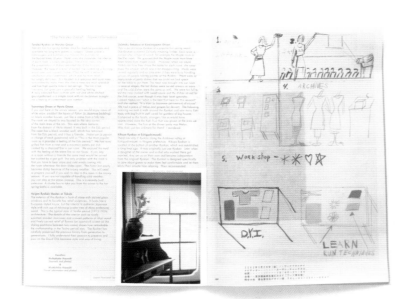

I DON'T UNDERSTAND

"THEATER, ART, LITERATURE, CINEMA MUST BE CLEANSED OF ALL MANIFESTATIONS OF OUR ROTTING WORLD"

I DON'T UNDERSTAND
ISSUE 1/FRANCE/11.61x16.54 in (295x420 mm)
"PRESENTS THE CASE FOR A JOURNALISM OF THE
UNEXPLAINABLE AND THE IRRATIONAL IN AN EFFORT
TO DEMOLISH ITS OBSOLETE VERBOSENESS"

±100%

Geneva - A 80 year-old patient is deceased which a healthy leg had been amputated in the last days at the Civic hospital of Lugano. The physician that had performed the intervention himself immediately denounce and suspended by the functions,

SWISS AMPUT ATES THE WRONG LEG, PATIENT DIES

MOSCOW — AN ELEPHANT HAS KILLED, CRUSHING HIM\IT, HIS\HER TAMER AFTER THE EXHIBITION IN A CIRCUS IN MOSCOW. "AN ELEPHANT HAS KILLED, TEREKHOV" TWO EMPLO YEES OF THE DUROV CIR CUS HAS SAID TODAY. YOU\HE\SHE HAS BEEN STAMPED ON TO DIED BY THE ANIMAL, THAT WAS BRINGING IN HIS\HER ENCLOSURE AFTER THE EVENING SHOW. "WE ARE STILL INVESTIGATING ON THE ACCIDENT". YOU\HE\SHE HAS TOLD ONE OF THE TWO, DEPENDENT OF THE AGENCY REUTERS SOME SERVICES OF AMBU LANCES HAVE CONFIRMED TO THE AGENCY INTERFAX THE DEATH OF THE TAMER.

HE BURNS HIS EX-WIFE. REJECTED FOR THE BAD BREATH

NEW DEHLI, INDIA

RAPE AND BURNS HIS EX WIFE. SHE JUST WANTED TO LEARN HOW TO DRIVE.

ISSUE

$10 US
Fall 2003, ISSUE 7

ISSUE
ISSUE 7/UNITED STATES/8.50x10.94 in (216x278 mm)
"CREATED THROUGH AN EVOLVING COLLECTION OF HIGHLY
ACCLAIMED CONTEMPORARY ARTISTS OF DIVERSE MEDIUMS."

1 3 3

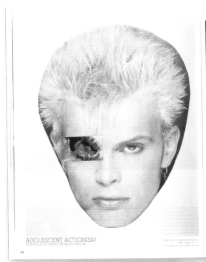

K&K
ISSUE 1/UNITED STATES/11.38x16.06 in (289x408 mm)
"AN OVERSIZED NEWSPRINT PUBLICATION
ABOUT FASHION, POP, AND ART"

K&K MAGAZINE
BERLIN NEW YORK
ISSUE N°1
SPRING SUMMER 2005
1000 YEN 8 EURO 10 $

CECI N'EST PAS UN MAGAZINE · BERLIN · NEW YORK · 2005

K&K

N°1

1.3.5

M Publication
ISSUE 3/GERMANY/8.27x10.63 in (210x270 mm)
"A METAPHOR, A MISSION, A MOVEMENT, AMUSEMENT,
AND A DISTILLATE OF PURE INSPIRATION."

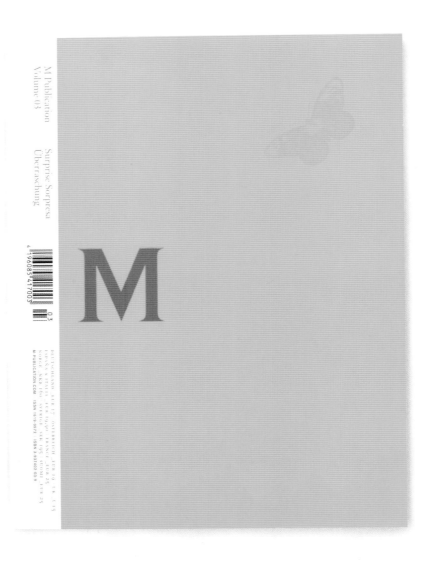

M Publication
Volume 03

Surprise Sorpresa
Überraschung

M

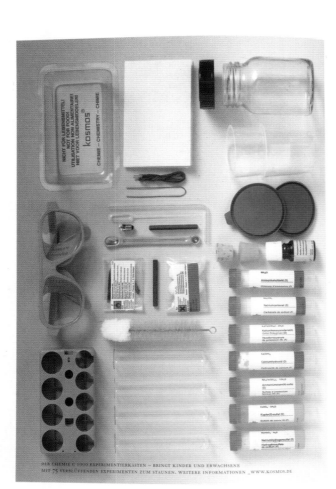

DER CHEMIE C 1000 EXPERIMENTIERKASTEN ~ BRINGT KINDER UND ERWACHSENE
MIT 75 VERBLÜFFENDEN EXPERIMENTEN ZUM STAUNEN. WEITERE INFORMATIONEN _WWW.KOSMOS.DE

BY BROCKHAUS

Experiment

[lat.] *das,* methodisch-planmäßige Herbeiführung von reproduzierbaren, meist variablen Umständen zum Zwecke wissenschaftlicher Beobachtung; wichtigste empirische Methode der Naturwissenschaften, aber auch anderer empirisch vorgehender Wissenschaften (z. B. Psychologie, zum Teil auch Soziologie). Während man in der Antike an der Beobachtung der möglichst ungestörten natürlichen Abläufe interessiert war, greift das moderne Experiment gezielt in die Natur ein. Heute ist ein grundsätzlich neues Verständnis des Experiments erforderlich, da sich die Beobachtungen in vielen Bereichen nur statistisch durchführen lassen und eine nicht zu eliminierende Wechselwirkung zwischen Beobachter und Beobachtetem besteht.

Bibliographisches Institut & F. A. Brockhaus AG, 2001
www.brockhaus.de

136

MARK - ANOTHER ARCHITECTURE
ISSUE 1 /THE NETHERLANDS/9.45x12.60 in (240x320 mm)
"A PLATFORM FOR THE PRACTICE AND PERCEPTION OF ARCHITECTURE
FLAVORED WITH A DIFFERENT KIND OF PHOTOGRAPHY."

Marmalade
ISSUE 0/UNITED KINGDOM/7.28x9.88 in (185x251 mm)
'MAPPING NEW IDEAS AND TRENDS AND EXPLORING
NEW DESIGN POSSIBILITIES'

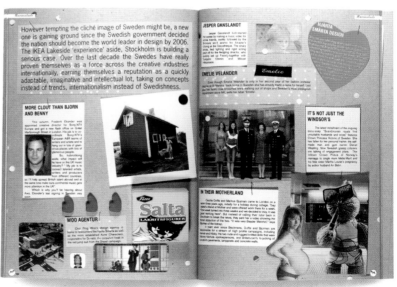

Modern Toss
(ISSUE 1/UNITED KINGDOM/5.83x8.27 in (148x210 mm)
"THE STINK OF EXCELLENCE IN A WORLD GONE TITS UP"

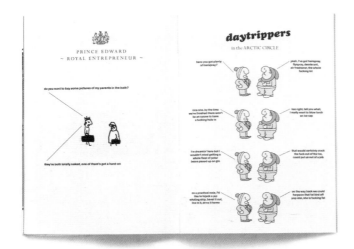

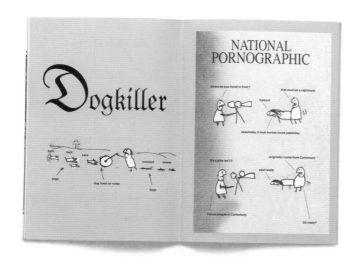

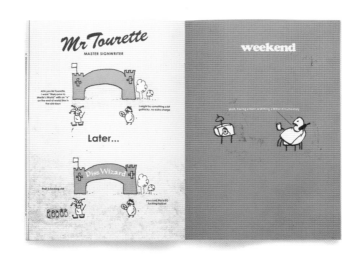

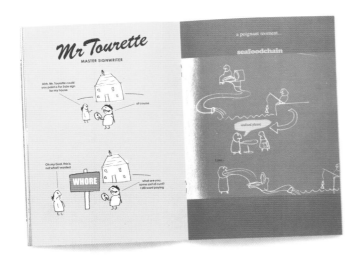

OJODEPEZ

FOTOGRAFIA DOCUMENTAL

0 1

OJODEPEZ
ISSUE 1/SPAIN/9.25x11.81 in (235x300 mm)
"AN UNDISCIPLINED VISION OF DOCUMENTARY
PHOTOGRAPHY AND JOURNALISM."

picnic

SUPERVIVENCIA Y BIENESTAR

TARGET

No.6
SEPTIEMBRE / OCTUBRE 2005

México **$55.00**
U.S.A. **$15 USD**
Europa **€12**

LOS CAZADORES

picnic
ISSUE 6/MEXICO /9.06x11.26 in (230x286 mm)
GIVES IN EACH MONOTHEMATIC ISSUE
"A PRISMATIC VISION OF OUR CONTEMPORARY WORLD"

7 52435 57305 4

06

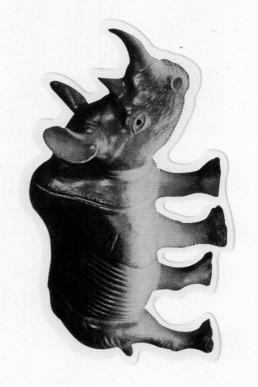

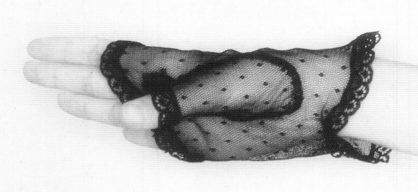

Plastic Rhino
ISSUE 1/UNITED KINGDOM/9.06x11.81 in (230x300 mm)
"COMPILATION OF VISUAL AND EDITORIAL
EXPERIMENTATION DOCUMENTING POPULAR CULTURE"

No. 01 August 2004 £3.50

Refill. A Keep Left and Another Production.   Print with Love.   ⌐

You are here `USE`   Cover Design created: Mon, Mar 17-2003, 18:29
                          Modified: Thu, Mar 20-2003, 10:55

`ISSUE` `OH` `START`   `PROCEED` `➡` `TX` `GR` `IMG`
        `ONE`   `RIGHT`

♥FORMAT: INTERNATIONAL ENGLISH   A MAGAZINE COVER IN 05 PARTS
CE☒CHECKED   PART 01 HERE
  TM

self service
ISSUE 23/FRANCE/9.06x11.77 in (230x299 mm)
'A PLATFORM FOR EXPERIMENTING WITH PHOTOGRAPHY,
STYLING, WRITING, GRAPHICS, TYPOGRAPHY, AND LAYOUT'

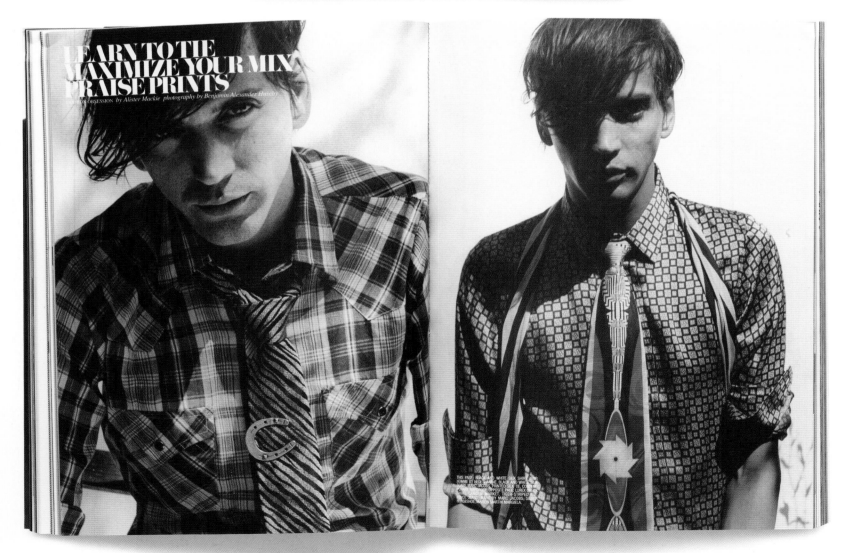

A BAD ECONOMY IS A BIG CHANCE FOR CREATIVITY

Helmut Lang, 2003, n°19

I USED TO CARE WHEN THEY SAID I WAS A MISOGYNIST, BUT THE MORE YOU MEET THESE PEOPLE, THE MORE YOU DON'T GIVE A SHIT, THEY DON'T KNOW FUCK ALL!

Alexander McQueen, 2002, n°16

WHY DO THINGS ONE WAY WHEN YOU CAN DO THEM DIFFERENTLY?

Desirée Heiss, 1999, n°10

I THINK A CAREER IN FASHION, OR IN MY CASE OBSERVING FASHION IS ONE NEAR PURE SELF-INDULGENCE

Ginia Bellafante, 2000, n°13

THE IDEA THAT CELINE DION CAN BE SIMULTANEOUSLY NUMBER ONE IN 46 COUNTRIES IS SURELY ENOUGH TO MAKE ANYONE WITH ANY INTELLIGENCE CONSIDER MURDER OR SUICIDE

Paul Davis, 1999, n°9

TOP 10 MOST CREDITS FOR A SINGLE DESIGNER IN ONE ISSUE

1. RAF SIMONS, 33 credits, n°8
2. YVES SAINT LAURENT
3. BALENCIAGA, 28 credits, n°12
4. CHANEL, 23 credits, n°11
5. HERMÈS, 22 credits, n°11
6. CHANEL, 22 credits, n°13
7. BALENCIAGA, 21 credits, n°15
8. BALENCIAGA, 20 credits, n°8
9. GUCCI, 19 credits, n°11
10. DIOR HOMME, 18 credits, n°11

TOP 10 FAVORITE VERBS

1. CELEBRATE 2. CHALLENGE 3. DEFINE 4. EMBRACE 5. EXPLORE 6. EVOLVE 7. INDULGE 8. INFLUENCE 9. PERSONALIZE 10. TRANSCEND

YOU ALWAYS HAVE TO LOOK IN THE MIRROR AND TRY TO RATIONALIZE YOUR STANDARD OF TASTE. TASTE IS REALLY THE FILTER THAT EVERY DECISION IS SEEN THROUGH.

Brian Grazer, 2004, n°20

TOP 10 MOST USED WORDS

1. ESTABLISHMENT
2. INTEGRITY
3. INFLUENCE
4. PERCEPTION
5. GENERATION
6. INDIVIDUAL
7. INFILTRATING
8. POWERFUL
9. PERSPECTIVE
10. STYLE

ABOUT COINCIDENCES AND 20 YEAR OLD BOYS, DO YOU KNOW THAT IN THE FIRST BEAUTY PICTURE EVER SHOT THE FACE OF THIS BEAUTIFUL WOMAN WAS NOT THAT OF A WOMAN BUT OF A YOUNG BOY CHOSEN FOR THE EXTREME PERFECTION OF HIS/HER FEATURES. THE PHOTOGRAPHER WAS BARON ADOLPHE DE MEYER AND THE PHOTOGRAPH WAS FOR ELIZABETH ARDEN.

Anna Piaggi, 1997, n°6

I MISS LOOKING OUT THE WINDOW AND SEEING A GRAY DAY.

Chris Cunningham, 2001, n°14

I GUESS I MUST HAVE 30 BLACK TURTLENECKS

Polly Mellen, 2002, n°17

I'VE ALWAYS HATED OVERTLY POLITICAL MUSIC. I THINK THE THING WITH MUSIC IS THAT IT WORKS ON A KIND OF PURELY EMOTIONAL LEVEL

Jarvis Cocker, 2003, n°19

I'VE LIVED THROUGH HELL AND I'LL KEEP ON GOING

Jeremy Scott, 2000, n°13

A WORK OF ART THAT ISN'T SHOCKING IS NO GOOD, WHICH MAKES MAKING ART A COMPLETE WASTE OF TIME

Jake Chapman, 2004, n°20

TOP 10 TOPICS OF CONVERSATION

1. ON CHAOS IN WONDERLAND, 2003, n°18 2. ON ACCIDENTAL ART AND BRANDING A SOCIAL CAUSE, 2004, n°21 3. ON BEING AN OUTSIDER ON THE INSIDE, 2004, n°21 4. ON HIDDEN PLEASURE GONE UNDERGROUND, 2003, n°18 5. ON HYBRIDS IN HOLLYWOOD AND DRESSING A NARRATIVE, 2004, n°21 6. ON THE REFUSAL TO BE CATEGORIZED AND UNDERMINED, 2002, n°17 7. ON NEGOTIATING INTANGIBLES, 2004, n°18 8. ON THE SUPERFICIALITY OF WANT-GARDISM, 2002, n°14 9. ON SEEKING PEACE FROM CONSUMERISM, 2003, n°18 10. ON DRESSING FOR THE REVOLUTION, 2002, n°17

WHEN I WORKED FOR FAIRCHILD, I WAS SEATED FIRST ROW AND EVERYBODY WAS KISSING MY ASS. WHEN I MOVED TO MIRABELLA, ALL OF A SUDDEN I WAS SEATED BETWEEN THE 3RD AND 5TH ROWS, AND COULDN'T GET A PR PERSON ON THE PHONE. I KNOW HOW THE SYSTEM WORKS

Richard Buckley, 2000, n°12

I THINK IT'S DIFFICULT TO BE CREATIVE FOR A LONG TIME IF YOU DON'T HAVE ZILLIONS OF REFERENCES

Karl Lagerfeld, 1999, n°11

YOU CAN'T BREAK MY SPIRIT

Polly Mellen, 2002, n°17

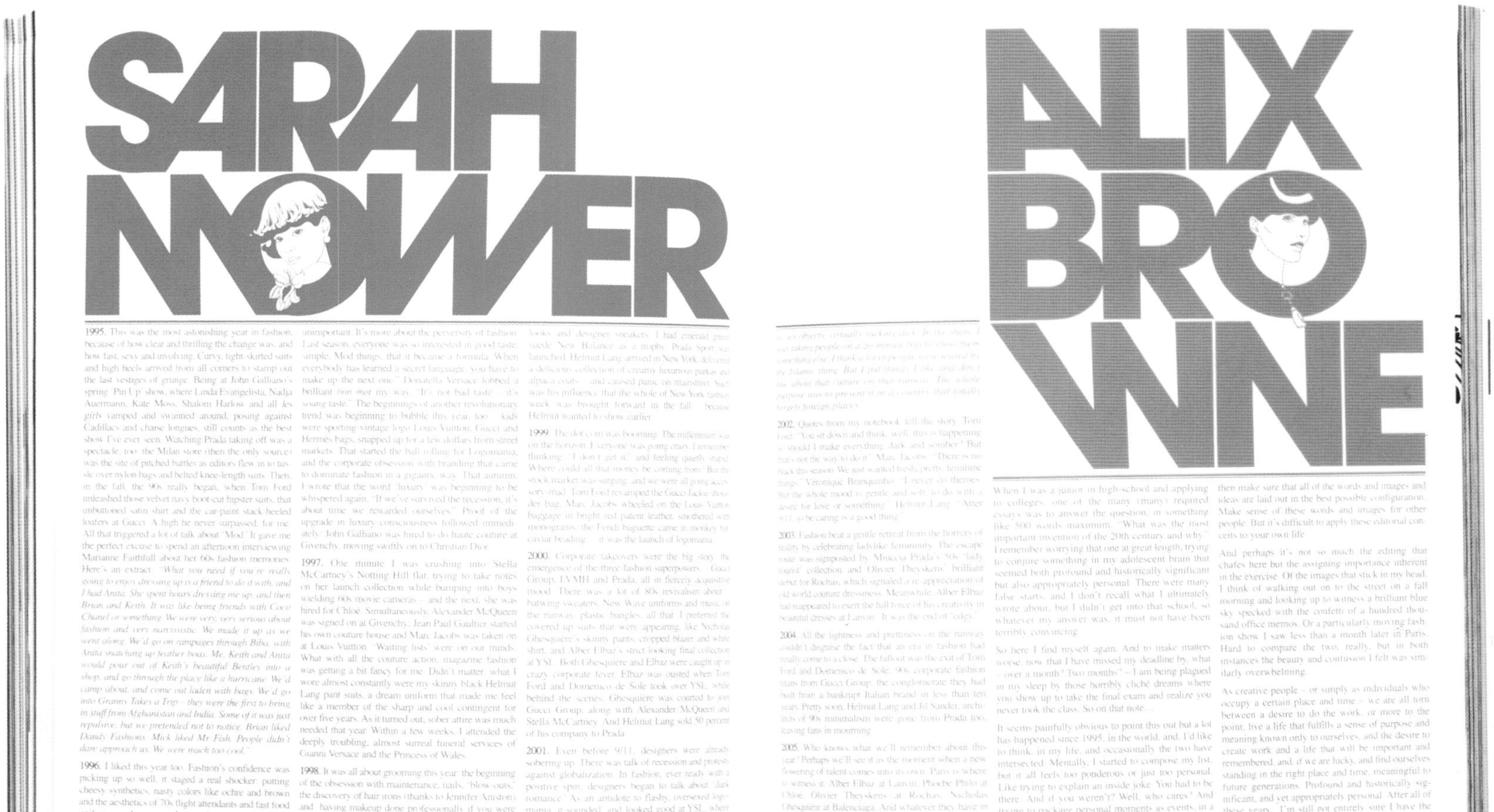

SARAH MOWER

1995. This was the most astonishing year in fashion, because of how clear and thrilling the change was, and how fast, sexy and involving. Curvy, tight-skirted suits and high heels arrived from all corners to stamp out the last vestiges of grunge. Being at John Galliano's spring Prêt Up show, where Linda Evangelista, Nadja Auermann, Kate Moss, Shalom Harlow and all les girls vamped and swanned around, posing against Cadillacs and chaise longues, still counts as the best show I've ever seen. Watching Prada taking off was a spectacle, too: the Milan store often the only source - was the site of pitched battles as editors flew in to snatch up nylon bags and belted knee-length suits. Then, in the fall, the 90s really began, when Tom Ford unleashed those velvet navy boot-cut hipster suits, that embittered satin shirt and the cut-paint slash-heeled loafers at Gucci. A high he never surpassed, for me. All that triggered a lot of talk about 'Mod'. It gave me the perfect excuse to spend an afternoon interviewing Marianne Faithfull about her 60s fashion memories. Here's an extract: "What you need if you're really going to crack dressing up is a friend to do it with, and I had Anita. She spent hours dressing me up, and then Brian and Keith. It was like being friends with Coco Chanel or something. We were very, very serious about fashion and very narcissistic. We made it up as we went along. We'd go on rampages through Biba, with Anita snatching up leather boas. Me, Keith and Anita would pour out of Keith's beautiful Bentley into a shop and go through the place like a hurricane. We'd camp about, and come out laden with bags. We'd go into Granny Takes a Trip - that's were the first to bring in stuff from Afghanistan and India. Some of it was just repulsive, but we pretended not to notice. Brian liked Dandy Fashions. Mick liked Mr Fish. People didn't dare approach us. We were much too cool."

1996. I liked the year too. Fashion's confidence was picking up as well: it staged a real shocker, putting cheesy synthetics, nasty colors like ochre and brown and the aesthetics of 70s flight attendants and fast-food uniforms on the runway. It was a breakout from insanely chrome minimalism, set by Miuccia Prada and her 'Bad Taste' collection; she'd sourced lots of her ideas from a store called Smylonylon on Lafayette Street, whose owner, Chris Brick, said he found his polyester delights by "scouring black cities, like Detroit." But my notes show that she wasn't the only instigator of the 'off' Marc Jacobs told me, "The issue of taste is

important. It's more about the perversity of fashion. Last season, everyone was so interested in good taste, nude. New Balance as a trophy. Prada Sport we launched Helmut Lang arrived in New York, defining a delicious collection of creamy luxurious parkas accessories - and caused panic on magazines. Suzy was his influence that the whole of New York fashion week was brought forward in the fall - because Helmut wanted to show earlier.

1997. One minute I was crushing into Stella McCartney's Notting Hill flat, trying to take notes on her launch collection while bumping into boys wielding 60s movie cameras - and the next, she was hired for Chloé. Simultaneously, Alexander McQueen was signed on at Givenchy, Jean-Paul Gaultier started his own couture house and Marc Jacobs was taken on at Louis Vuitton. Waiting lists were on our minds. What with all the couture action, magazine fashion was getting a bit fancy for me. Didn't matter: what I wore almost constantly were my skinny black Helmut Lang pant suits, a dream uniform that made me feel like a member of the sharp and cool contingent for over five years. As it turned out, sober attire was much needed that year. Within a few weeks, I attended the deeply troubling, almost surreal funeral services of Gianni Versace and the Princess of Wales.

1998. It was all about grooming this year: the beginning of the obsession with maintenance, nails, blow-outs, the discovery of hair irons (thanks to Jennifer Aniston) and having makeup done professionally if you were going out. I suppose that was the more mortal reflection of the arrival of 'red-carpet dressing', a construct that reared onto our consciousness as soon as haute couture started doing business with young Hollywood aristocracy. Uma Thurman in Prada, Nicole Kidman in Dior, Gwyneth Paltrow in Dolce & Gabbana - celebrity style really kicked off here. None of which prevented the simultaneous craze for sportswear in utility

looks and designer sneakers. I had coined a phrase inside New Balance as a trophy.

[remaining 1999–2005 text continues in columns]

Sarah Mower is a fashion journalist and contributing editor to Style.com and Vogue US. She lives in London with her husband and their children.

ALIX BROWNE

When I was a junior in high-school and applying to colleges, one of the many (many) required essays was to answer the question, in something like 300 words maximum, "What was the most important invention of the 20th century, and why." I remember worrying that one at great length, trying to conjure something in my adolescent brain that seemed both profound and historically significant but also appropriately personal. There were many false starts, and I don't recall what I ultimately wrote about, but I didn't get into that school, so whatever my answer was, it must not have been terribly convincing.

So here I find myself again. And to make matters worse, now that I have missed my deadline by what - over a month? Two months? - I am being plagued in my sleep by those horribly cliché dreams where you show up to take the final exam and realize you never took the class. So on that note...

It seems painfully obvious to point this out but a lot has happened since 1995, in the world, and, I'd like to think, in my life, and occasionally the two have intersected. Mentally, I started to compose my list, but it all feels too ponderous or just too personal. Like trying to explain an inside joke. You had to be there. And if you weren't? Well, who cares? And trying to package personal moments as events, in a way that makes them seem like small universal truths, strikes me as just plain old pretentious.

What is more: including some things automatically means excluding others. Editors have to make these kinds of judgment calls all day long - decide that one word or image or idea is better or more appropriate or simply more appropriate than another, and

then make sure that all of the words and images and ideas are laid out in the best possible configuration. Make sense of these words and images for other people. But it's difficult to apply these editorial concepts to your own life.

And perhaps it's not so much the editing that chafes here but the assigning importance inherent in the exercise. Of the images that stick in my head, I think of walking out on to the street on a fall morning and looking up to witness a brilliant blue sky specked with the confetti of a hundred thousand office memos. Or a particularly moving fashion show I saw less than a month later in Paris. Hard to compare the two, really, but in both instances the beauty and confusion I felt was similarly overwhelming.

As creative people - or simply as individuals who occupy a certain place and time - we are all torn between a desire to do the work, or move to the point, live a life that fulfills a sense of purpose and meaning known only to ourselves, and the desire to create work and a life that will be important and remembered and of a way that will both ourselves standing in the right place and time, meaningful to future generations. Profound and historically significant, and yet appropriately personal. After all of these years, I'm still not entirely sure I have the answer to that one, but I can say, with real confidence that in my own case, the opportunity to get to know and work with Ezra and Suzanne and Self Service has had something to do with it.

Alix Browne is a journalist and editor at The New York Times. She lives in Manhattan.

sherman

ART AND FASHION WINTER 2002/2003 NUMBER 1

US $9.95 CA $12.95 EU €12

01>

7 87838 96947 0

sherman
ISSUE 1/UNITED STATES/8.98x12.01 in (228x305 mm)
SINGLE ISSUE NEW YORK MAGAZINE WITH INNOVATIVE DESIGN

...HEE IJA ALLARD 5 NIC HESS 6 HEE J
...ANG 8 GHADA AMER 10 SWETLANA
...EIJA-LIISA AHTILA 14 CAROL BOVE
...JULIA CHIANG RYAN MCGINNESS 16
...NNE WILSON 17 CLAUDE CLOSKY 18 S
...O INDIGO PEOPLE 22 SANJA IVEKOVI
...B PETE MOSS 24 JOSEPH GRIGELY 2
...NITED BAMBOO 27 ROBERTO CUOGH
...CHELE MACCARONE 28 LILA SUBRA
...O LUIS GISPERT 32 PHIL COLLINS 4 K
...LLARD 5 NIC HESS 6 HEE JIN KANG 8
...HADA AMER 10 SWETLANA HEGER 12
...UA-LIISA AHTILA 14 CAROL BOVE 15
...ULIA CHIANG RYAN MCGINNESS 16 AI
...WILSON 17 CLAUDE CLOSKY 18 SEVEN
...O INDIGO PEOPLE 22 SANJA IVEKOVI
...B PETE MOSS 24 JOSEPH GRIGELY 2
...NITED BAMBOO 27 ROBERTO CUOGH
...CHELE MACCARONE 28 LILA SUBRA
...O LUIS GISPERT 32 PHIL COLLINS 4 K
...LLARD 5 NIC HESS 6 HEE JIN KANG 8
...HADA AMER 10 SWETLANA HEGER 12
...UA-LIISA AHTILA 14 CAROL BOVE 15
...ULIA CHIANG RYAN MCGINNESS 16 AI
...WILSON 17 CLAUDE CLOSKY 18 SEVEN
...O INDIGO PEOPLE 22 SANJA IVEKOVI
...B PETE MOSS 24 JOSEPH GRIGELY 2

SODA
ISSUE 18/SWITZERLAND/8.66x10.63 in (220x270 mm)
"MAGAZINE FOR VISUAL CULTURE."

CHF 28.–
EUR 25.–
USD 26.–

18

9 771424 671008

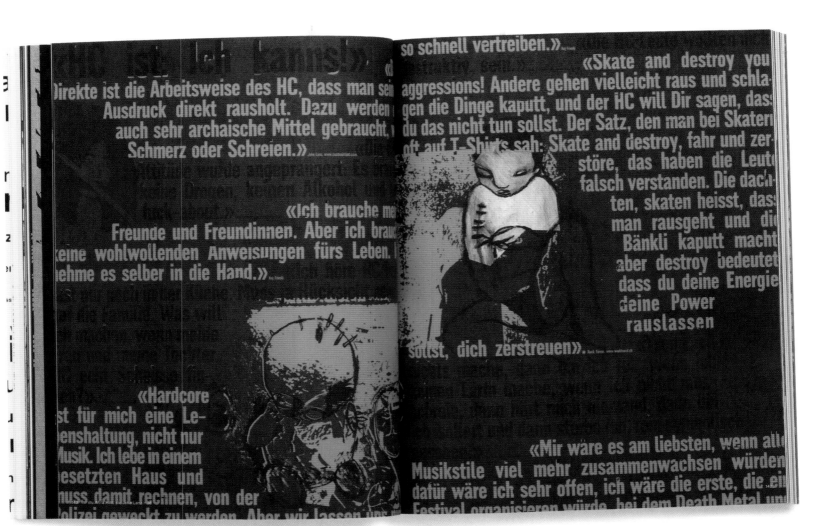

«HC ist: Ich kanns!».

...irekte ist die Arbeitsweise des HC, dass man sein... Ausdruck direkt rausholt. Dazu werden... auch sehr archaische Mittel gebraucht,... Schmerz oder Schreien.»

«Ich brauche me... Freunde und Freundinnen. Aber ich brau... keine wohlwollenden Anweisungen fürs Leben.... ...ehme es selber in die Hand.»

«Hardcore ...st für mich eine Le-...enshaltung, nicht nur ...usik. Ich lebe in einem ...esetzten Haus und ...uss damit rechnen, von der ...olizei geweckt zu werden. Aber wir lassen uns...

...so schnell vertreiben.»

«Skate and destroy you... aggressions! Andere gehen vielleicht raus und schla-...gen die Dinge kaputt, und der HC will Dir sagen, dass... du das nicht tun sollst. Der Satz, den man bei Skater... oft auf T-Shirts sah: Skate and destroy, fahr und zer-...störe, das haben die Leute... falsch verstanden. Die dach-...ten, skaten heisst, dass... man rausgeht und die... Bänkli kaputt macht... aber destroy bedeutet... dass du deine Energie... deine Power... rauslassen... ...sollst, dich zerstreuen».

«Mir wäre es am liebsten, wenn alle... Musikstile viel mehr zusammenwachsen würden... dafür wäre ich sehr offen, ich wäre die erste, die ein... Festival organisieren würde, bei dem Death Metal un...

FREIHEIT MACH DIR...

BIT WELBOW, YOU CAN TURN AROUND FUCK OUTA HERE,

Eine kleine Auswahl an grossen Momenten, grossen Gitarristen und kleinen Gesten:

Fred "Sonic" Smith/Sonic's Rendez Vous Band – "City Slang", 1977
Dass sich der Umfang des Technikeinsatzes durchaus reziprok zu dem durch ihn erzielten Effekt verhalten kann, wird nirgends so deutlich wie hier: Ex-MC5-Gitarrist und Patti-Smith-Ehemann Fred Smith führt in diesem Song perfekt vor, wie eine Gitarre ökonomisch zu handhaben ist. Kurz gehalten, kleine Ausreisser machend, um über Umwege das zu erreichen, wonach jeder strebt: Transzendenz! In dieser wunderbaren Einfachheit nur noch von Ron Asheton (Stooges, "Destroy all Monsters") zu toppen. Detroit metal is the real meat. Sound: Mosrite Gitarre durch einen Marshall Stack.

Greg Sage/Wipers – "When it's over", 1981
Von allen Gitarristen zwischen 1979 und 1986 ist mir Greg Sage der Liebste. Niemand verstand sich so gut auf eine derartige Verflechtung zwischen Rhythmus und Leadgitarre und war doch so sehr Gitarrist im klassischen hendrixschen Sinne. Auf "When it's over" kommt Sages Vorliebe für epochale Arrangements voll zum Tragen, allein die nackten Fakten, wie etwa eine Songlänge von 6:30 Min. bei einer Punkband im Jahre 1981, sprechen Bände. Live am besten. Sound: Gibson SG Junior mit selbstgebautem Amp, der einen der markantesten Sounds produzierte, den es bis heute gibt.

J. Mascis/Dinosaur Jr. – "Raisans", 1987
Hier stimmt einfach alles. Ein doppelter struktureller Spannungsaufbau, der sich einerseits über eine Rücknahme der Dynamik und andererseits über eine akustische Öffnung des Raumes speist. Danach nicht einfach das simp-le Einlösen, sondern erst nochmal das Riff präsentieren, um dies dann auf wunderbare Weise zu toppen. Der fantastische Sound stammt aus J. Mascis Fender Jazzmaster, die in Kombination mit dem Big Muff Verzerrer unglaublich gut klingt und für Distinktion sorgt. Wie jedes gute Solo hat auch dieses seinen Platz im Song und ist zusätzlich durch eine zweite dynamische Struktur gekennzeichnet. Hut ab!

spector cut + paste
ISSUE 1/GERMANY/9.21x11.61 in (234x295 mm)
'SEEKS TO PROMOTE RECIPROCAL COMMUNICATION
AND COLLABORATION BETWEEN MANY AREAS
OF CONTEMPORARY ARTISTIC OUTPUT.'

155

スプ ラウト
2002 7
VOL 01
ISBN 4-9901171-0-7

SP ROUT

Fashion, Design and Visual Art

Photography. Drawing. Product Design. Experimental Graphics. Beauty

SPROUT
ISSUE 1/JAPAN/9.06x11.65 in (230x296 mm)
"CONTEMPORARY ART IN THE CONTEXT OF GLOBALISM"

Sugo
ISSUE 2/ITALY/9.06x11.81 in (230x300 mm)
"A BALANCED MIX OF VARIOUS INGREDIENTS, EACH OF THEM
WITH THEIR OWN CHARACTERISTICS THAT, TOGETHER,
MAKE AN INVITING, ALWAYS DIFFERENT, MAGAZINE."

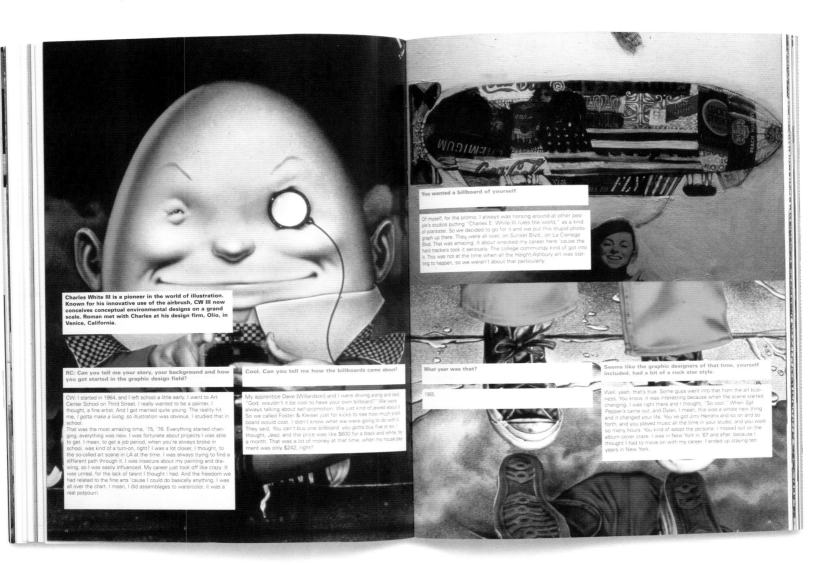

Charles White III is a pioneer in the world of illustration. Known for his innovative use of the airbrush, CW III now conceives conceptual environmental designs on a grand scale. Roman met with Charles at his design firm, Olio, in Venice, California.

RC: Can you tell me your story, your background and how you got started in the graphic design field?

CW: I started in 1964, and I left school a little early. I went to Art Center School on Third Street. I really wanted to be a painter, I thought, a fine artist. And I got married quite young. The reality hit me, *I gotta make a living*, so illustration was obvious. I studied that in school.

That was the most amazing time, '75, '76. Everything started changing, everything was new. I was fortunate about projects I was able to get. I mean, to get a job period, when you're always broke in school, was kind of a turn-on, right? I was a lot closer, I thought, to the so-called art scene in LA at the time. I was always trying to find a different path through it. I was insecure about my painting and drawing, so I was easily influenced. My career just took off like crazy. It was unreal, for the lack of talent I thought I had. And the freedom we had related to the fine arts 'cause I could do basically anything. I was all over the chart. I mean, I did assemblages to watercolor, it was a real potpourri.

Cool. Can you tell me how the billboards came about?

My apprentice Dave [Willardson] and I were driving along and said, "God, wouldn't it be cool to have your own billboard?" We were always talking about self-promotion. We just kind of jawed about it. So we called Foster & Kleiser just for kicks to see how much a billboard would cost. I didn't know what we were going to do with it. They said, *You can't buy one billboard, you gotta buy five or six.* I thought, *Jeez*, and the price was like $600 for a black and white, for a month. That was a lot of money at that time, when my house payment was only $242, right?

You wanted a billboard of yourself.

Of myself, for the promo. I always was horsing around at other people's studios putting "Charles E. White III rules the world," as a kind of prankster. So we decided to go for it and we put this stupid photograph up there. They were all over, on Sunset Blvd., on La Cienega Blvd. That was amazing. It about wrecked my career here 'cause the hard trackers took it seriously. The college community kind of got into it. This was not at the time when all the Haight-Ashbury art was starting to happen, so we weren't about that particularly.

What year was that?

1965.

Seems like the graphic designers of that time, yourself included, had a bit of a rock star style.

Well, yeah, that's true. Some guys went into that from the art business. You know, it was interesting because when the scene started changing, I was right there and I thought, "So cool." When *Sgt. Pepper's* came out, and Dylan, I mean, this was a whole new thing and it changed your life. You've got Jimi Hendrix and so on and so forth, and you played music all the time in your studio, and you work so many hours. You kind of adopt the persona. I missed out on the album cover craze. I was in New York in '67 and after, because I thought I had to move on with my career. I ended up staying ten years in New York.

The difference between art and design
by Andy Simionato

Design

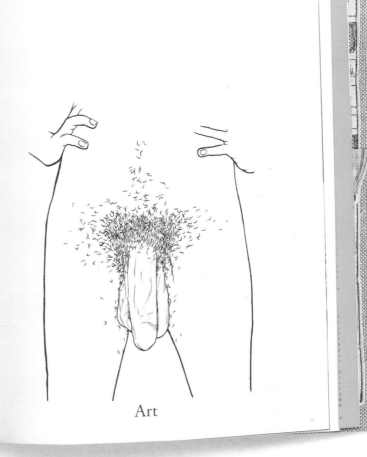

Art

tank
ISSUE 7/UNITED KINGDOM/5.83x6.97 in (148x177 mm)
A PIONEERING STYLE PUBLICATION THAT HAS BEEN IN SEVERAL
FORMATS OVER THE PAST NINE YEARS

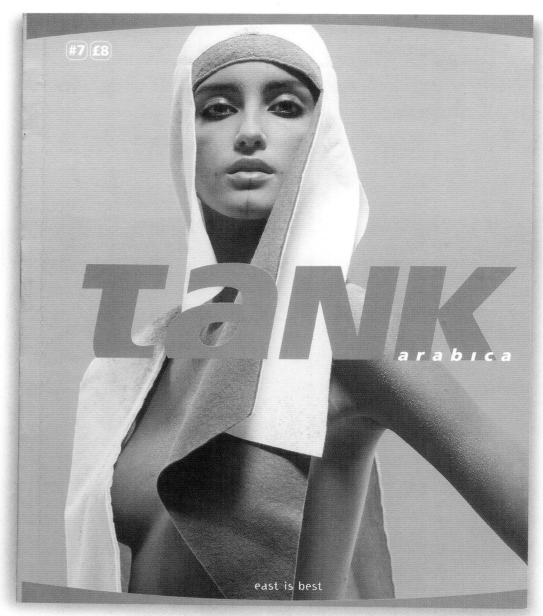

Textfield Magazine
Volume 01 Issue 01

10 US 10 Euro 15 CHF
Limited Edition:1 of 1000

Textfield
ISSUE 1 /UNITED STATES/8.46x10.94 in (215x278 mm)
LOS ANGELES BASED. "ART, ARCHITECTURE,
DESIGN, AND FASHION"

160

THE INTERNATIONAL
ISSUE 1/JAPAN/8.19x11.65 in (208x296 mm)
BUILT AS A VISUAL STORY.

POPEXPLOITATION

3-MINUTES
B&W SILENT

IS ALL THAT
REMAINS.
SOME BIOGRAPHI-
CAL DATA IS
STILL MISSIG,
LIKE WHO WAS
BORN WHEN
OR DIED WHEN,
OR IF IT'S STILL
EARLY AUTUMN.

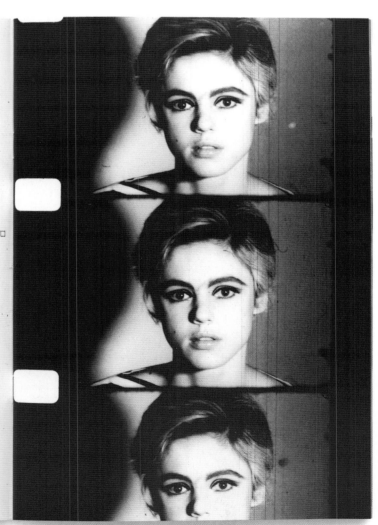

FUCKING IS WHAT I LOVE. IT'S THE ... IN YOUR FACE,

THE ARCHITECT
URE
OF
REASSURANCE

UOVO
ISSUE 9 /ITALY /6x9.45 in (150x240 mm)
"INTERVIEWS OF INTERESTING PERSONALITIES ON
THE INTERNATIONAL ARTS SCENE SET IN A DESIGN SETTING THAT
ILLUSTRATES, ENRICHES, AND BECOMES THE SUBJECTS."

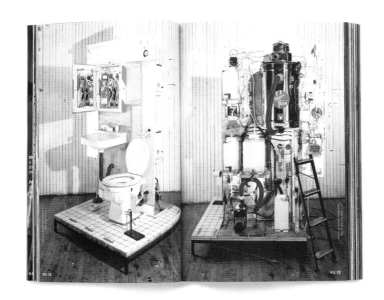

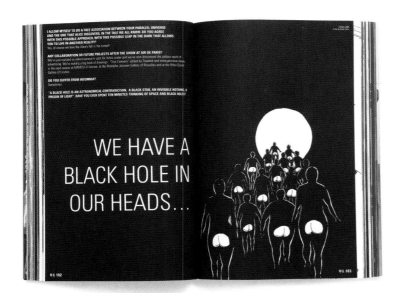

WE HAVE A BLACK HOLE IN OUR HEADS…

FAUSTO GILBERTI
INTERVIEW BY NORMA MANGIONE

IN THE LAND OF SHADOWS
BY LARA FACCO

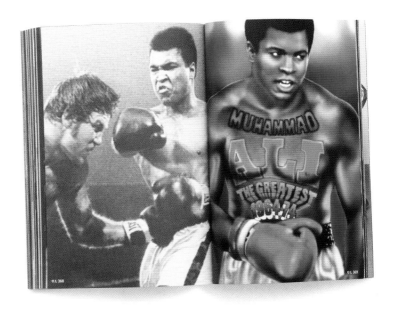

164

vorn
ISSUE 1 / GERMANY / 8.23 x 11.65 in (209x296 mm)
"THE MAGAZINE FOR FREE DESIGN, ALLOWING
ABSOLUTE CREATIVE FREEDOM, WITHOUT BOUNDARIES,
BRIEFS, OR THEMES."

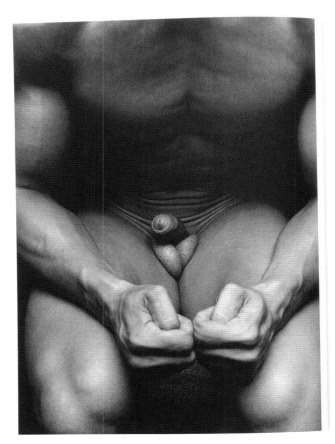

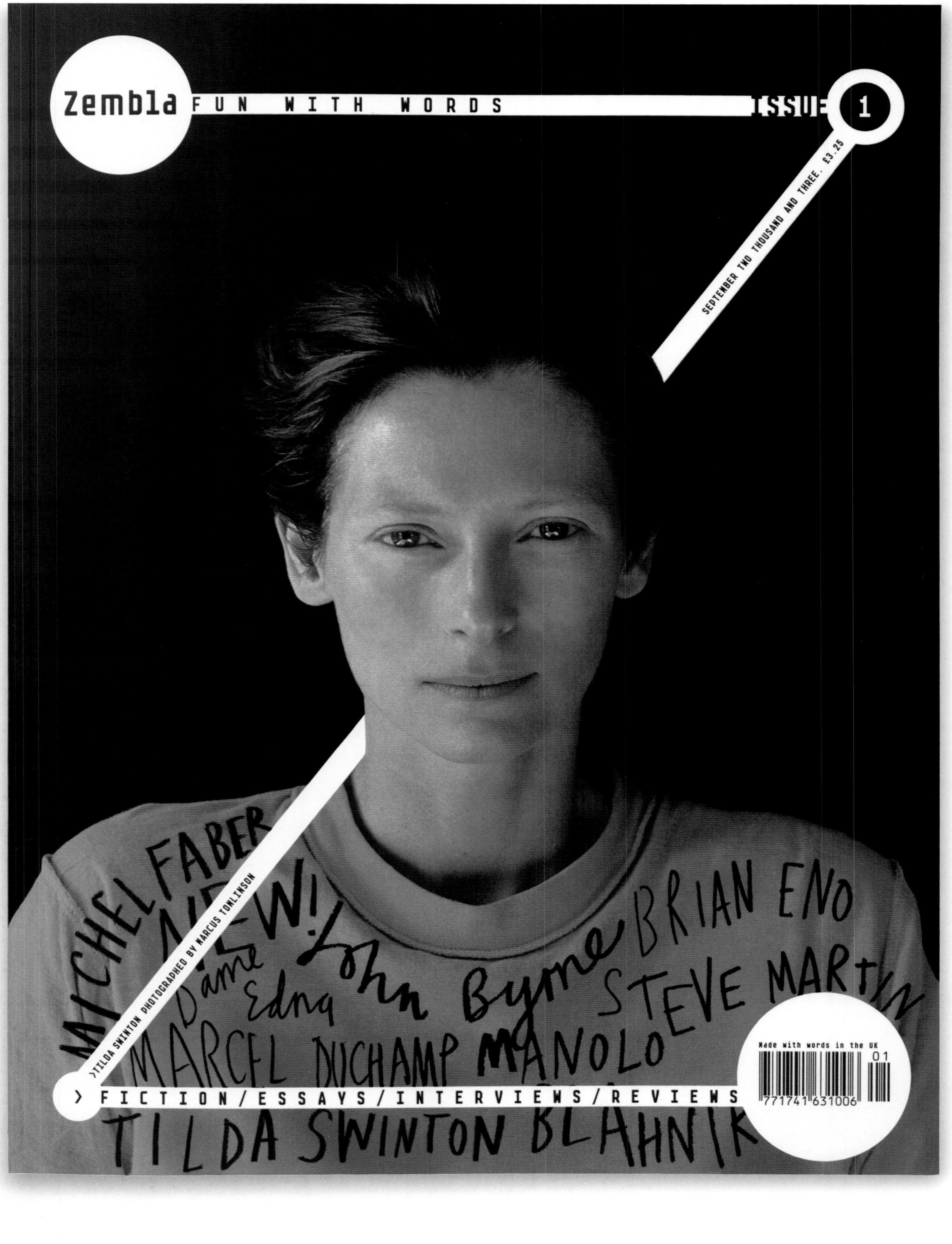

Zembla FUN WITH WORDS ISSUE 1

SEPTEMBER TWO THOUSAND AND THREE. £3.25

TILDA SWINTON PHOTOGRAPHED BY MARCUS TOMLINSON

MICHEL FABER
NEW!
Dame Edna John Byrne BRIAN ENO
STEVE MARTIN
MARCEL DUCHAMP MANOLO
TILDA SWINTON BLAHNIK

> FICTION/ESSAYS/INTERVIEWS/REVIEWS

Made with words in the UK
01
7 71741 631006

Zembla
ISSUE 1/UNITED KINGDOM/9.1x11.8 in (231x300 mm)
"FUN WITH WORDS"

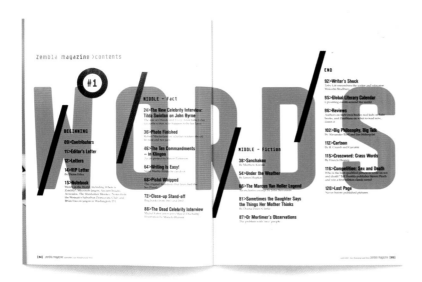

Zembla magazine > contents

#1

BEGINNING

09> Contributors
11> Editor's Letter
12> Letters
14> VIP Letter
By Diane Edny

15> Rulebook
How's the World including Where is Zembla?, Microsoft jargon, Ancient Roads, Avocados, The Manhattan Memos; Notes from the Wetlands Suburban Democratic Club; and Brian Eno on anger in Washington, 171

MIDDLE – Fact

24> The New Celebrity Interview: Tilda Swinton on John Byrne
Our star on Glasgow and renewal of ways that her favourite artist also happens to be her father

30> Photo Finished
The original Manhattan matchbook artefacts should be tried and tested

45> The Ten Commandments – on Klingon
As contracted by Marcel Patterson

64> Writing Is Easy!
By Martin Amis the overshoot

68> Pistol Whipped
The original manuscript that spun April over Jim Ptobam

72> Close-up Stand-off
Big Icons from 1967 and 2002

88> The Dead Celebrity Interview

MIDDLE – Fiction

38> Sanehaken
By Matthew Kneale

54> Under the Weather
By James Hopkins

66> The Marcus Van Heller Legend

81> Sometimes the Daughter Says the Things Her Mother Thinks
By R. Cronoth and Lucians

87> Dr Mortimer's Observations
The problem with Vera's people

END

92> Writer's Shock
Soho Life sometimes the writer and educator Malcolm Bradbury

95> Global Literary Calendar
Upcoming events around the world

96> Reviews
Authors on their own books and kids or kids' books, and Zemblans on what to read now, Issues 6

102> Big Philosophy, Big Job
By Alexander Bard and Jan Söderqvist

112> Cartoon

115> Crossword: Crass Words
By Francis Heaney

118> Competition: Sex and Death
Who is the UK's published philosopher-condiment and who is our dead? Sex-obsessed publisher Steven Pinch and was a few hidden classic novel?

120> Last Page
Seven-button published pictures

letters page

and out of it is. But we letter issues as a world like to have yet taken.
Please send us at 6 Ledbury Road, London W11 2AE.

ZEMBLA

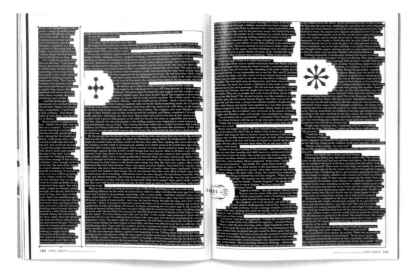

FICTION TWO

UNDER THE WEATHER
BY JAMES HOPKIN

bugs

BIG PHILOSOPHY by Alexander Bard

ZOO
ISSUE 4/GERMANY/9.06×11.7 in (230×297 mm)
FASHION AND ART MAGAZINE FROM BERLIN.

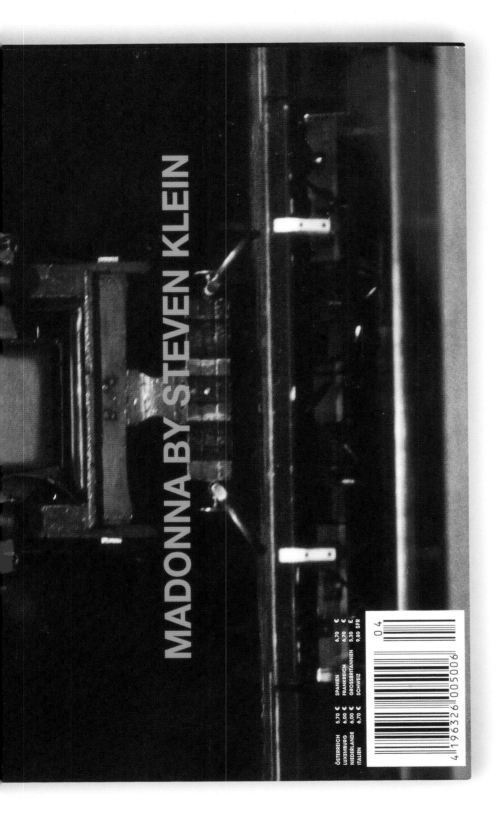

MADONNA BY STEVEN KLEIN

ÖSTERREICH 5,70 €
LUXEMBURG 6,00 €
NIEDERLANDE 6,00 €
ITALIEN 6,70 €

SPANIEN 6,70 €
FRANKREICH 6,70 €
GROSSBRITANNIEN 5,30 £
SCHWEIZ 9,80 SFR

04

4 196326 005006

CONTENT

Like their predecessors, but with a far less political and militant approach, the stylepress stretch the frontiers of content compared to the "story-" and news-based mainstream titles. They continue to challenge the limits of what is "possible" and acceptable in order to have their voices "heard." Timeliness is not as important as creating something (a collection or a single piece) that will be relevant today, two years ago, and ten years from now. // Though these categories are the same as they have been for years the treatment is not: the photography of *THE PHOTO ISSUE*, *crème*, and *BRANSCH*; the artistry of *PERMANENT FOOD*, *rojo*, and *Faesthetic*; the fashion of *doingbird*; the culture of *blag* and *THE COLONIAL*; the objects of *carl's cars*, *Our Magazine*, and *FOUND*; the sex of *Richardson* and *DELICIAE VITAE*; and the texts of *The Illustrated Ape* and *THE PURPLE JOURNAL*.

Why are magazines created to be disposable?

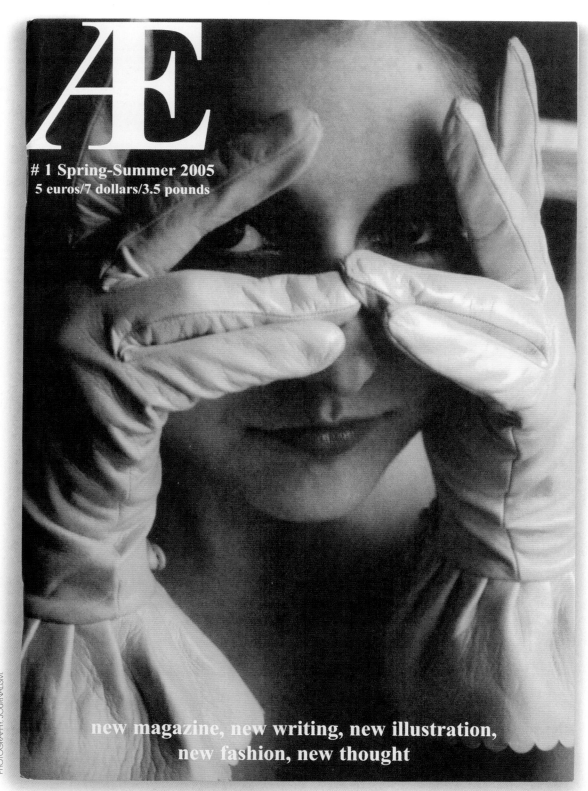

ÆE

 # 1 Spring-Summer 2005
5 euros/7 dollars/3.5 pounds

new magazine, new writing, new illustration,
new fashion, new thought

ÆE ISSUE 1/FRANCE/5.83x8.27 in (148x210 mm)
"A GRASSROOTS QUARTERLY DEDICATED TO THE EXPOSURE
OF ASPIRING AND EMERGING TALENT IN WRITING, ILLUSTRATION,
PHOTOGRAPHY, JOURNALISM."

10:30pm

by Manolo Martinez
Illustrated by Jeanne Detallante

It's getting colder   Beautiful Amanda is   Don't talk about that, hang on for a second. Hang on for a second:

I'm lying on the sofa, a streetlamp reflected on the blue wall in front of my house, putting my living-room between brackets, so to speak. I was saying Beautiful Amanda is; but no. I'm napping legs under a blanket, that's it; napping or plainly sleeping: it's half past ten pm. Not sleeping-sleeping: I'm aware of the blue light, if only. Then, say no more, beautiful Amanda,

Of course not: the street noises, that's it: steps among the puddles, rustling anoraks, throats expelling air; this is hopeless. The neon sign, that's that: reflected on the blue wall too, each letter cyclically —because I know them to be letters, otherwise it's just changes on the blue wall, zone by zone sequential unspecified changes. How do I even know the streetlamp; I

remember, of course. If I didn't, the blue wall shining and beating along a horizontal line would be enough -therefore it'd be enough; and therefore I'd be merely napping or sleeping-sleeping; but no: it is the streetlamp through the bracketed living room, the bracketing streetlamp, then, yes. How do I know. I merely; if I were to move my legs from beneath the blanket, go look through the window, the streetlamp, the neon sign letter by letter then I'd know and then, cascading, the puddles the anoraks and whatnot, beautiful Amanda even I may.   But no, I've left my glasses somewhere on the sofa, of course not: I don't remember the glasses as such, not even merely, an unspecified reverberation over the blanket, a non-propositional something a force field connected to my knee as it were: move your knee and you'll break your glasses. Wait, non-propositional: move it then crack, or even a reverberating don't move; this is hopeless. Not even remembering this time, then, merely a non-propositional link between my knee and some probability distribution on the blanket and the sofa. Don't move. If you wish, wiggle your toe, of course; or think, that's movement too, if only, as if. Probability distribution of my glasses over the sofa, then drops sharply to zero in the edge of the sofa, but that'd be. A bland overflow of my glasses beyond the sofa on to the corner behind, that's better. Wait, what better, that'd be, instead; that's it: that'd instead. Not the glasses, the force field, the reverberating non-propositional something, but it's so the glasses themselves blandly reaching for the corner, intenting the corner, long arms caressing ever so slightly the corner of the living-room behind me and the sofa, lenses forcing perspectives; this is programmatic.

The corner of the living room-behind me and the sofa. If I stood up some-how, went to see it with my very eyes, as if. No question, of course, but the shadow, the laws of perspective, the sad sad sad trihedron and there we are: the corner of the living room in all its —not all, merely some of its. There's no fact of the matter as to how much of its is *all* of its; it could be thought of as a calculus couldn't it baby. Whom, wait, Amanda the beauti-ful, but no way, no, wait. No corner behind me and the sofa: I have this suspicion of glasses on the blanket and if I move then. It's getting colder, that's a fact.

"Glory", was it so difficult.

The puddles downstairs too. *Down*stairs? and down*stairs*? how dare I,

---

The Wonder Years
By Christopher Lewis

1980 – 1991
I walked, ran, jumped this path. We met at my awakening to the world outside my family. It has seen my failings, anger, dreams, worries, happiness. It has witnessed my growth. I have left. I have returned. Twenty-four years it has not changed.

Spring 1985
He called me the colored boy. We were on the D line. He was drunk. Fat. Irish. He called me the colored boy. I felt ashamed. Embarrassed. I felt I did something wrong. No one said anything. They watched. I didn't know what to do. I got off there. It wasn't my stop. I was thirteen.

1986 – 1990
Her locker was next to mine. She had a soft smile. I thought of her often. She was quiet. Her sneakers were usually untied. She dated one of my friends, Dan. Her lips were full. Sometimes wet. Her face is still fresh in my mind. She killed herself some time after high school. Stephanie.

Fall 1981
His name was Ray. He was my brother's friend. He sat on me. He poked a needle in my testicles. He was heavy. I couldn't move. He laughed. He did it more than once. I was angry. I wanted to cry. I held it in. It was on the second floor. I was nine.

210 x 297

A4

A'CZTERY magazyn * format na życie

international
miesięcznik
numer 01 2003
cena 7,50 pln
(w tym 7% vat)
issn 1731-1454

9 771731 145001

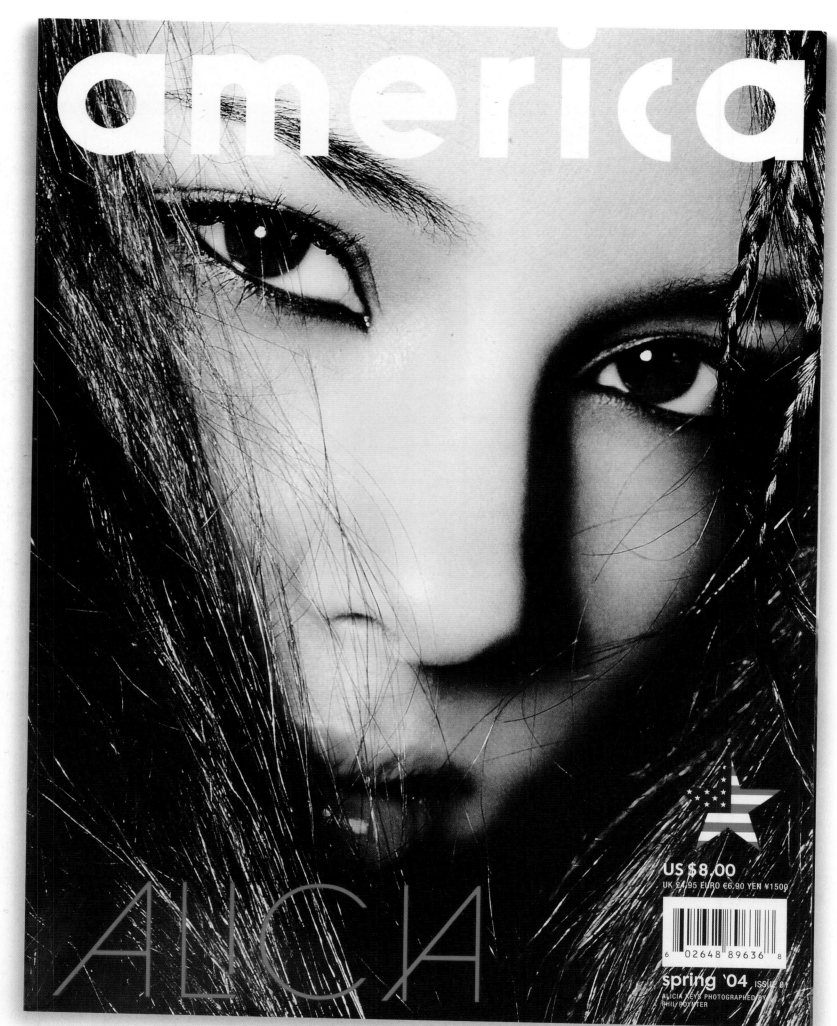

america

ALICIA

US $8.00
UK £4.95 EURO €6.90 YEN ¥1500

spring '04 ISSUE 01
ALICIA KEYS PHOTOGRAPHED BY PHIL POYNTER

america
ISSUE 1/ UNITED STATES/9.02x11.69 in (229x297 mm)
"THE HIP-HOP NATION HAS MATURED AND SUCCEEDED -
AND IS ENJOYING A LIFESTYLE OF FAME AND FORTUNE"

ARKITIP
ISSUE 31 / (UNITED STATES) / 9.02x11.50 in (229x292 mm)
"SUPPORT THE ARTS. PROMOTE FREEDOM OF EXPRESSION.
MAKE ART AFFORDABLE AND ACCESSIBLE."

blag
ISSUE NA/UNITED KINGDOM/9.65x11.89 in (245x302 mm)
"A DOWN-TO-EARTH CULTURAL TASTE MAGAZINE"

BRANSCH
ISSUE 1/GERMANY/9.06x11.81 in (230x300 mm)
LARGE-FORMAT PHOTOGRAPHY MAGAZINE.

carl★s cars

a magazine about people

carl's cars
ISSUE 1 / NORWAY / 9.06x10.98 in (230x279 m)
"ABOUT PEOPLE'S CREATIVITY, ALL THE STRANGE THINGS PEOPLE
SAY, ALL THE RANDOM STUFF THEY DO, AND THE CARS THEY DRIVE"

Nordic champion of reverse driving with a camper

photo: Lars Bollen

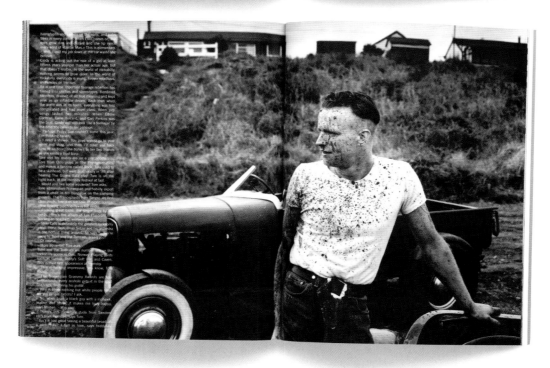

Charley
ISSUE 1/UNITED STATES/5.91x7.91 in (150x201 mm)
'A MACHINE FOR REDISTRIBUTION. A PRE-DIGESTED COMBINATION,
WITH CONTENT AND A FORMAT COMPLETELY RENOVATED AT
EACH APPEARANCE.'

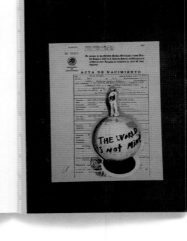

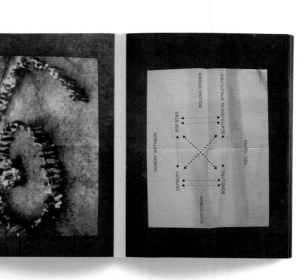

commons&sense

man

commons&sense man
ISSUE 1 / JAPAN / 10.08 x 14.33 in (256 x 364 mm)
OVERSIZE MEN'S FASHION MAGAZINE.

commons&sense man ISSUE00 FEBRUARY 2006

Continuous Projects
ISSUE 7 / UNITED STATES / 17.05 x 10.98 in (433 x 279 mm)
"BEGAN WITH A DESIRE TO RELEASE 'ISSUES'. LIKE A MAGAZINE, BUT
TO SOMEHOW STAND OUTSIDE OF THE NORMAL PROCESS OF
MAGAZINE MAKING".

Avalanche

Fall 1970

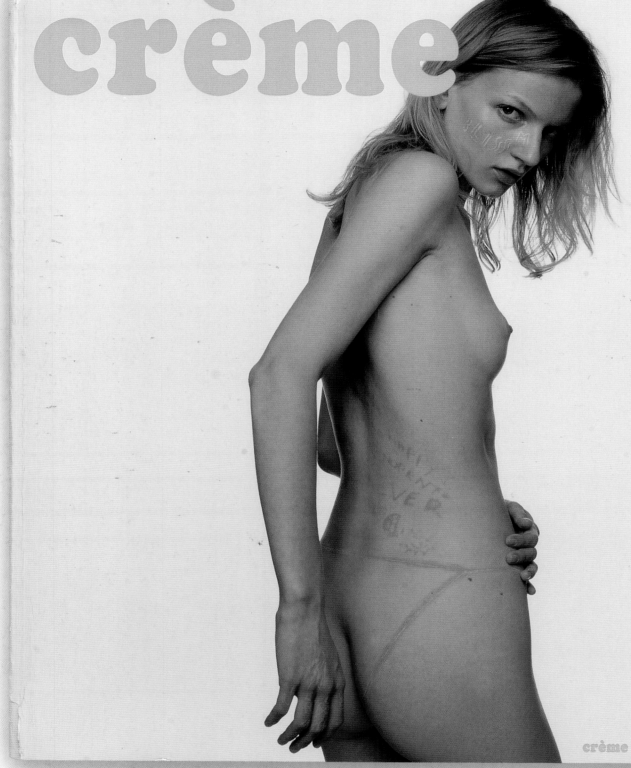

crème n° 1   skin with pleasure

crème
ISSUE 1 / LUXEMBOURG / 10.28x10.16 in (261x258 mm)
PHOTOGRAPHY AND STYLE.

PREMIERE FOIS
DEdiCate 01
12 Euros

DEdiCate
ISSUE 1/FRANCE/9.45x11.61 in (240x295 mm)
"ANOTHER PERSPECTIVE ON TODAY'S PASSIONS."

№ 03096

DEdiCate

Edito.

This side up

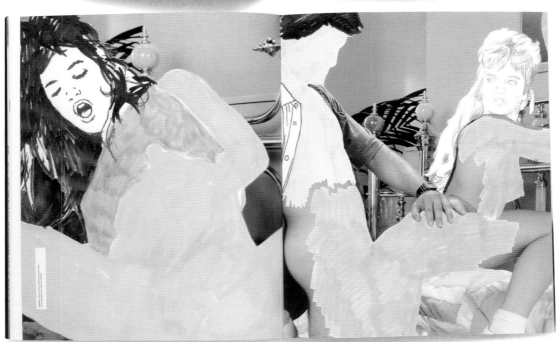

spr
i n
n g
2 0 0 1
n. 0 1
£ 10

DELIC VITAE IAE

DELICIAE VITAE
ISSUE 1 /ITALY /8.86x11.65 in (225x296 mm)
'DELIBERATE, UNASHAMEDLY LUXURIOUS EXCESS. AUTONOMOUS.
AND UNCONSTRAINED IN A WORLD OF EVER MORE INCREASING
CONGLOMERATE FASHION.'

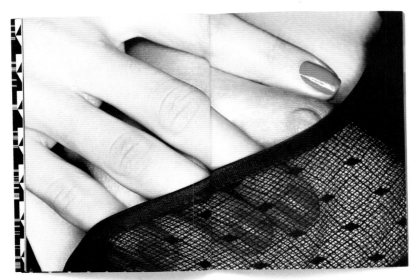

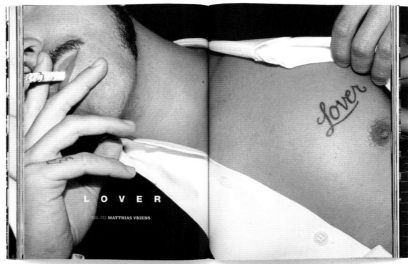

LOVER

120–133 MATTHIAS VRIENS

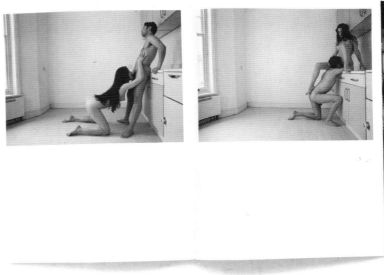

global street art connection from osaka japan

digmeout | 05

e n a

m a r i   k u b o t a

Z A n P o n

n e k o s h o w g u n

m i o   m a t s u m o t o

p c p

digmeout
ISSUE 5/JAPAN/8.66x11.65 in (220x296 mm)
AN OSAKA-BASED "VISUAL ARTIST EXCAVATION PROJECT"

194

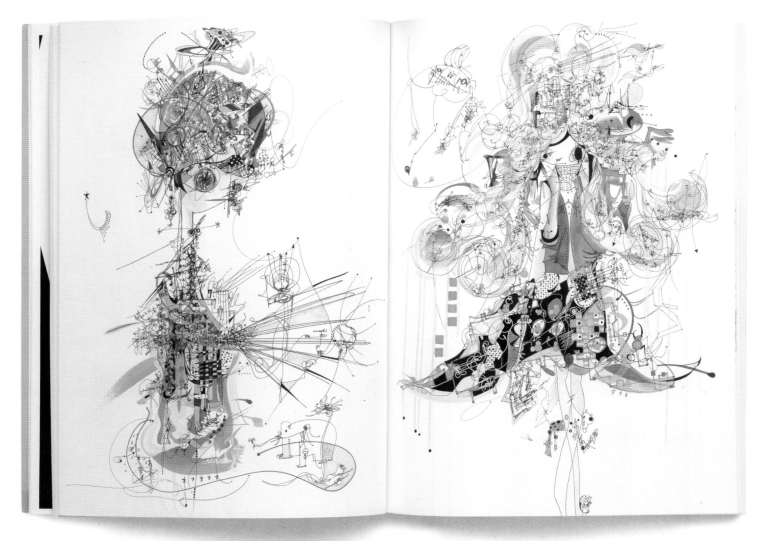

doingbird
ISSUE 1/AUSTRALIA/8.27x10.83 in (210x275 mm)
"FASHION AND ARTS PUBLICATION".

ISSN 1444-7312

01

9 771444 731003

doingbird #one

SOMEBODY WENT TO Faesthetic AND ALL I GOT WAS THIS STUPID MAGAZINE.

Faesthetic
ISSUE 4/UNITED STATES/8.27x10.51 in (210x267 mm)
"PROVIDES AN AFFORDABLE, ACCESSIBLE SHOWCASE FOR
SOME OF THE BEST CREATIVITY AND NEW ART THE WORLD
HAS TO OFFER."

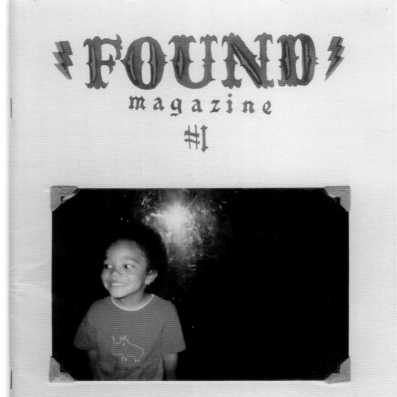

FOUND
ISSUE 1/UNITED STATES/8.27×10.91 in (210×277 mm)
"FOUND STUFF ANYTHING THAT GIVES A GLIMPSE
INTO SOMEONE ELSE'S LIFE. ANYTHING GOES..."

FOUND magazine #1

2nd Printing
15 all-new
pages!!!

amazingly... only
5 BUCKS!!

Attention friends! Our new mailing address is 3455 Charring Cross Rd., Ann Arbor, MI 48108-1911 USA.
Our new email is: info@foundmagazine.com. Peace!

HAPPY BIRTHDAY

HAPPY HAPPY BIRTHDAY TOINE

HAPPY BIRTHDAY TOINE

No player-Hating Permitted

Don't Miss Out!

bebe

When Dec. 12, 1999

9:00 PM until

A Morning

IT'S A PAJAMA PARTY

Where
2655 BIRNEY PLACE #12 S.E.
b'Anacostia
SUBWAY

Come! Party! wit a grown Man!

GBU
MAIN, TAZ, TOINE
Lowery

2nd Annual

PURPLE PARTY

In Connection with "Get wit it Productions"!

A GROWN MAN

FOUND by Gulliver Gold

South-East Washington, D.C.

4

YOU LIKE SPORTS, I LIKE SPORTS

I found this flyer taped up next to a drinking fountain on the U. of M. campus in April of 1998. O.K., I know it would be really easy to make fun of this dude, and I'm not too sure if I like his tone at times -- "I have a hearty sense of humor (those who do not, need not apply)" -- but all the same I've got to say that in a strange, desperate way, wallpapering every stairwell and kiosk on campus with these personal ads feels to me a courageous act.

FOUND by Gulliver Gold

Looking for love?
(I sure am.)

But what is love anyway? Is it just the physical nature of the beast? Perhaps. But more so, it's being able to watch a scary movie with someone knowing that if something happens, you'll be there to protect them. It's being able to call that person in the wee hours of the morning "just cuz" and know that person won't get angry at you for calling so late. It's brushing that stray piece of hair from their face, not because it bothers you, but because it hides their true beauty.

Sure, that's what I want. It's so easy isn't it? If it is that easy, I wouldn't have to write this......

So here goes. I'm 5'8"(-ish) Asian guy looking for someone to watch a movie and eat ice cream with. You like sports? I like sports. Pool, darts, rock climbing, racquetball, snowboarding, ultimate, skating, you name it. I have a hearty sense of humor (those that do not, need not apply), and I like aminals. If anything, we can always go have hot chocolate(since I never got used to the taste of coffee) and reminisce about the 80's.

There I said it.

- lovelost@umich.edu

5

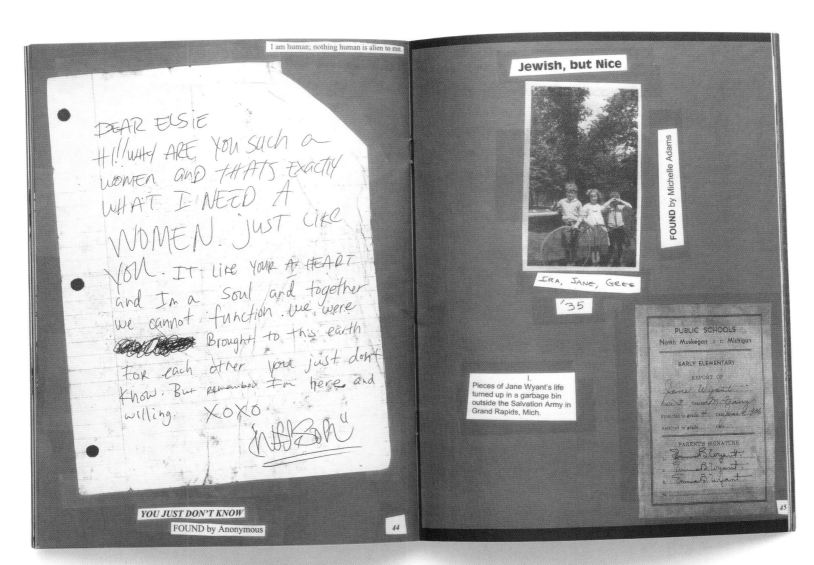

DEAR ELSIE
HI!! WHY ARE YOU SUCH a
WOMEN and THATS EXACTLY
WHAT I NEED A
WOMEN. JUST LIKE
YOU. IT LIKE YOUR A HEART
and Im a soul and together
we cannot function. we were
~~Brout~~ Brought to this earth
FoR each other you just don't
KNOW. But remember Im here and
willing. XOXO

YOU JUST DON'T KNOW
FOUND by Anonymous
44

Top right page:

Jewish, but Nice

FOUND by Michelle Adams

IRA, JANE, GREE
'35

1.
Pieces of Jane Wyant's life
turned up in a garbage bin
outside the Salvation Army in
Grand Rapids, Mich.

PUBLIC SCHOOLS
North Muskegon :: :: Michigan

EARLY ELEMENTARY

REPORT OF

45

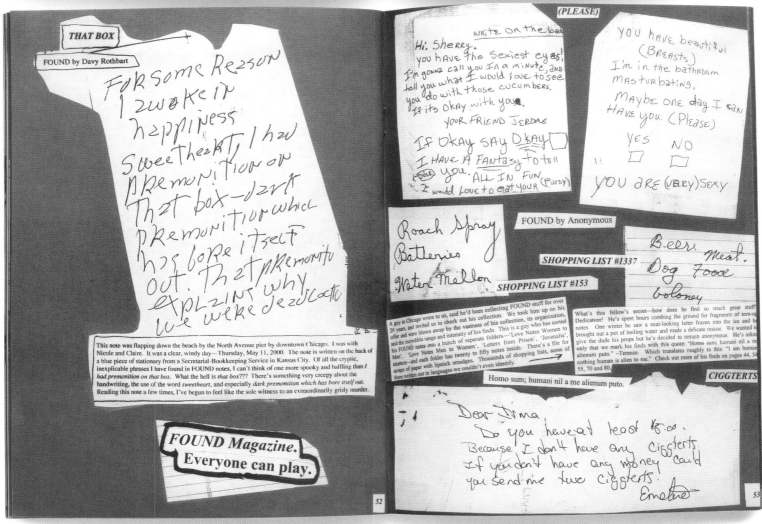

THAT BOX
FOUND by Davy Rothbart

FOR SOME REASON
I awoke in
happiness
Sweetheart, I had
Premonition on
That box—dark
Premonition which
has bore itself
out. That premonitio
explaint why
we were dedicate

This note was flapping down the beach by the North Avenue pier by downtown Chicago. I was with Nicole and Claire. It was a clear, windy day—Thursday, May 11, 2000. The note is written on the back of a blue piece of stationary from a Secretarial-Bookkeeping Service in Kansas City. Of all the cryptic, inexplicable phrases I have found in FOUND notes, I can't think of one more spooky and baffling than *I had premonition on that box*. What the hell is *that box*??? There's something very creepy about the handwriting, the use of the word *sweetheart*, and especially *dark premonition which has bore itself out*. Reading this note a few times, I've begun to feel like the sole witness to an extraordinarily grisly murder.

FOUND Magazine.
Everyone can play.

52

(PLEASE)

write on the back
Hi. Sherry.
you have the sexiest eyes!
I'm gonna call you In a minute, and
tell you what I would love to see
you do with those cucumbers.
If its okay with you.
YOUR FRIEND JEROME

IF OKAY SAY OKAY ☐
I HAVE A FANTASY to tell
(okay) you. ALL IN FUN (Pussy)
I would love to eat your

YOU HAVE beautiful
(BREASTS)
I'm in the bathroom
masturbating.
Maybe one day I can
HAVE you. (Please)

YES   NO
☐   ☐

YOU ARE (VERY) SEXY

FOUND by Anonymous

Roach Spray
Batteries
Water Mellon

SHOPPING LIST #153

SHOPPING LIST #1337

Beer. Meat.
Dog Food
boloney

A guy in Chicago wrote to us, said he'd been collecting FOUND stuff for over 20 years, and invited us to check out his collection. We took him up on his offer and were blown away by the vastness of his finds. This is a guy who has sorted the incredible range and intensity of his finds. This is a guy who has sorted his FOUND notes into a bunch of separate folders—'Love Notes Women to Men', 'Love Notes Men to Women', 'Letters from Prison', 'Juvenalia', etcetera—and each folder has twenty to fifty notes inside. There's a file for scraps of paper with lipstick smudges. Thousands of shopping lists, some of them written out in languages we couldn't even identify.

What's this fellow's secret—how does he find so much great stuff? Dedication! He's spent hours combing the ground for fragments of torn-up notes. One winter he saw a neat-looking letter frozen into the ice and he brought out a pot of boiling water and made a delicate rescue. We wanted to give the dude his props but he's decided to remain anonymous. He's asked only that we mark his finds with this quote: "Homo sum; humani nil a me alienum puto." —Terence. Which translates roughly to this: "I am human; nothing human is alien to me." Check out more of his finds on pages 44, 54, 55, 70 and 80.

Homo sum; humani nil a me alienum puto.

CIGGTERTS

Dear Irma,
Do you have at least $8.00.
Because I don't have any ciggterts.
If you don't have any money could
you send me two ciggterts.
Emeline

53

happening

fashion photography architecture community education

1

biannual june 2003

happening
ISSUE 1 /TAIWAN /9.06x11.57 in (230x294 mm)
"TO INSPIRE AND ENCOURAGE SO THAT READERS CAN MAKE
THE THINGS THEY BELIEVE IN HAPPEN."

influence

$10. ISSUE 01, 2003 (15) WESCHLER, Lawrence (15) ANDERSEN, Kurt (19) NERI, Louise (24) MEATYARD, Ralph Eugene (44) WILCOX, Emma (50) BESHTY, Walead (64) MIRER, Daniel (80) COOKE, Nigel (88) MAIER-AICHEN, Florian (92) LUNDIN, Ulf (114) GOODWIN, Danny (114) BRAWLEY, Louis (120) HAWKINS, Stuart (124) RICHTER, Gerhard (125) VERMEER, Johannes (132) MARCOPOULOS, Ari (140) BELIN, Valérie (144) VAN LAMSWEERDE, Inez and MATADIN, Vinoodh

influence
ISSUE 1/UNITED STATES/9.49x11.97 in (241x304 mm)
"NUMEROUS EXAMPLES OF THE INSPIRATIONS AND INFLUENCES
ON THE CUTTING EDGE OF CREATIVE DISCUSSION"

0 1 >

7 25274 57024 9

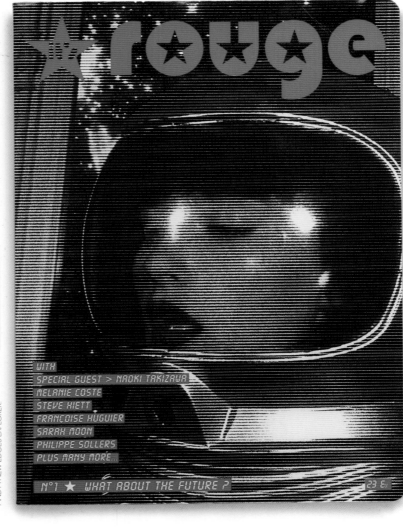

it's rouge
ISSUE 1/FRANCE/9.06x12.13 in (230x308 mm)
'AN ATTEMPT FOR VISUAL BRAINSTORMING,
AND A NEW EDGES EXPLORER'

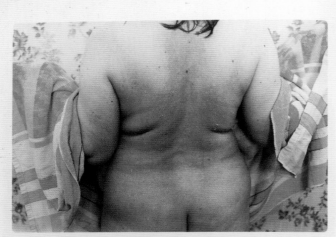
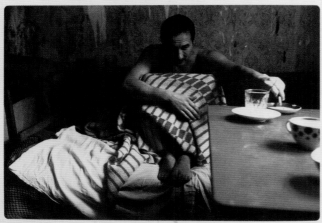

The *Issue* Journey

Magazines, magazines, and more magazines. Pretty much anyone who has worked in a creative field or has had creative ambitions has thought about starting a magazine. This is quite simply because being creative is about expressing things in an altered, deviate way: presenting a shining piece that can stand out and give away the whole puzzle or at least an idea of the puzzle that you would like people to believe. What better place than a magazine to feature these "pieces," adding commentary, substantiation, and legitimacy—and leaving out whatever contradicts them? Magazines are like fantasy microcosms into which you can project your viewpoint and ideals. No one can truly claim to take full creative satisfaction in their expressive endeavors even if they are highly successful. Though, when you make a magazine you feel psychologically that you can attain that goal. It is this myth that lures us all into this media. Thanks to the fleeting nature of magazines, and their periodicity, reality never quite hits until you wake up one day and realize you have a business to run. Your precious gift to society becomes nothing more than an expensive ego trip, which only lasts as long as those tripping with you want to hang on. ■■■■■■ For as long as it lasts or can last, this is essential. The magazine is one of the few truly collaborative art forms where unlikely collisions can take place, where the collaborators' faults and talents balance each other out and fit together to build the puzzle. Ideas flow freely out of necessity to make things exist, to fill the blanks, to just do—and these ideas surprisingly, when they are unmediated, bring something new and inspirational to others, bring so many possibilities to light. Baring all and standing with bright eyes—that is what we all do, that is what the readers and contributors feel, and all is transparent and radiance shines through. It is like partaking in a naturalist community where conventions, structures, rules, and money don't apply, but where people, ideas, and ideals can exist. ■■■■■■ Of course, you have camps, cliques, all sorts of people doing their thing their own way. Each group has its own little island and believes that what they are doing is best. Some are more structured, free, provocative, liberal, pretentious, naive, inventive, full of shit, conventional, visual, intelligent, viable, or whatever. Then sometimes people move from one island to another for the greener grass or because of the bad weather—and set up their own island, stage a coup d'état, or go back to the mainland of mass-market publishing to cash in, sell out, or seek pardon for having deserted. ■■■■■■ Marginal magazines, niche, specialty, or whatever you want to call them, are nothing more than micro societies, and the end result is a testimony, a chronicle. Such magazines are not produced; they are lived. Having published *Issue* on and off for the last six years (1999–2006), I have been living in *Issue* Land. Everything I eat, live, breathe, love, and die for is in *Issue* Land. *Issue* is dedicated to the celebration of creative thought and development in all industries, including visual arts, photography, music, film, architecture, culture, and style. It is probably quite apparent that my ruling policy embodied a certain utopian approach in *Issue* Land. My strength as an editor was not my knowledge of art and culture, but rather my ability to pinpoint the less obvious choices of "those in the know." Content was created through an evolving collection of skilled contributors and highly acclaimed contemporary artists working in diverse mediums. We garnered a unique reputation for our successful collaborative skills in breeding trust and creative energy. It was my mission to know damn well why a big name would be included, aside from the obvious publicity angle, as well as to find out exactly what would pique this contributor's interest in collaborating.

by Jan-Willem Dikkers

The energy from all this cross-fertilization was then bottled up and published in the magazine. My goal was to create the catalyst and then editorialize the yield, staying as true and honest to the source as possible, and package the content so that the reader could feel included and breathe the magic.

Accuracy in this regard rewarded *Issue* with its distinction as a chosen forum for expression. ▬▬▬▬ Having worked in the heart of fashion and image building in the quite peculiar moment of the mid-1990s, I was privy to the blurring lines between the not-so-distant worlds of art, culture, design, photography, film, magazines, and all that. I aimed to give these correlations a voice and for boundaries to be crossed, to allow for leaders of different camps to show their similarities and share their fascinations for one another. This approach rubbed off on many contributors, who would in turn solicit further collaborations or seek interactions with each other. *Issue* became a sort of creative agency through which projects and relationships could be developed—producing books and exhibitions, establishing a performance space, managing artists, and much more. The energy from all this cross-fertilization was then bottled up and published in the magazine. My goal was to create the catalyst and then editorialize the yield, staying as true and honest to the source as possible, and package the content so that the reader could feel included and breathe the magic. I was the fascinated reader living it in real time, being thrown into one world after another, sitting and listening to the less-told stories of the likes of Bob Richardson, Larry Clark, Paul McCarthy, Jack Pierson, Christopher Wool, Bill Owens, Ari Marcopoulos, Tom Wood, Peter Fend, or Pipilotti Rist . . . having strange visits from an MI6 agent, reading autobiographies that may never be published, getting complimentary letters from Karl Lagerfeld on his Monaco stationery, seeing collaborative work we initiated hanging at Luhring Augustine Gallery, helping artists to find work on other commercial or editorial projects, having a method —the *Issue* way of collaborating—that allows us to nurture fruitful relationships and new ideas throughout countries on all continents. It was because of all this that I could not just run a picture alongside a quick interview or critical essay, but rather thought harder about how I could share all this with those who did not have this chance. How to give justice to both contributors and readers, how to give more and reach further. The willingness to hold together a network of hundreds of people with ties crossing through *Issue* made collaborations with and between artists and contributors the way of *Issue*. This is all overwhelmingly exciting and time-consuming, for a very small, constantly evolving, micro underpaid or nonpaid staff, with no backers or conscious effort to sell advertising. ▬▬▬▬ Now, in a period of transition due to circumstance and economic realities, no longer allowing myself to hold things together the way I had hoped, where do I belong? I find myself lost in a foreign land with nothing more than the clothes on my back and memories of the old country. How many Factories should one create? Will the magic be there each time? Is it possible to exist on the outside and function from within? Why do such magazines never last? I look at some of my favorite magazines from the past, like *Horizon* (U.S.) or *Opus* (France), and in awe witness some of the most incredible encounters and collaborations of their time—the beginnings, dreams, and first expressions of those who became the greatest thinkers, artists, filmmakers, and writers of our time. I notice that they tried in their own way to adjust periodicity and editorial formulas, but refused to embrace the beast of change fully, and eventually died out. It is quite ironic that for the price of just one ad in magazines that are celebrating their fiftieth and one hundredth anniversaries, which no one actually reads or holds on to, most marginal magazines could publish multiple issues. Stepping out of the ivory tower, you realize that their reflections are nothing more than echoes of the way everything in society functions. If you want things to change, then—with blood, sweat, and tears—make the change happen the way you can. And although in the larger scope things might never shift, you will have tried, and that is what is necessary—these testimonies are the ones that give hope to those who believe that it is worth fighting for what you believe in, and that another way is possible. It is this strength that we all need to keep alive the dreams we had when we were thirteen-year-old kids.

Magazines are like fantasy microcosms into which you can project your viewpoint and ideals.

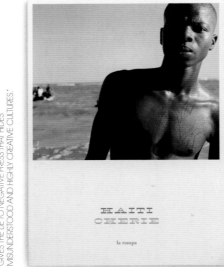

la rampa
ISSUE 2/CANADA/10.04x13.98 in (255x355 mm)
"GIVES THE LIE TO NEGATIVE PRESS THAT HIDES
MISUNDERSTOOD AND HIGHLY CREATIVE CULTURES."

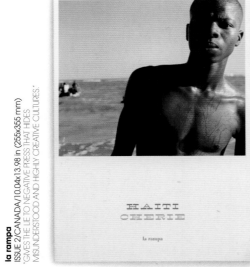

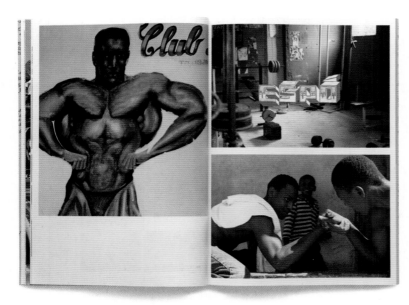

M_00

MODA E CONTEXTO
AGOSTO 2001 | Nº 00

R$ 15,00

ISSN 1519-7948

next level
ISSUE 1/UNITED KINGDOM/9.25x11.02 in (235x280 mm)
'AIMS TO BRING AWARENESS TO CONTEMPORARY ISSUES FROM A
VISUAL AND TEXT-BASED PERSPECTIVE'.

104/5   Josef Koudelka

Our Magazine
ISSUE 1 / SWITZERLAND / 7.48×9.76 in (190×248 mm)
"EACH ISSUE IS DEDICATED TO A DIFFERENT TOPIC,
FEATURED AS THE TITLE, AND SHOWCASES WORK
OF VARIED NATURE AND PROVENANCE."

PERMANENT FOOD
ISSUE 1/UNITED STATES/ITALY/7.17x9.96 in (182x253 mm)
"A SECOND-GENERATION MAGAZINE" WITH PAGES COMING
FROM MAGAZINES AROUND THE WORLD.

FOR ALL THOSE
WAITING FOR THE
PERFECT BALANCE OF
HAND CRAFTSMANSHIP,
ADVANCED TECHNOLOGY,
AND A LOOK THAT'LL
KNOCK THE WIND
RIGHT OUT OF YOU...

TALES OF THE UNIVERSE

Living in the asphalt jungle

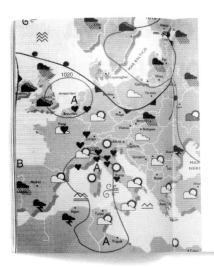

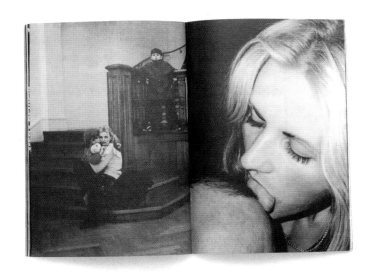

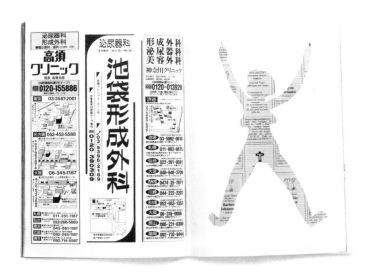

POLISHED T
ISSUE 1/UNITED KINGDOM/8.27x10.43 in (210x265 mm)
"A VIRTUAL GALLERY SPACE"

purple

FASHION, PROSE, SPECIAL, FICTION, INTERIOR
75 FF, $14, 11 EUROS
NUMBER 4, WINTER '99-'00

9 782912 684127 >

purple
ISSUE 4/FRANCE/6.10x8.46 in (155x215 mm)
A DIFFERENT TAKE ON FASHION AND PHOTOGRAPHY.

216

PURPLE SEXE

NUMBER 4
SUMMER 1999
60F $10 9EUROS
ADULTS ONLY
13 TOPICS

9 782912 684110

PURPLE SEXE
ISSUE 4/FRANCE/6.10x8.43 in (155x214 mm)
A DIFFERENT TAKE ON SEX.

Quadrafoil

Quadrafoil
ISSUE 1 / UNITED STATES / 10.87 x 13.74 n (276x349 mm)
"BRINGS ARCHETYPES TO THE FOREFRONT, DISTILLED INTO
MULTIPLICITY, TOTALITY, AND UNITY."

RANK

RANK F'SHION ISSUE 00
DECEMBER/JANUARY £7.95
ISSN 1472-6548

9 771472 654008

RANK
ISSUE 0/UNITED KINGDOM/9.45x12.60 in (240x320 mm)
'A FASHION AND PHOTOGRAPH JOURNAL'

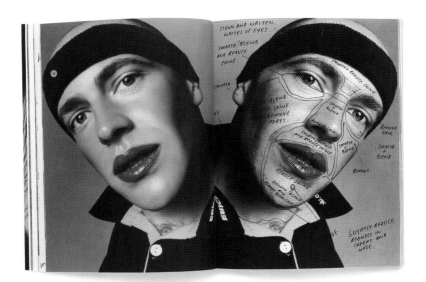

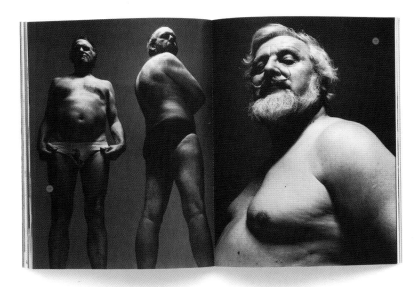

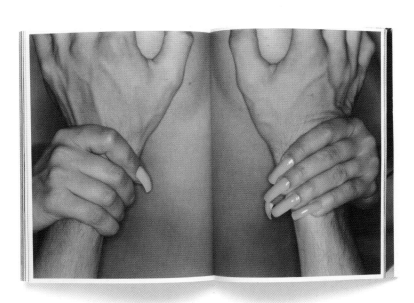

Richardson

SNOOZER 12月号増刊

ISSUE A1 DECEMBER 1998　1998年12月1日発行第2巻第7号（通巻11号）

A1

世界同時発売
世界初の
ヴィジュアル系ポルノ
マガジン

テリー・リチャードソン
グレン・ルッチフォード
ハーモニー・コリン他

Richardson
ISSUE 1 / UNITED STATES / 8.82x12.01 in (224x305 mm)
"AN ART/SEX PUBLICATION"

love letter to Amerika Takashi Homma

Photographed by Takashi Homma
Model Sayaka Yoshino
Stylist Misa Tennai
H.M. Asashi Yamaguchi

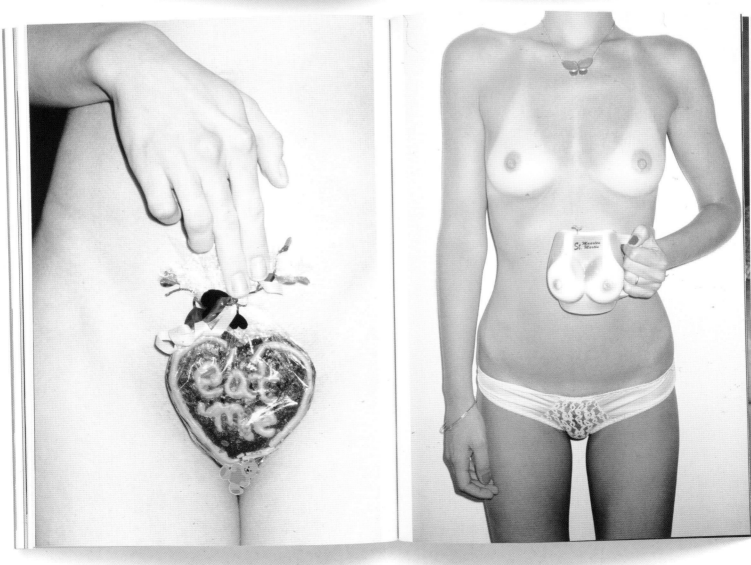

rojo
ISSUE 19/SPAIN/8.27×11.02 in (210×280 mm)
"EXCLUSIVELY MADE OUT OF CONTRIBUTIONS"

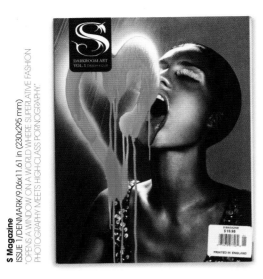

S Magazine
ISSUE 1/DENMARK/9.06x11.61 in (230x295 mm)
"OPENS A WINDOW ON A WORLD WHERE SUPERLATIVE FASHION PHOTOGRAPHY MEETS HIGH-CLASS PORNOGRAPHY."

ZANNE SOELE PIPER

**2
2
4**

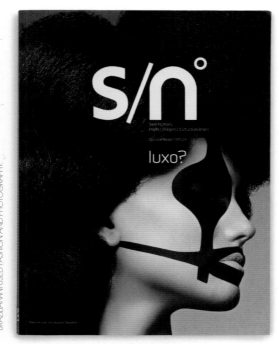

s/n° ISSUE 1 / BRAZIL / 9.45x12.56 in (240x319 mm)
BRAZILIAN-INFUSED FASHION AND PHOTOGRAPHY.

SEPP.

FOOTBALL **FASHION**

1

$10.00 U.S.

25 >

0   74470   56900   8

SEPP
ISSUE 1/UNITED STATES/GERMANY/8.07 x 10.83 in (205x275 mm)
"A FASHION INSIDER'S VIEW OF THE WORLD'S
MOST POPULAR SPORT, SOCCER"

STARE
ISSUE 1/UNITED STATES/7.28x9.17 in (185x233 mm)
"THROUGH THE USE OF ORIGINAL PHOTOGRAPHY,
ARTWORK, QUOTES, AND FACTUAL CAPTIONS, THIS PUBLICATION
COVERS MODERN LIFE AND EXPERIENCES."

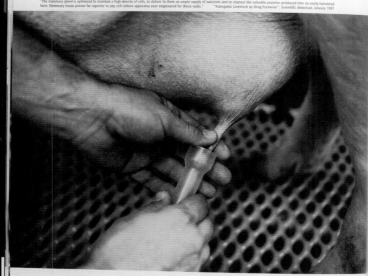

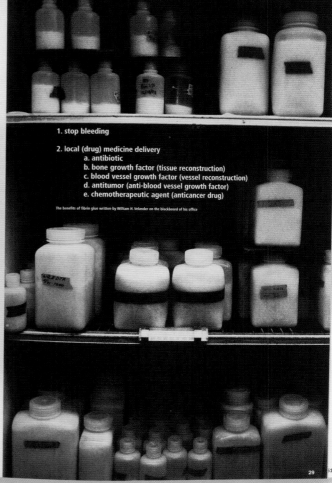

Fibrinogen and other similar proteins are present in human blood, but in very small amounts. The existing process of extraction and purification is difficult and expensive, and can lead to contamination with infectious agents. By creating these human blood proteins with transgenic livestock, the Red Cross is on the path towards efficient mass production.

"The mammary gland is optimized to maintain a high density of cells, to deliver to them an ample supply of nutrients and to channel the valuable proteins produced into an easily harvested form. Mammary tissue proves far superior to any cell-culture apparatus ever engineered for these tasks."   "Transgenic Livestock as Drug Factories", Scientific American, January 1997

1. stop bleeding

2. local (drug) medicine delivery
   a. antibiotic
   b. bone growth factor (tissue reconstruction)
   c. blood vessel growth factor (vessel reconstruction)
   d. antitumor (anti-blood vessel growth factor)
   e. chemotherapeutic agent (anticancer drug)

The benefits of fibrin glue written by William H. Velander on the blackboard of his office

"Red Cross scientists, working with the U.S. Army, have developed revolutionary bandage and foam devices that utilize two human plasma proteins, fibrinogen and thrombin, to stop bleeding within seconds."

"Fibrinogen and thrombin interact to form fibrin, the major component of a blood clot."

Extracted from American Red Cross press releases

Storage of milk from transgenic mouse

territory
ISSUE 3 /MALAYSIA/9.45x11.38 in (240x289 mm)
"OUR MISSION IN LIFE IS TO PUSH THE ENVELOPE FURTHER
WITH THE SOLE AIM OF CREATING SOMETHING NEW"

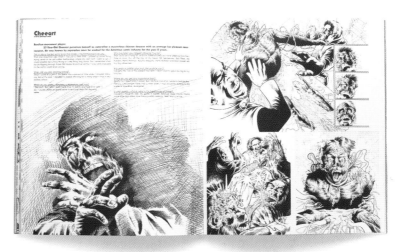

THE BLOW UP
ISSUE 1/UNITED STATES/7.95x9.96 in (202x253 mm)
"ABOUT IMPORTANT ISSUES/INNOVATIONS IN ART,
POLITICS, MUSIC, AND FASHION".

THE BLOW UP

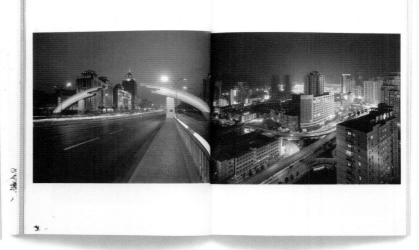

WE ARE
ALL
PEOPLE

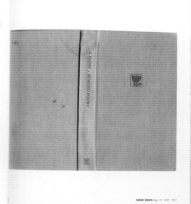

THE COLONIAL

#1: Sound and Music | Fall/Winter 2005 | 8 USD

BOB DYLAN
Ian Svenonius

YELLOW SWANS
& JOHN WIESE
Oliver Hall

LAFMS
Rick Potts

MATHIAS POLEDNA
Diedrich Diederichsen

ROBERT BRESSON
Kent Jones

TEXT OF LIGHT
Alan Licht

MARK E. SMITH
Michael Bracewell
& Jon Wilde

WYNDHAM LEWIS
Stuart Bailey

+

Richard Prince
Anders Edström
Ira Cohen
Finnish folks
Steve Dore
The Shady Ladies
Terence Koh
Ron Rege Jr.
Anagram Record Reviews

THE COLONIAL
ISSUE 1/UNITED STATES/7.01x8.98 in (178x228 mm)
"ART JOURNAL GENERALLY FOCUSED ON MUSIC THEMES"

THE CURVE
ISSUE 1/UNITED KINGDOM/9.84x7.48 in (250x190 mm)
"A HIGH-OCTANE MIX OF AUTOMOTIVE POWER MEETS FANTASY."

THE CURVE
A BIGFRANK PRODUCTION FOR 2002
ISSUE 1: AUTOMOTIVE *IT'S THE FEEL OF THE SPEED THAT COUNTS* **£10**

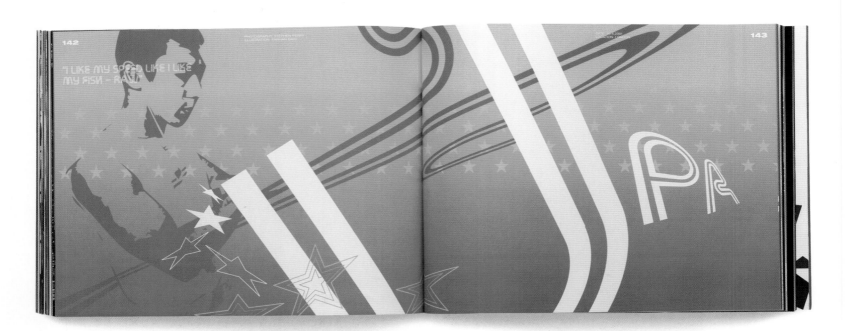

The Illustrated Ape
ISSUE 19/UNITED KINGDOM/10x12.24 in (245x300 mm)
'CULTURAL MAGAZINE THAT CONTAINS POETRY ILLUSTRATIONS,
SHORT FICTION, ESSAYS, DESIGN IDEAS, AND MORE'

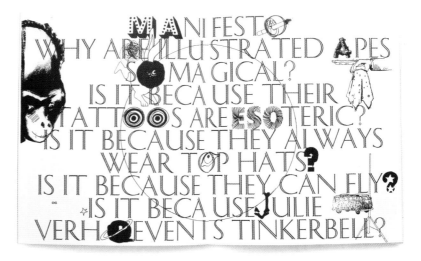

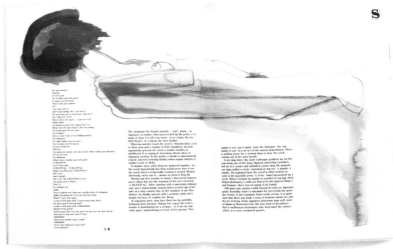

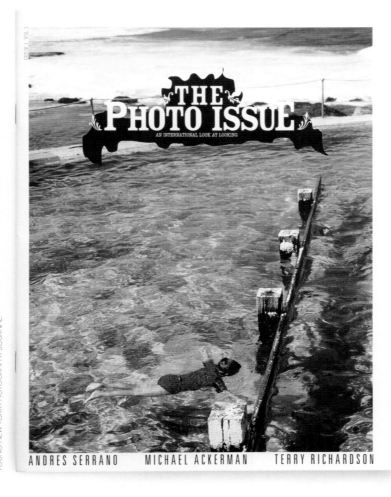

THE PHOTO ISSUE
ISSUE 1 / UNITED STATES / 8.07x9.92 in (205x252 mm)
YOUNG NEW YORK PHOTOGRAPHY JOURNAL

THE PURPLE JOURNAL

ENGLISH VERSION.
PUBLISHED EACH SEASON.
NUMBER 1. SUMMER 04.
7.5 EUROS (FRANCE)

This is our first issue: joy, hope. Starting out or beginning again (the journal Hélène *and the magazine* Purple*)—anyway, it's a first appearance. A path we'll travel together, we, the editors, and you, the readers. We will show reality as we see it through encounters with people, places, landscapes, artworks. Writing and photographs, original voices. The journey is not mapped out in advance, we'll discover it (as it reveals itself) with the changing seasons.*

THE PURPLE JOURNAL
ISSUE 1/FRANCE/8.27x10.83 in (210x275 mm)
"IS A PLACE IN WHICH TO ESCAPE THE MONOTONE REPETITIONS
OF THE WORLD MEDIA—A LIVELY MAGAZINE THAT RESISTS
DEAD ENDS AND DIVISIONS."

Anouschka, une des étudiantes de Arnheim qui a participé à la réalisation du film.

48

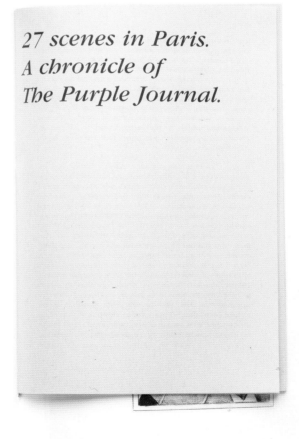

27 scenes in Paris.
A chronicle of
The Purple Journal.

49

TRUCE
ISSUE 1/SWITZERLAND/9.06x11.42 in (230x290 mm)
"PURSUES OUTSTANDING CREATIVE CONTENT FROM
INTERNATIONALLY ACCLAIMED ARTISTS,
PHOTOGRAPHERS, AND WRITERS."

Wish u were here xxx
ISSUE 1/UNITED STATES/8.27×10.59 in (210×269 mm)
TRAVEL MAGAZINE FEATURING PERSONAL SHOTS FROM
PHOTOGRAPHERS AWAY ON A SHOOT

⊗ 2 (A et B).
 ‗ NEVADA / 01/2000.
 ‗ LOOKING FOR PHOENIX AIRPORT. BACK TO PARIS for LOUIS
   VUITTON.
 ‗ ZEN, CLEAR ..... PLENTY of ....

yummy

junkfoodesignmagazine

yummy
ISSUE 1/FRANCE/8.39x10.83 in (213x275 mm)
"JUNK FOOD DESIGN MAGAZINE"

Snacks

Céreales & Biscuits

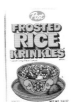

zing magazine
curatorial crossing

zing
ISSUE 20/UNITED STATES/8.46x11.02 in (215x280 mm)
ECLECTIC ART MAGAZINE FROM DOWNTOWN NEW YORK.

ISSUE 20/UNITED STATES $15.00 / SPECIAL EDITION 22 • CANADA $20.00 • SHELVE UNTIL MARCH 2006

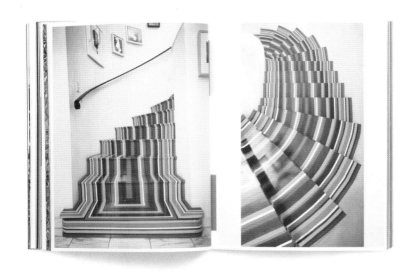

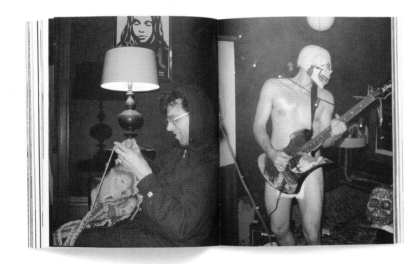

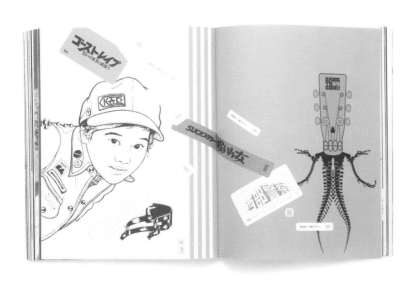

COM
MUN
ITY

The stylepress are created by individuals and small groups for slightly larger social tribes. Their purpose is not fueled by the desire to appeal to all within a category, as in the traditional magazine paradigm. Instead, they are harbingers and mediators of taste and quality for others who play the same role. Advertising revenue flows, when it does, to the stylepress not because of elaborate yet unreliable cpm data, but because of these tribal tastemakers: their attention has a multiplying effect. / / This community focus can take on a wide variety of forms. From Virgin Atlantic's upper-class *CARLOS* and an independent film's *ANNA SANDERS* to *Me*, filling its pages with the featured artist's friends, the pseudo-autobiographical *RE-*, and the mock *Daniel Battams Fan Club*. From the gay, art and culture *They Shoot Homos Don't They?* and *BUTT* and the surf and architecture infused *PROPHECY* to the Middle Eastern, German, and Los Angelino groupuscules of *bidoun*, *ACHTUNG*, and *PUTA*, the young amateur artist-focused *LOOK LOOK*, and the ever-changing creative direction of *Big*.

Why does a magazine have to be programmed to the lowest common denominator?

2
4
4

A BIT SPECIAL
ISSUE 4/UNITED KINGDOM/5.75x8.3 in (146x210 mm)
"FOR HOMOS INTO ANYONE. NOT USER-FRIENDLY HOMO
VERY RANDOM. FLIP IN ANTICIPATION."

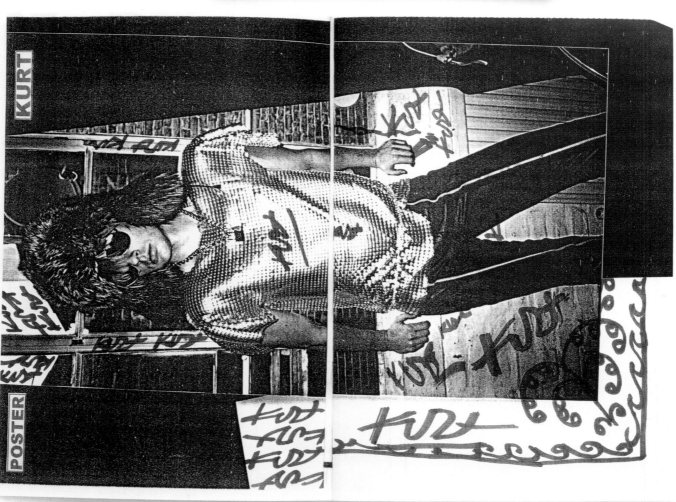

ACHTUNG
ISSUE 1 / GERMANY / 8.8x11.75 in (224x299 mm)
"REPRESENTS WHAT HAPPENS CREATIVELY IN FASHION IN
GERMANY, SWITZERLAND, AND AUSTRIA."

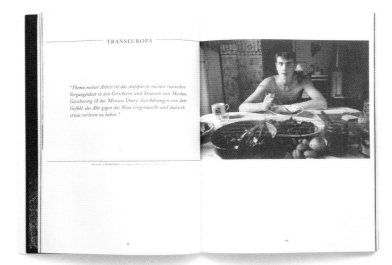

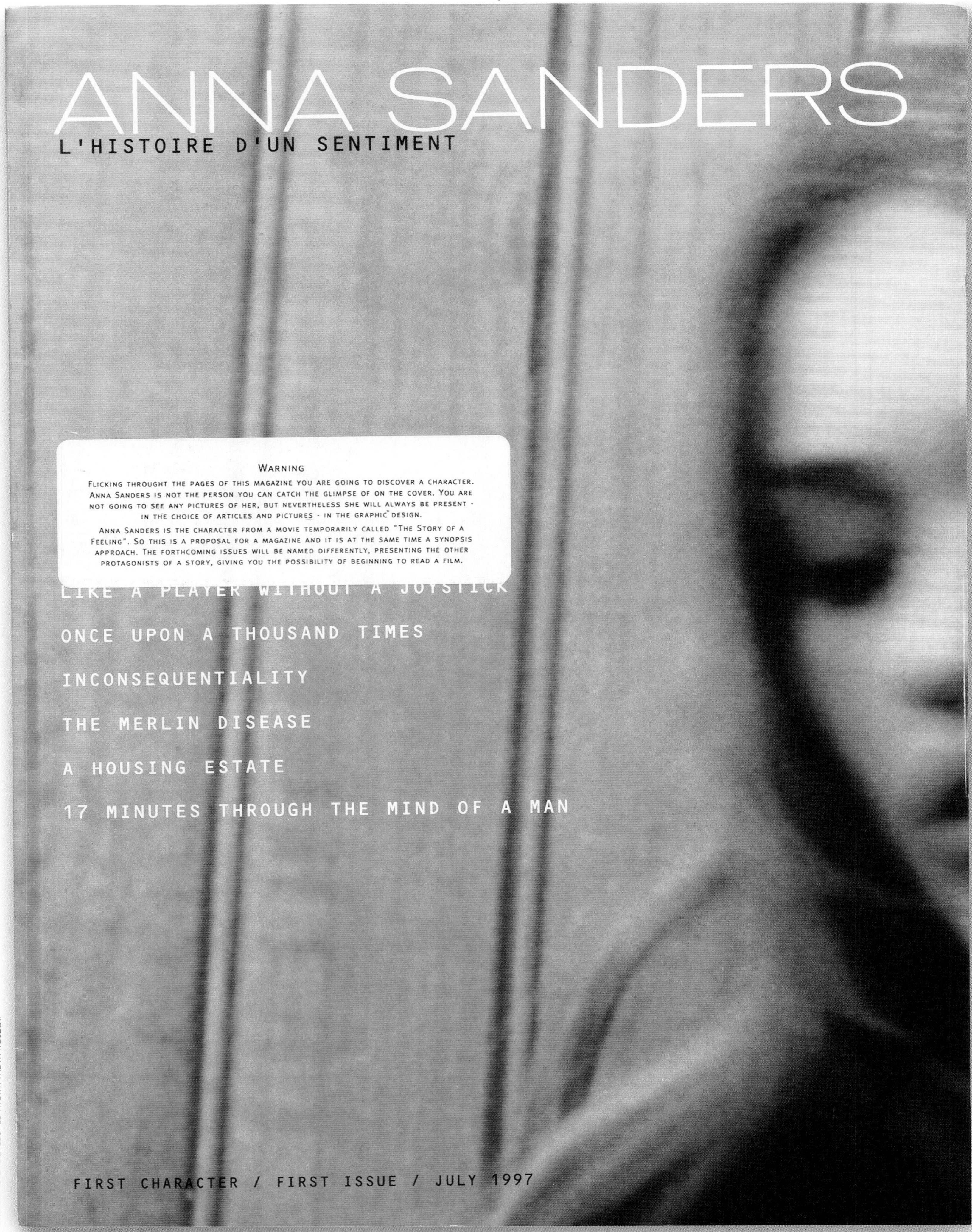

ANNA SANDERS

L'HISTOIRE D'UN SENTIMENT

WARNING

FLICKING THROUGHT THE PAGES OF THIS MAGAZINE YOU ARE GOING TO DISCOVER A CHARACTER. ANNA SANDERS IS NOT THE PERSON YOU CAN CATCH THE GLIMPSE OF ON THE COVER. YOU ARE NOT GOING TO SEE ANY PICTURES OF HER, BUT NEVERTHELESS SHE WILL ALWAYS BE PRESENT - IN THE CHOICE OF ARTICLES AND PICTURES - IN THE GRAPHIC DESIGN.

ANNA SANDERS IS THE CHARACTER FROM A MOVIE TEMPORARILY CALLED "THE STORY OF A FEELING". SO THIS IS A PROPOSAL FOR A MAGAZINE AND IT IS AT THE SAME TIME A SYNOPSIS APPROACH. THE FORTHCOMING ISSUES WILL BE NAMED DIFFERENTLY, PRESENTING THE OTHER PROTAGONISTS OF A STORY, GIVING YOU THE POSSIBILITY OF BEGINNING TO READ A FILM.

LIKE A PLAYER WITHOUT A JOYSTICK

ONCE UPON A THOUSAND TIMES

INCONSEQUENTIALITY

THE MERLIN DISEASE

A HOUSING ESTATE

17 MINUTES THROUGH THE MIND OF A MAN

FIRST CHARACTER / FIRST ISSUE / JULY 1997

ANNA SANDERS
ISSUE 1 / FRANCE / 8.26x10.95 in (210x278 mm)
A CHARACTER DEVELOPED FROM A FILM PROJECT.

A PAGE TORN OUT OF A MAGAZINE.
LEND REALITY TO THE PICTURE OF A
MAGAZINE, AND SEE HOW THIS
CHARACTER CAN EXIST. CARRY ON THE
GAME WITH PICTURES OF PLACES IN
WHICH SHE CAN EVOLVE, AND GOINGS-
ON WITH EVENTS WHICH SHE CAN BE
INVOLVED IN. COLLECTING THESE
PICTURES TO BUILD A STORY.
A LIAISON BETWEEN DIFFERENT PICTURES
WHICH APPARENTLY MAKE SENSE
TOGETHER, A PRIORI, BUT ALL THAT CAN
JUST AS WELL BE A FLOP.

a page torn out of a magazine

UNE PAGE ARRACHÉE D'UN MAGAZIN
DONNER À CETTE IMAGE UNE RÉALIT
VOIR COMMENT CE CARACTÈRE PE
SE METTRE À EXISTE
POURSUIVRE LE JEU AVEC DES IMAG
DE LIEUX DANS LESQUELS ELLE PE
ÉVOLUER, DES ÉVÉNEMENTS QU'E
PEUT TRAVERS

Fait à la maison
★ BRONX (Paris)
34 BD Bonne Nouvelle
75 010 Paris
Tel. 01 47 70 70 00

248

bidoun
ISSUE 1/UNITED STATES/8.85x10.65 in (225x270 mm)
"A PLATFORM FOR IDEAS AND AN OPEN FORUM FOR EXCHANGE,
DIALOGUE, AND OPINIONS ABOUT ARTS AND CULTURE
FROM THE MIDDLE EAST."

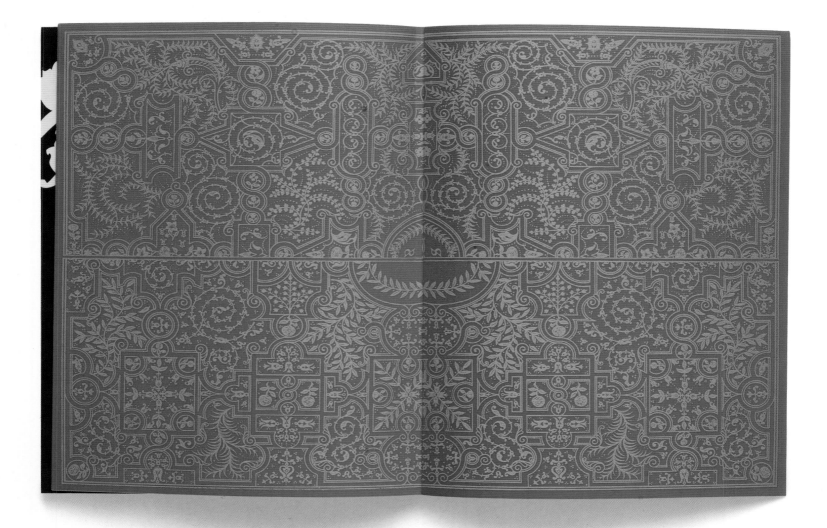

Previous page: Marc Garanger, Femme Algérienne, 1960.
Above: Jananne Al-Ani, 'Untitled', 1996. Left: AES art
group, 'New Freedom 2006, AES - The Witness of the
Future', 1996.

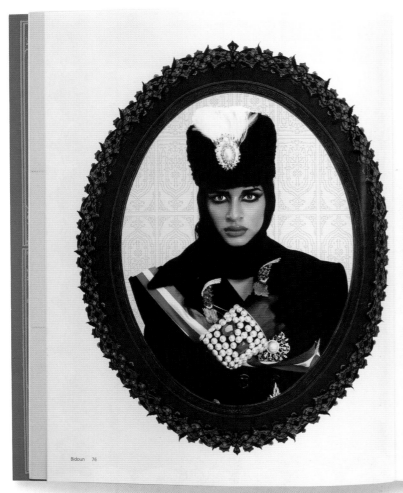

250

Big
ISSUE 26/UNITED STATES/9.45x12 in (240x304 mm)
"PRODUCES EACH ISSUE IN A DIFFERENT COUNTRY,
WITH DIFFERENT TEAMS OF CONTRIBUTORS."

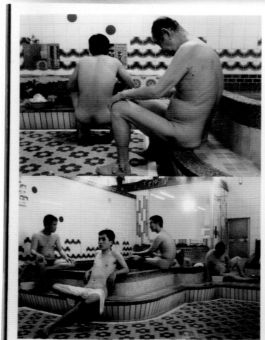

DR. STRANGELOVE
or: How I Learned to Stop Worrying and Love the Image of Japan

Nude

photographed by Daido Moriyama

YOKOSUKA

How to Take a Japanese Bath

by Leonard Koren · Illustrations by Suehiro Maruo

INTRODUCTION

BUTT
ISSUE 1 /NETHERLANDS/6.6x9.45 in (168x240 mm)
"POCKET-SIZE MAGAZINE FOR AND ABOUT HOMOSEXUALS."

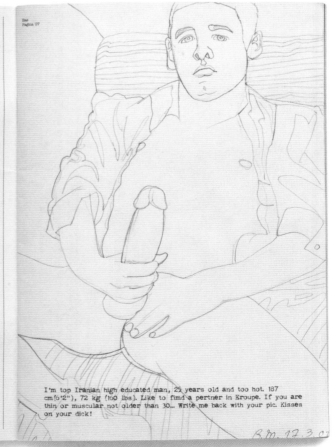

BART JULIUS PETERS FOTOGRAAF DRAAGT VERSACE EN ONTMOET ZONDER BRIL BEROEMDE AMERIKAANSE ACTEUR IN HOMO-SAUNA

door Gert Jonkers
foto Bart Hendriks

Geen opening van een expositie, modeshow of ander art event is compleet zonder Bart Julius Peters, de steevast in pak gestoken, twee meter lange jongeman die dankzij z'n buitensporig model bril en verbaasde blik ook wel 'Bart Bril' of 'Andy Warhol' wordt genoemd. Hij heeft altijd een camera bij zich, maar heeft ooit iemand een foto van zijn hand gezien? Ja. Wie bij Bart Peters op bezoek komt krijgt een grote map vol contactafdrukken op schoot, en daarna een doos vol foto's van chique dames, en een stapel pasfoto's van leuke jongens.

Laten we bij het begin beginnen. Waar je vandaan komt.
'Ik ben geboren in Koeweit, mijn vader bouwde er een haven. Daar hebben we tot mijn elfde gewoond, en toen tot mijn twintigste in het Gooi.'
Vandaar die aardappel in je keel?
'Aardappel? Ik vind niet dat ik bekakt praat. Ik praat netjes. Ik kan mijn spraak trouwens prima aan de situatie of 't milieu aanpassen.'
Je bedoelt dat je in bed niet netjes praat?

'In bed praat ik nooit. Of in ieder geval niet veel.'
Heb je kunstacademie gedaan?
'Ja, zeven jaar Rietveld Academie. De eerste drie jaar liep ik daar illegaal rond, want ik werd nooit aangenomen. Een van de docenten zag wel iets in mijn werk dus daarbij mocht ik de lessen volgen zonder dat ik echt op school zat. Daarnaast deed ik de opleiding tekenen en schilderen aan de Lutmastraat. Toen kreeg ik een Braziliaans vriendje en daar ben ik na een half jaar achteraan

---

FRANÇOIS-XAVIER COURRÈGES FRENCH ARTIST MAKES VIDEO WITH BOYS SAYING I LOVE YOU

Text and Photography by Sisc Cartier

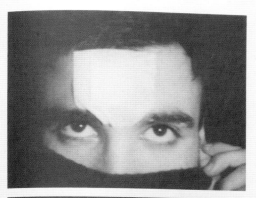

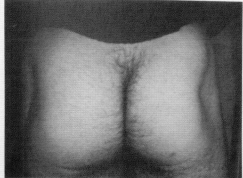

It is early March in Paris, people are having lunch outside in the sunshine, I meet up with François-Xavier Courrèges (well the name is beautiful, that's simple), an aspiring, charming French artist. We sit with our drinks on the sidewalk in the 11th, still bundled up, but it feels like spring, we talk, mostly in English though sometimes taking refuge in French, to be more or less exact.

SC: Could you tell me about your 2 installations that were on show simultaniously the last time I met you here, what they were about and how they relate?
FXC: I had these 2 soloshows in Paris, the first one was at Alain Gutharc's gallery and it was called 'Nuancier', it is a video installation consisting of 20 TV-screens which are installed like a circle, it shows 19 guys simply saying 'je t'aime,' to the camera (laughs) The spectator is encircled by these guys, who are filmed from a fixed point, full-face, each one is a possible lover. This installation is

about Love. The other one 'Dancing for joy' which was shown at the Caisse des dépôts is about Love too, this 2nd one consists of just one video which is diffused in individual virtual helmets, it insinuates itself into the spectator's body and vision, slipping into this intimate universe like a dream or a flash. In a sense that second video was my reaction to what I did in the first, so they came in an order, it could be like a diptych but they can live seperately too.
SC: What I wondered about was the blue screen in the first installation, you confront your audience with these 19 guys declaring

CARLOS
ISSUE 6/UNITED KINGDOM/6.7×9.45 in (170×240 mm)
"AN IN-FLIGHT MAGAZINE THAT ISN'T A FAUX NEWSSTAND TITLE. THE
DESIGN, CONTENT, AND FORM OF CARLOS
IS DEFINED BY ITS ENVIRONMENT."

THE STYLE-HIGH CLUB

SMART-COMFY: THE NEW JET SET CHIC

BY
JESS CARTNER-MORLEY

42

Try to imagine Grace Kelly stepping off a yacht in a tracksuit. Or Jackie Onassis. Impossible. Until very recently, no one with best-dressed aspirations would have been seen dead in casual wear.

Now take a look around you. Frankly, the more tracksuits you can count in the surrounding rows, the more A-list this flight. A quick trawl through arrival lounge paparazzi shots makes it clear that for today's chic young things, a Juicy Couture tracksuit is the new Chanel suit. Kate Moss has one in black, Gwyneth has one in chocolate brown, Britney has one in baby pink (naturally) and Jade Jagger favours the same style, but in scarlet cashmere.

Smart-comfy has replaced smart casual as fashion's boom sector. Smart casual was all about looking polished enough for the office but not too fusty to go straight out to drinks or dinner. Smart-comfy, on the other hand, is about feeling comfortable enough to relax on the London to LA flight but smart enough to hold your head up in the lobby of the Standard when you arrive. It's about

going to a yoga class and then out to brunch. It's about what to wear on a spa weekend, as you pad between the massage parlour and the juice bar. In other words, it is about showing yourself to be the sort of lady who takes a seriously upscale lifestyle in her French pedicured stride.

Smart-comfy is not quite dressing up, but it is certainly not dressing down. It is, in fact, the art of dressed-down dressing up.

Confused? Don't be. Kooky as it sounds, smart-comfy makes perfect sense. In an era when most of the cash-rich are time-poor, downtime is the ultimate luxury — et voila, the market for luxe loungewear is born.

Juicy Couture is the brainchild of LA girls Pam Skaist-Levy and Gela Taylor — Fluffy and Fluffy to their friends, I kid you not — who have become arguably the first velour millionaires, by taking the Waynetta out of tracksuits. The secret is in the cut, which shows off the LA gym-honed body to perfection. (This is very important. Smart-comfy must always, always be flattering.) The tracksuit top

is cut to emphasise the waist and to reveal a sliver of tummy; the hipster bottoms flatter the backside, are cut straight rather than baggy, and are long enough to be worn over, say, a pair of Ibizan jewelled kitten heeled flip-flops. They are not, reps at not, designed to be worn for sport, they are much more at home at a breakfast meeting. Apparently, Kate Beckinsale was once spotted wearing one to go jogging in Santa Monica, but then she's British, and therefore probably a bit eccentric.

But there is more to smart-comfy than LA power tracksuits. The trend can be traced back to that Nineties icon, the pashmina. The pashmina was essentially a blanket, but by virtue of costing several hundred pounds was considered to have enough cachet to be worn at parties. Of course, six months after every fashionable woman declared she could not imagine life without a pashmina, it went the way of all must-have accessories. Its legacy, however, was an enduring obsession with cashmere, which has become a pillar of the smart-comfy lifestyle; cashmere socks for wearing on planes, cashmere

covers for your hot water bottle, cashmere cushions for the sofa. Expensive and cosy, cashmere is smart-comfy in a nutshell. The latest designer to have benefited from our lust for the belly hair of goats is Ralph Lauren, whose latest global hit is a version of his classic, sporty three-button cotton polo shirt in — you guessed it — cashmere. (Being neither too warm nor too cool, these are very popular on planes. Award yourself extra fashion points if you can spot any in your row.) In Britain, the Toast mail order company has earned a loyal following with its elegant yet slouchy, upscale yet downhome aesthetic. In the catalogue, the wearers of the cashmere-and-linen mix cardigans (£110) and high-heeled espadrilles (£49) are either meandering past faded palazzos at midnight or sipping espressi from tiny white cups under dappled shade. It is all soft edges and inner glow. In short, it's a sort of porn mag for the overworked middle-class couples to leaf through at bedtime. Smart-comfy — it's practically the new sex. END

Jess Cartner-Morley is Fashion Editor of The Guardian.

ILLUSTRATED BY
JO RATCLIFFE

43

---

44. Two decades ago, the New Romantic heroes of British pop music wowed the USA just as The Beatles had 20 years before. The second British invasion owed its success to style, the emergence of MTV and one killer haircut. Peter York was there to salute...

HOW THE WEDGE WAS WON

BY
PETER YORK ILLUSTRATED BY JAMIE GULLY

DANIEL BATTAMS FAN CLUB
FAN CLUB©
MAGAZINE

Issue 5 / Spring 2005 / $8.00 US / Eur 5.99 / £2.95

INSIDE:
DIZZEE!
LUDES!
DANIEL!

ISSN 1742-1799

MOBILITY • ART • SARCASM

9 771742 179019   05>

DANIEL BATTAMS FAN CLUB
ISSUE 5/UNITED KINGDOM/5.85x8.25 in (149x210 mm)
"DEDICATED TO AN ORDINARY PERSON FROM LONDON."

MEMBERS NEWS

LUCKY WINNER

Julia Mealing of Keynsham, near Bristol is the lucky winner of our competition on the Channel 4 web site www.ideasfactory.com. She guessed correctly that the first ever Daniel Battams Fan Club Magazine was based on the size of Daniel's Jobseekers Allowance booklet. Her prize is a Scooter print and Fan Club T-shirt from Made Up Studios. Congrats!

SEPARATE WE FROM THE CHAVS

DB

Fan Club associate Linda Angel hasn't joined ex-Libertine Carl Barat's super group with someone from Razorlight. She has joined a band called 'The Chavs' who had to threaten Carl Barat with a lawsuit for trying to nick their name.

"They were forced to change it because we had proof that we were performing under the name The Chavs way before them" she says, proudly. "We are the Chavant Garde. We separate the wheat from the Chav."

Download 'Angry Sex' at www.the-chavs.com or buy it direct from angel@the-chavs.com for £10.

IN CONVERSATION WITH DIZZEE RASKIT

In the Winter, DBFCM bore the name *Charles Saatchi* on the cover. Now in Spring it's the turn of LDN upstart Dylan 'Dizzee Rascal' Mills to get that fame for his name. But what did Dizzee do to earn the privilege? Let's just say that it pays to nurture your personal network of friends and associates, as the following email extract will testify:

From: Dizzee Rascal
RE: Dizzee who?

Dizzee is for everyone mate! Glad you feel it.

Stay safe,
Diz

BEHIND YOU

We met Ingrid Pitt, England's 'first lady of Horror' and star of 'Hammer' film classics The Vampire Lovers, Countess Dracula, The House That

Dripped Blood, The Sound of Horror, The Omegans and Wickerman, two years ago.

Sitting behind her stall at a rather nerdy record fair in Wembley, north London, Ingrid was inviting folk to sign up to her own Fan Club – the 'Pitt of Horror'. As we had not heard of her before, we jokingly mentioned to her about Daniel Battams Fan Club. But she didn't wish to subscribe.

We hadn't seen one of Ingrid's films until last week, when The Wickerman was shown late at night on BBC. It was definitely scary, with Ingrid giving an excellent performance as a librarian and omnipresent leader of da gang.

Join Ingrid at
www.pittofhorror.com

NEW MEMBERS!!!

Mairead Queens of Noize
Member #000161
Gillian Ali
Member #000156
Beatrice Galilee
Member #000166
Tony Blair
Member #000167
William Shakespeare
Member #000168

Below
Nina Member #000148 meets Robert Kilroy-Silk, Non-Member, formerly of the BBC.

Top Right
Niall Cullinane, Member #000093, sent this self portrait inspired by Dan's new logo.

Above
Glen Matlock, Member #000105, discusses the Sex Pistols on a BBC3 documentary.

Right
KT Shillingford, Member #000102, welcomes Molaroid, Member #000162, to the club.

Fan File: Vladimir Putin, Member #000169
Age: 52
Location: Kremlin, Moscow, Russian Federation
Occupation: President
Company: Government of the Russian Federation
Member since: February 2005
Favourite Member: All equal
Favourite TV/Film: NTV, RUTV, Vremya
Favourite Group/Pop star: Tchaikovsky, Rachmaninoff, Prokofiev, Rimsky-Korsakov
Favourite Pizza topping: Cheese and Tomato
What would you buy if you had £100 to spend? Official Daniel Battams Fan Club T-shirt, buss pass
If you could meet anyone famous who would it be? Peter the Great, Vladimir Ilyich Lenin, Kliment Voroshilov, Mikhail Suslov, Konstantin Chernenko, Tsar Nicholas II Romanov, Tsarina Ekaterina

Fan File: Namalee Bolle, Member #000160
Age: 27
Location: Brixton, London, United Kingdom
Occupation: Stefan's Superstore Superstar
Website: Not yet, soon!
Member since: 31/12/2004
Favourite Member: KT Shillingford, Member #000102
Favourite TV/Film: The Muppet Show (always and forever)
Favourite Group/Pop star: Me
Favourite Pizza topping: Ham, Pineapple and Woolworths pick 'n' mix
What would you buy if you had £100 to spend? Official Daniel Battams Fan Club T-Shirt
If you could meet anyone famous who would it be? God
Notes: You can now buy Daniel Battams Fan Club Magazine at Stefan's Superstore, 66 Railton Rd, Brixton, London SE24

DANSK
ISSUE 1/DENMARK/9x10.65 in (230x270 mm)
"AN INTERNATIONAL FASHION MAGAZINE, BUT (ONE WHICH VIEWS
THE WORLD FROM A DANISH PERSPECTIVE."

258

FANTASTIC MAN
ISSUE 1/NETHERLANDS/9×11.8 in (230×300 mm)
'A GENTLEMEN'S STYLE JOURNAL'

FANTASTIC
MAN

A GENTLEMEN'S STYLE JOURNAL ... FIRST ISSUE ... SPRING & SUMMER 2005

MR. RUPERT EVERETT
The charming film star in Miami, page 50...

MR. MALCOLM McLAREN ... MR. ROY BLAKEY ... MR. DENNIS FREEDMAN ... MR. THOM BROWNE
THE BEST SUMMER FASHIONS ... THE MOST ELEGANT LOOKS

FANTASTIC
MAN

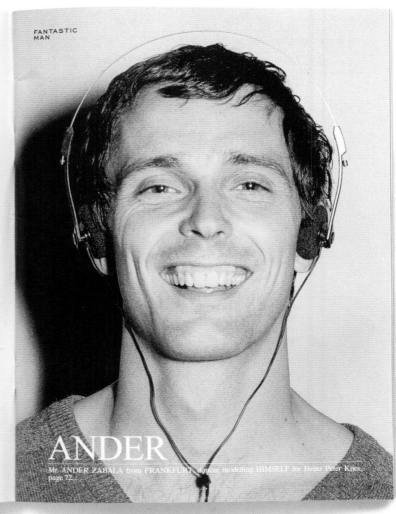

BART
Mr. BART JULIUS PETERS, artist and photographer from AMSTERDAM, revealing his marvellous
wardrobe, page 27...

ANDER
Mr. ANDER ZABALA from FRANKFURT, dancer, modelling HIMSELF for Heinz Peter Knes,
page 72...

– 6 –

Mr. THOM BROWNE from NEW YORK, modelling his own designs on the next pages...

— 14 —

MISTER

THOM
BROWNE

NEW YORK CITY TAILOR IS MEATPACKING DISTRICT'S BEST KEPT SECRET...

PHOTOGRAPHY MARCELO KRASILCIC • STYLIST HAIDEE FINDLAY-LEVIN
INTERVIEW GERT JONKERS

— 15 —

— 72 —

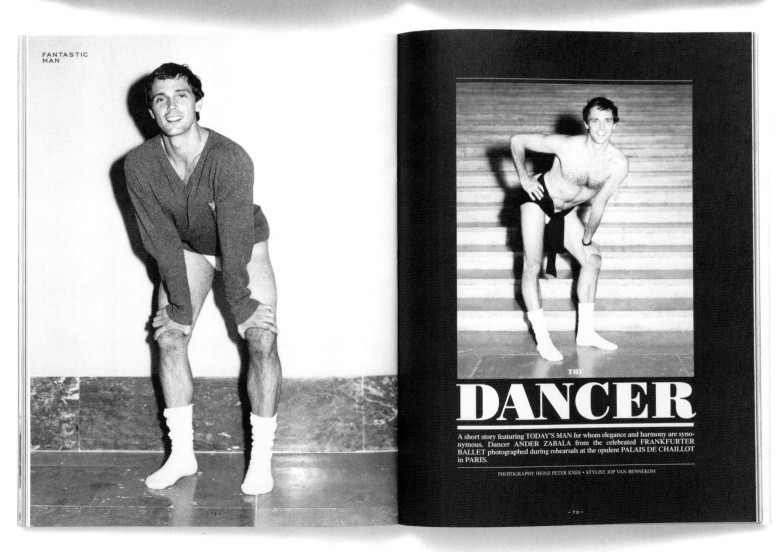

THE
DANCER

A short story featuring TODAY'S MAN for whom elegance and harmony are syno-
nymous. Dancer ANDER ZABALA from the celebrated FRANKFURTER
BALLET photographed during rehearsals at the opulent PALAIS DE CHAILLOT
in PARIS.

PHOTOGRAPHY HEINZ PETER KNES • STYLIST JOP VAN BENNEKOM

— 73 —

Beyond Printed Matter

Beyond printed matter ▮▮▮▮▮▮ People wonder what I do. Yes, maybe I create a magazine that looks a bit out of the ordinary. I might even do that on a semiregular basis. Yet the format changes, the theme changes. And the circulation goes from thousands of copies in thirty countries to five copies to be passed from one person to another across the world. ▮▮▮▮▮▮ A magazine, in my humble opinion, is much more than printed matter. It can be found in the traces of tension between editorial content and inspiration for readers. It can be considered an internal newsletter for well-defined social tribes. It's all that—and more. ▮▮▮▮▮▮ In all human interaction one has to consider collaborating. Well, a magazine is a collaborative project par excellence. And I have chosen the magazine as a template for human interaction. Can we do this? Yes. We should. *We live in a borderless world. Is that a way to chaos or an open road to a new renaissance?* ▮▮▮▮▮▮ **Freedom of speech. Freedom of market.** ▮▮▮▮▮▮ Maybe the most diversifying aspect of "our kind of magazine" is that we do not want to listen to the market—the rules, the deals, the obvious obstacles, and hidden traps. "Creative magazines" exist because we act as individuals who want to make a point of some sort. Freedom of speech takes as many shapes as there are formats of paper and typefaces. ▮▮▮▮▮▮ In spite of all the rational behavior of markets, segments, business plans, or other such trivia, we seem to want to create with our hearts rather then our minds. We flirt with economic rules, sometimes going bankrupt or maybe breaking even, yet most of the time far from a glance of profitability. This is not a reasonable business attitude. ▮▮▮▮▮▮ How do you think our distributor reacted when I told them I'd like to bring chaos theory to magazine editing? Having a magazine pass from one hand to another. Having readers become editors, adding their views on the subject and contributing to the content before passing it on. Growing organically. Eventually, this approach would mean being able to reach as many readers as before; it would just take much more time and effort. ▮▮▮▮▮▮ Obviously, experiments like this may seem mad to some—well, most—of the audience. They are important for us. ▮▮▮▮▮▮ **The magazine as an art form** ▮▮▮▮▮▮ Let's define it as art—that's the easiest way of looking at it. So we "don't have to understand it." Art is considered legitimate. And it's true. Magazines provide printed inspirational surroundings on a regular basis. That could be a new definition of "our kind of magazine." ▮▮▮▮▮▮ **The financial aspects: a Don Quixote feeling** ▮▮▮▮▮▮ Now here is a bugger. My bank account proves that with *Ad!dict* I have been working on the edge of what is doable. What am I saying? Way beyond that. ▮▮▮▮▮▮ It's painful to see how much money the big publishing houses spend to find a hole in the market. Big-shot marketing studies by big-shot agencies trying ruthlessly to define a certain underserved audience that needs another printed layer added to their busy life and—we should stress that with a number of slick Powerpoint slides—is willing to undergo continuous advertising bashing. This is, let's face it, the only reason some magazines make it through the chain of command. Big publishing houses work within certain boundaries, self-created boundaries—that is, from a commercial point of view. ▮▮▮▮▮▮ A strong contrast with what you're

9

by Jan Van Mol

If I didn't know better, I'd think that sometimes the accountant or financial director is in the editor's seat, comparing the square centimeters of content to the advertising space sold. All this, as if there could be a mathematical approach to creativity *tout court*.

Freedom of speech takes as many shapes as there are formats of paper and typefaces.

discovering here. The big publishing houses can't create these kinds of inspirational beauty. Looking at the bulk of their publications, you stumble into a well-defined range of characters and fonts, and images in calculated sizes to illustrate the content. If I didn't know better, I'd think that sometimes the accountant or financial director is in the editor's seat, comparing the square centimeters of content to the advertising space sold. All this, as if there could be a mathematical approach to creativity *tout court.* ████████ "Creative magazines" focus on the content aspect. *On the experience of content, rather than splitting it up into predefined templates and boredom.* ████████ These magazines offer ways to go behind each article. To dive into the different layers as they are presented to you by the writer, the editor, the graphic language, the art direction, or, at best, a combination of all that and more. You're allowed to enter via the artists' entrance and discover a bit of the how and the why—the editorial environment in which the magazines are created, the contact with others, its dynamic community. ████████ "How can you do this?" you may ask. "How can you have the guts not to draw within the existing template, not to play by the existing rules?" I guess be naive or stubborn, or just plain stupid. During the almost ten years that I have been doing this, I should have stopped more times than the number of *Ad!dict* magazines I created. ████████ Someone once said that the most positive and inspiring thing about *Ad!dict* is simply that we still exist after all these years. There is a lot of truth in that. It is sad to see how many other beautiful magazines have not been able to survive. The stories I could tell you about their or our finances would take you from James Bond–like scams in Málaga to a Kuwaiti prince wanting to buy *Ad!dict* as a birthday gift for his mother back home, who loves art. ████████ **Part of a visual culture** ████████ The visual strength, the power to stop the eye, a true cover policy—it all adds up to the visual identity of your magazine. Too many times I see people stopping there: limiting our creations to that of "eye candy" and coffee-table books. One should expect, or at least hope, that readers will dive into our content and follow us in the editorial decisions we take. There is work to be done. ████████ But it is clear that by forcing art directors, graphic designers, photographers, and journalists to think beyond what they are used to, you create a world on its own, a mix of texts and images, blurring into one another yet developing a very distinctive language. ████████ **Tangible** ████████ Through the years, we have had the opportunity to work with different paper suppliers. I am talking not only about printed experiences—divine mixes of visual, graphic, and editorial abundance—but also the feeling of paper. For us, that will never disappear. We want to touch, smell, taste, eat. The Internet is obviously more than just an interesting tool. An article published in Australia described *Ad!dict* as the Internet turned into flesh. The possibilities for community building, exchange, and interaction using the Internet can only make the experience grow and the concept clearer. ████████ Big publishing houses look for business opportunities and allow the commercial value to decide the process. At the current cost of the Internet, you'll see their content distribution shift from printed matter to digital platforms, including PDAs, and other yet-to-be-created gizmos and tools. ████████ And thus, hurray, tangible paper comes back into our hands, the hands of the "creative magazines." The added value of paper enriches and embraces the beauty of its content. It becomes part of it. It's the canvas of the magazine artist. *Someone hold me down before I get carried away.* But honestly, the moment the copies arrive from the printer, the first glance at your creation after deadline rushes, compromises, experiments—that first smell of fresh ink and touch of the magazine—well, it's divine. ████████ **Critics, anyone?** ████████ I consider one's drive to be the most important fact to take into consideration. Nothing is as important to democracy as freedom—and thus the possibility to experiment. I like to listen to critics, but only if what they say is about the direction and the speed in which we're going, rather then the actual created objects. At the moment the magazine has been created, there are tons of mistakes we've made and an astronomical number of paths we didn't take.

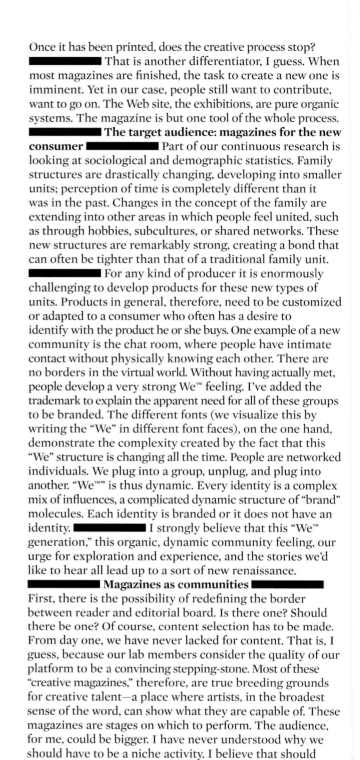

Once it has been printed, does the creative process stop? ▬▬▬▬▬▬ That is another differentiator, I guess. When most magazines are finished, the task to create a new one is imminent. Yet in our case, people still want to contribute, want to go on. The Web site, the exhibitions, are pure organic systems. The magazine is but one tool of the whole process. ▬▬▬▬ **The target audience: magazines for the new consumer** ▬▬▬▬▬ Part of our continuous research is looking at sociological and demographic statistics. Family structures are drastically changing, developing into smaller units; perception of time is completely different than it was in the past. Changes in the concept of the family are extending into other areas in which people feel united, such as through hobbies, subcultures, or shared networks. These new structures are remarkably strong, creating a bond that can often be tighter than that of a traditional family unit. ▬▬▬▬▬▬ For any kind of producer it is enormously challenging to develop products for these new types of units. Products in general, therefore, need to be customized or adapted to a consumer who often has a desire to identify with the product he or she buys. One example of a new community is the chat room, where people have intimate contact without physically knowing each other. There are no borders in the virtual world. Without having actually met, people develop a very strong We™ feeling. I've added the trademark to explain the apparent need for all of these groups to be branded. The different fonts (we visualize this by writing the "We" in different font faces), on the one hand, demonstrate the complexity created by the fact that this "We" structure is changing all the time. People are networked individuals. We plug into a group, unplug, and plug into another. "We™" is thus dynamic. Every identity is a complex mix of influences, a complicated dynamic structure of "brand" molecules. Each identity is branded or it does not have an identity. ▬▬▬▬▬ I strongly believe that this "We™ generation," this organic, dynamic community feeling, our urge for exploration and experience, and the stories we'd like to hear all lead up to a sort of new renaissance. ▬▬▬▬▬ **Magazines as communities** ▬▬▬▬▬ First, there is the possibility of redefining the border between reader and editorial board. Is there one? Should there be one? Of course, content selection has to be made. From day one, we have never lacked for content. That is, I guess, because our lab members consider the quality of our platform to be a convincing stepping-stone. Most of these "creative magazines," therefore, are true breeding grounds for creative talent—a place where artists, in the broadest sense of the word, can show what they are capable of. These magazines are stages on which to perform. The audience, for me, could be bigger. I have never understood why we should have to be a niche activity. I believe that should change. Consumers are ready. ▬▬▬▬ **Where does Ad!dict fit in all this?** ▬▬▬▬▬ The Internet era has changed our way of thinking. The new world is about a global

It's not what
product we produce,
but what experience we offer.

sensibility—not one contained by national or ethnic borders. What if we use the crossover possibilities of the World Wide Web to start up thinking processes? Our Ad!dict Creative Lab is marshaling thinkers around the world on a wide range of projects. Virtual surroundings are turned into flesh and become breeding grounds for innovation. I have taken time to build arguments to prove my view, reflections on the process, and projects to test it. In fact, *Ad!dict* is not a finished product. It is a template, an attempt to define a creative structure and learn about the semantics and paradigms involved. It's a vision to accelerate local talent, brands, regions, countries, and the world as we know it. A vision to blend economy, culture, education, and more— all of which are too valuable to be left only in the hands of politicians. ███████████ Yet maybe there's nothing new under the sun. No new vision, but a mere repetition of thinking processes from ancient times. "Our kind of magazine" is a communicative tool, proof of the dynamics of our different social groups, and clear proof of a world that is turning global. Shall we announce a new renaissance? ███████████ Because in the end, we all like new cultural initiatives in an increasingly homogenized world, ones that are able to surprise us with refreshing ideas. I refuse to provide ready-made solutions, but want to implement *Ad!dict*'s methodology to generate increased self-awareness and a more accurate perception of positioning in the market. ███████████ *(Not creating a magazine* ███████████ *Ad!dict Creative Lab generates ideas on a global scale. Visualized by a lookalike Mendeleyev Table (the Periodic Table of the Elements), the structure of Ad!dict is an international network of creative people, our lab members, brought together in a multidisciplinary database as well as on the Ad!dict Lab Web site. Depending on the nature of the project, Ad!dict assembles a team from our database that we judge to be able to generate the best ideas. Our concept of "creativity is chemistry" reveals how organizations can become a place where bright ideas are bounced across a global network. Working this way is a completely new approach to creation for many long-standing companies that keep repeating the same working patterns of past generations.)* ███████████ **Magazines as breeding grounds for new creative resources** ███████████ The social relevance of the magazine (shall we call it "commuzine"?) is probably its most important aspect. When done properly, magazines can't help but be true fertile grounds for new talent. In fact, it is in these surroundings that you can spot the real good ones. Photographers, graphic designers, visual artists, journalists . . . All that talent deserves a spot in the sun, or at least a drip of ink. Preserving independent magazines means preserving the enormous richness of our culture. ███████████ **The bigger picture** ███████████ Yet one should always see it in a global context. It's not what product we produce, but what experience we offer. As readers, consumers, designers, producers, press, and people— as a society—our approach should be to rethink the creative process. When we create, we can't think just about the product we are creating but must also think about the surroundings that change because we are creating. Using the knowledge and findings emanating from our heritage, creating—and we all do this—becomes a complex, yet challenging activity. It makes the world turn. ███████████ Creativity is the "oil" of the twenty-first century. There is a certain overkill in using the C-word, but it is the future's main asset: I believe it is mankind's hope for social interaction, innovation, and general improvement. Consider "creative magazines" as manuals to that process.

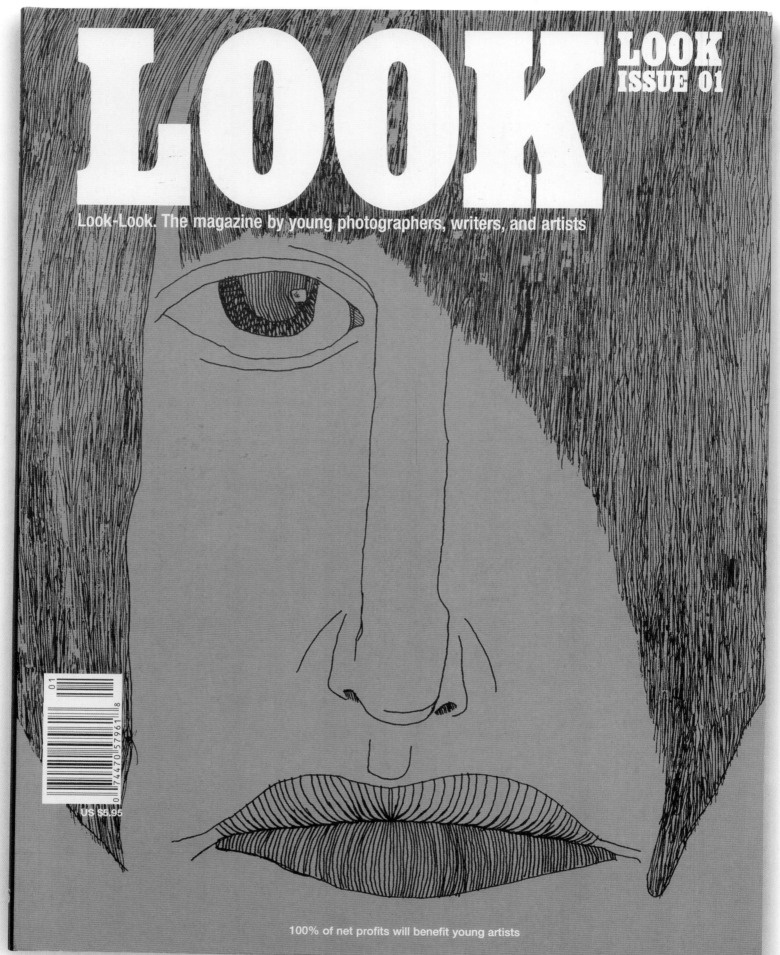

LOOK

Look-Look. The magazine by young photographers, writers, and artists

US $5.95

100% of net profits will benefit young artists

LOOK LOOK
ISSUE 1 / UNITED STATES / 8.35x10.85 in (212x275 mm)
"SHOWCASES AND CELEBRATES THE UNCENSORED ART PHOTOGRAPHY, IDEAS,
POETRY, AND PROSE OF AMATEUR YOUTH (AGES 14-30)".

ADAM BRAGG, RICHMOND, VA

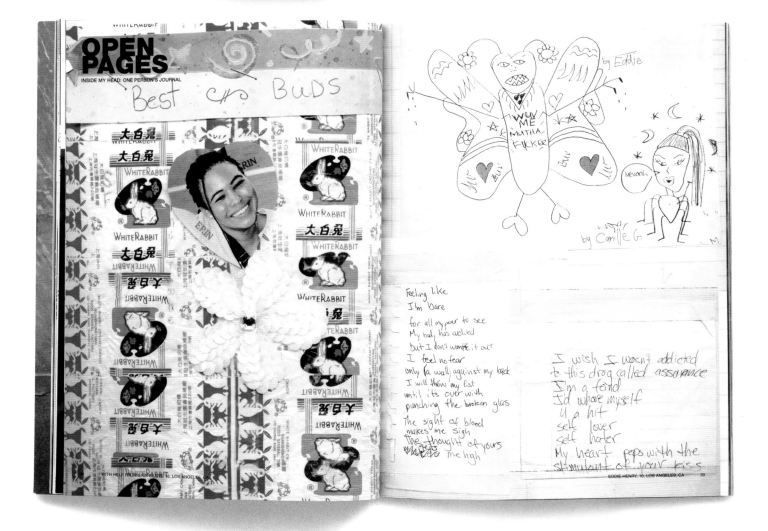

Best ⊂⊃ BUDS

by Eddie

by Camille G.

Feeling like
I'm bare
for all my peer to see
My body has evolved
but I don't want it out
I feel no fear
only (a wall) against my back
I will throw my fist
until its over with
punching the broken glas

The sight of blood
makes me sigh
the thought of yours
makes me high

I wish I wasn't addicted
to this drug called assurance
I'm a feind
I'd whore myself
4 a hit
self lover
self hater
My heart pops with the
stimulent of your kiss

EDDIE HENRY, 16, LOS ANGELES, CA   39

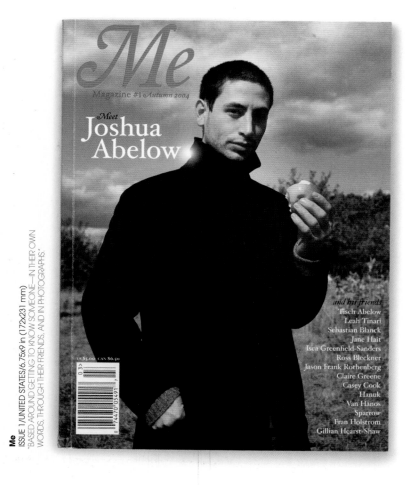

Me
ISSUE 1/UNITED STATES/6.75x9 in (172x231 mm)
"BASED AROUND GETTING TO KNOW SOMEONE—IN THEIR OWN WORDS, THROUGH THEIR FRIENDS, AND IN PHOTOGRAPHS."

Claire Greene

Age 19 *Birthday* November 30, 1984
Occupation Art Student *Based in* Soho

When and where did you meet Joshua? I met Josh in 1999 in Putney, Vermont, where his sister Tisch and I went to high school. *What was it about Joshua that made you interested in him?* When I was young and impressionable, Josh was the first metrosexual I'd ever met. I was intrigued to say the least. *What is the most embarrassing story you two share together?* When Josh and I went to Costa Rica together, he forced me to pretend that we were dating. That was pretty humiliating. *What are your favorite hang-outs?* Josh's studio. *Favorite music?* The Violent Femmes, Cage, Smog, and, of course, Louis. *Favorite movies?* M, Rear Window, Nanook of the North, Sunset Boulevard, Street Wise, Vivre Sa Vie, and anything by Errol Morris. *Favorite stores?* Cinema Nolita and Cupcake Cafe. *What is your favorite..?* I like cowboy boots and cookies (oatmeal cookies with dried cranberries). *If you had $20, what would you spend it on?* Ingredients for a nice brunch. Then, I would invite my friends over and have a feast. *What is your philosophy on life?* Bake cookies and be happy. *If there were no limits or barriers, what would you be doing right now?* Raising a family. *What is your most memorable moment?* Walking to the cow barn alone at 5 a.m. in December in Vermont, when the air is thin and icy clear, and everything—including the mountains in the distance, the trees and even the red barn—is blue.

Sparrow

Age 21 *Birthday* October 14, 1982 *Occupation* Photographer
Based in NYC, Hollywood, & Scottsdale, AZ

When and where did you meet Joshua? Two years ago at Ross Bleckners' studio. He was the first Jew I'd ever met. Naturally, I was intrigued. (Just to keep thinks straight... Ross is Jewish. I didn't know this until after I had found out Josh is Jewish, which why I say he's the first Jew I ever met.) *What was it about Joshua that made you interested in him?* His narcissism rivals only my own. *What is the funniest or most embarrassing story you two share together?* No embarrassing moments. I have no shame. But the funniest was when we got stuck in a taxi/mini van in the Hamptons in the middle of a blizzard. It was midnight on a Tuesday (who does this on a Tuesday!), and our driver was furious. We smoked so much while we waited that I thought, for sure, Indians were going to see the smoke signals, resurrect from the ground and scalp us. After almost three hours we were finally dug out. *What are your favorite hangouts?* Hmm, so many places I can shamelessly plug... In NYC: Bungalo 8, Scores, Maritime Hotel, Milano's (51 East Houston between Mulberry and Mott, the best dive bar EVER!), Josh's studio, of course... In LA: El Centro, Fubar, Concorde, Mauro's Cafe at Fred Segal, The Griddle, Baja Fresh on Sunset Boulevard... In Scottsdale: BS West, Dos Gringos (The best place to get anyone in a fraternity drunk. Let the hazing begin.), Four Peaks Brewery (They have a beer that tastes like blueberry pancakes). *Favorite music?* Bonnie Raitt is the shit, the CDs that Josh burns me... legally of course, also Lynyrd Skynrd, Black Gospel, Prince, Elephant and The Rolling Stones. *Favorite movies?* *The Last American Virgin*, *Drop Dead Gorgeous* (I love Kirsty Alley! I even like her Pier 1 commercials.), anything with Jennifer Coolidge, *Passion of the Christ*, *Fahrenheit 911*, *Jennatalia*. *Favorite stores?* In NYC: Hollywould, Helmut Lang, Rite Aid, Steven Alan, Housing Works, Salvation Army, Radio Shack, the new Calvin Klein underwear store, for obvious reasons... In LA: Fred Segal in Santa Monica, most stores on Melrose, Barneys, Jet Rag. *What is your favorite...?* Bush twin: Barbra. Worthy Cause: Jews for Jesus. *If you had $20, what would you spend it on?* I would feed a child in need for a year (or a supermodel for a lifetime). *What is your philosophy on life?* When life hands you a bag a lemons, make lemonade... or use the bag to beat the shit out of someone. *If there were no limits or barriers, what would you be doing right now?* I would be buying Martha Stewart's apartment in the Richard Meier building... *Ten years from now?* ...running a brothel out of it, pimping out all my friends out to major NYC and Hollywood players, getting caught, going to jail, hatching a plan in the slammer with Martha Stewart to recreate the Trojan horse out of 350 count linens (as a gift to the D.A.) so we could bust out, then dying of an O.D. Very chic right now. *What is your most disappointing moment?* Joining Friendster, and the day I woke up and realized I was uneducated poor white trash. *What is your most memorable moment?* Ditto.

36

Things I Like...

Favorite stores
• Steven Alan
• Jack Spade
• A.P.C.
• Fresh
• Serve Yourself and Save
• Sky Frames
• Vasari
• Soho Art Materials
• Pearl Paint
• My dad's carpet store
• Opening Ceremony

66

ONE ONE NINE
ISSUE 1/UNITED STATES/7 x 8.6 in (178 x 218 mm)
"A GRAPHIC DESIGN/ART ZINE COLLABORATION."

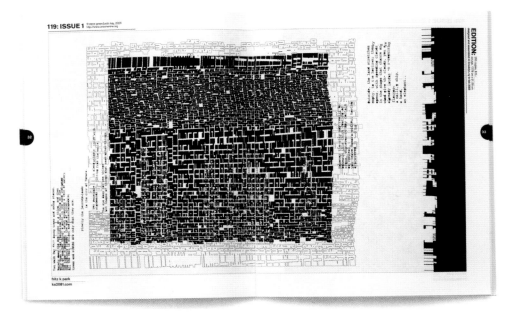

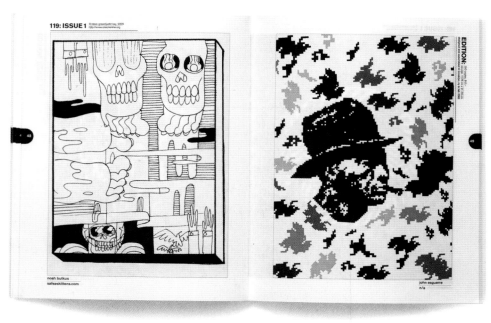

270

pablo internacional magazine
macho not rough
art, men and architecture
issue 0
spring 2005

1   portrait
     they call him pablo by mauricio guillén.

4   art on parade by pablo lafuente.

12   interview
     inside mental landscapes. federico herrero.

24   centrefold
     roman, a french builder changes broken windows.

34   fashion
     david waddington wears polo

40   architecture
     sonho de casa própria.

46   tourism
     robert smithson's hotel palenque.

54   fitness
     morning exercise. raimundas malasauskas.

58   advertisement

pablo international
ISSUE 0 /MEXICO/UK/5.5x8.45 in (140x215 mm)
'PERIODICAL OF ART, MEN AND ARCHITECTURE'

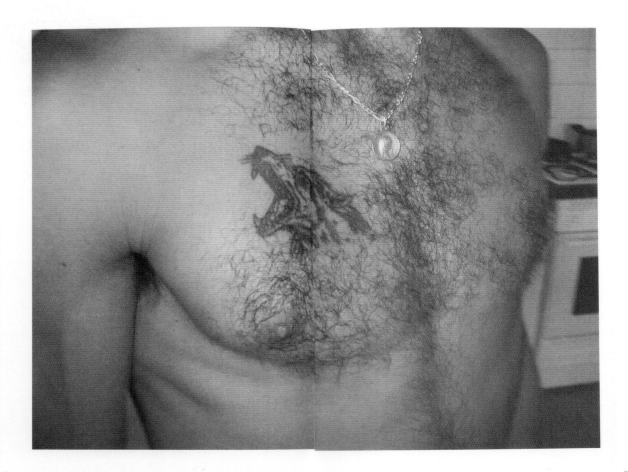

PROPHECY

1966-2001

PROPHECY
ISSUE 1/UNITED STATES/8.4x10.85 in (213x275 mm)
FUSES ARCHITECTURE, FASHION, MUSIC, ART,
CULTURE AND SURFING

PU/A

Put.Up.Truant.Art.
Issue#1

MISSING.

PUTA
ISSUE 1 /UNITED STATES/8.25x10.85 in (210x275 mm)
LOS ANGELES-BASED "PUT UP TRUANT ART"

RVN: CAPTURE OF TWO UA
HELICOPTER PILOTS IN
QUANG NAM PROVINCE/
Viet Cong Shoot Down U.S.
opter and capture its
rewmembers.
: RVN

s: LS; Aircraft
d; Quang Nam
Province

MIA

RE-
ISSUE 6/NETHERLANDS/8.65x11.65 in (220x296 mm)
"AN INTERSECTION OF VISUAL CULTURE AND EDITORIAL
EXPERIMENTATION. EACH ISSUE IS ABOUT THE LIFE OF ONE PERSON."

Nat.

RE—

Re-Magazine #6
From Amsterdam NL
Spring 2001
The Manic Issue
Hfl. 17,50 / 8 Euro

Page 1 continues on page 2.

The book is called 'Pain-free'.
I decided to order it after all, it's quite simple with easy exercises.

Listen.

Listen, the world is trying to cross me in everything I do. Honest, it's a conspiracy. Everything I now have, I've accumulated with enormous difficulty, an individual achievement. The rest of the world doesn't deserve any credit. They may all look very innocent; the bus driver with his synthetic suit, the dental assistant constantly smiling at me, the sales representative in the train with his socks down around his ankles. But I'm certain that, behind my back, they're all talking about me.

I = JEALOUS

I mean if not me, who else do they talk about? I'm like, so fucking good. I'm so good that David Fincher asked me to do the special effects for Aliens 3. So good that Stanley Kubrick came by and asked me to do the art direction for his latest film. Even though I'm only 22. And I'm good friends with Madonna.

I hate Chris Cunningham!

I hate everyone who at a premature age makes things that are too good. Makes such good work that David Fincher asks if you'll do the special effects for Aliens 3. Makes such good work that Stanley Kubrick drops by and asks you to do the art direction for his latest film. Even though you're only 22. I want to be good friends with Madonna.

I'm very cross that Madonna didn't invite me to her wedding.
Very cross.

• The Turkish Madonna slightly deconstructed.

I'm completely possessed by Madonna.
I've been a fan since I was 8 and started play-backing and imitating my idol at 9.

I look like Madonna.
If you visit our town and ask for Madonna, they'll give you directions to where I live.

The Turkish Madonna is called Yonca Evcimik.
www.yoncaevcimik.com

I'm strolling the evening streets of Tribeca and I hear someone shouting: "Madonna's coming!" I have a camera with me and manage to bluff my way through the crowd to the press enclosure. When she comes past I click away hysterically. Not even with the intention of getting her picture but more because I'm in the press enclosure and have to prove I'm a photographer or something. I'm so busy with the camera and she goes by so fast that I hardly catch a glimpse of her. The print I have made is blurred. Also that night was the first time she showed up with a black hairdo instead of her usual blonde, so nobody recognized her on the photo.

I had already kicked a hole in the cupboard door. Something had to give.
I was angry, I tore my new $300 shirt to shreds.
I'd only worn it once.

Generation Not.
This is our program:

My parents gave me new front teeth for my birthday.

The man on the photo is ... (Please look this up!), the political leader of a right-wing extremist party which was very successful during the last elections in Rumania. It's difficult to know how exactly you should interpret those glasses. And as a voter, how can you vote for such a man! I mean this isn't meant to be hip, this sort of hipness is by definition leftwing and that can't be the object.

People who fall off the edge of a photograph.

• Tudor is the name of the political leader of a right-wing extremist party in Rumania.

Perhaps it's more a question of glamour, the people around him all lack glasses. I mean sunglasses are primarily an instrument for keeping people at a distance. Pop stars. And all those fashion editors who visit fashion shows wearing sunglasses. Even though with sunglasses you can hardly differentiate between colors; by wearing sunglasses, they dictate a black and white collection.

The glasses remind me especially of my grandmother. She died and on the day of her funeral I'm sitting with my family in a sort of waiting room at the undertakers. Waiting till we can bury her. My mother cries. My grandfather is absent. He said that he loved her when she was alive and has no wish to see her now she's dead. My mother's feeling of shame for the absence of her father is greater than the grief she feels for the death of her mother.

TRIVIAL

During funerals a whole range of emotions suddenly lie very close together. Trivial things gain significance and significant things are completely empty.

My aunt, a sister-in-law of my mother, made a morning visit to my grandfather to collect a handwritten poem he'd written. It's a very dark and grim poem with imagery like: life consists of peaks and hollows etc. She had still quickly typed it out on the computer because she was afraid otherwise the minister wouldn't be able to read it. There was no signature under the poem so my aunt had written...Your husband, Cor. My mother has just seen the poem and is incredibly angry with her sister-in-law. Why hadn't she phoned her to discuss what salutations should be added under the poem. After all, wouldn't it have been much better if it had been 'your loving Cor'? The undertaker comes in and asks if anyone still wishes to take leave of Maaike, my grandmother. I get up and my father goes with me. We come to a small room where the coffin is. I take a step forward in order to inspect the body. My father is standing behind me and both of us, at the same time, see that my grandmother is still wearing her watch and that the hands are still moving. "Her watch is still ticking," my father says and I see he finds this difficult to beat. She's also still wearing her glasses. She has the largest pair of glasses I've ever seen on a human being. With reactolights. More glasses than face. I want to take a photo of this image, my grandmother dead in her coffin. I take out my Polaroid camera. The camera flashes and while I flutter the photo to and fro, I see in the slowly emerging picture that her glasses have reacted to the flashlight and taken on a darker hue.

I think the worst thing was that her name was 'Maaike',
so at odds with her character.

Not.

I MEAN:
~~IF SOMEBODY CLOSE TO YOU DIES,~~ CAN YOU SKIMP ON THE FUNERAL EXPENSES?

Can You?

I mean, if somebody close to you dies, can you skimp on the funeral expenses? I mean, if you turn the funeral into a sort of do-it-yourself ceremony in order to make it a personal farewell, can you use the money you save for a trip to Euro Disney? I mean, if somebody close to you dies and you take some time to think about how you want to bid them farewell, do you also have the time to compare the different undertaker firms? I mean, if you've got an insurance policy that offers cover in kind, do you get the chance to pick your own funeral directors? I mean, if you're looking for extras not available as part of the standard package, do you have to pay a supplement? I mean, for example, that should you want to have champagne and caviar once it's all over rather than coffee and cake, can you present the bill to the insurance company? I mean, if you can't afford champagne and caviar, but only sparkling wine and sturgeon roe, are you cheating the dead? I mean, is only the best good enough?

I mean, do Dutch shrimps know they're Dutch shrimps? I mean, have they got a Dutch passport or something? I mean, wouldn't it be better to settle for good coffee or a crematorium with a cappuccino-corner? I mean, wouldn't it just be far more sensible to settle for a funeral policy that pays out in cash? I mean, wouldn't it be even more sensible to put the money aside yourself and rake in the interest. I mean, if you decide against taking out a policy at all isn't that the most sensible course of action? I mean, if you take out a policy when you're 35 and you're well into your seventies before you die aren't you paying far too much? I mean if you take out a policy when you're 35 and two weeks later you end up being run over by a car does that mean you're lucky? I mean, what does a life insurance policy insure you against anyway. I mean, if there's an earthquake and you end up buried beneath the rubble and no one finds you, when do you turn into a source for viral infections, cholera or other health hazards? I mean if these days you fall into the crevice of a glacier could it still take thousands of years before your body was discovered? I mean, if that's the case wouldn't it be better to put on clean underwear before going skiing? I mean if you decide to go out skiing that morning with a butt plug up your ass would that result in all kinds of conclusions being drawn about the culture in which we live today? I mean, aren't you best off donating your body to science? I mean, if they cut you open and don't find anything, has it all been for nothing? I mean, if you send out mourning cards, should they state clearly where and when the funeral or cremation is to take place and the identity of the deceased? I mean, if you make the cards yourself, can you go and photocopy them down the copyshop? I mean, if you say you're making a batch of mourning cards, are you likely to get a discount? I mean, if you distribute 500 cards does that mean to say that the deceased was a popular person with a wide social circle? I mean, if you haven't got a big house capable of receiving 500 guests, can you arrange for a gathering at your local bar? I mean, if drink was the cause of death and it's something the surviving relatives suffered under, should they put that to one side in tribute to the spirit of the deceased? I mean, if there's no particular reason to, should you wash the body from head to foot? I mean, if it's a man will a shave and combing his hair suffice, or should you clean the dirt from under his fingernails as well? I mean, if a woman wore no make-up during her lifetime, but she looks too pale in death, should you resort to powder or rouge? I mean, if you've got a van or caravan of your own, can't you use it to drive the coffin to the cemetery? I mean, if your neighbor helps you in making the coffin and his wife helps you lay the body out and bake the cake, then doesn't that constitute a happy memory that in the long term can help you to come to terms with your loss? I mean, isn't coming to terms with your loss over the long term simply a euphemism for forgetting? I mean, if you face death with an appropriate degree of nonchalance, is that likely to help your relatives to accept their loss? I mean, if you take photographs at the funeral, will you later be able

THEY
SHOOT
HOMOS
DON'T THEY?
001

****
RRP
AUS $12.50
USA $10.00
EUR $8.50

THEY SHOOT HOMOS DON'T THEY?
ISSUE 1 / AUSTRALIA / 5.85x8.25 in (148x210 mm)
"AN ART LOOK BOOK FOR MEN AND THEIR ADMIRERS DIRECT
FROM THE BROTHERHOOD TO YOUR BACKDOOR"

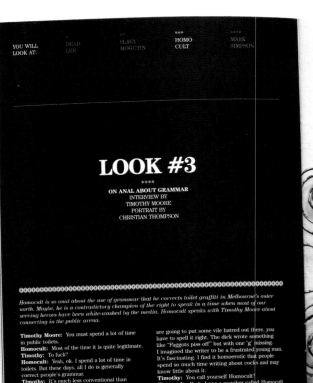

LOOK #3

••••

ON ANAL ABOUT GRAMMAR
INTERVIEW BY
TIMOTHY MOORE
PORTRAIT BY
CHRISTIAN THOMPSON

Homocult is so anal about the use of grammar that he corrects toilet graffiti in Melbourne's outer north. Maybe, he is a contradictory champion of the right to speak in a time when most of our serving heroes have been white-washed by the media. Homocult speaks with Timothy Moore about connecting in the public arena.

Timothy Moore: You must spend a lot of time in public toilets.
Homocult: Most of the time it is quite legitimate.
Timothy: To fuck?
Homocult: Yeah, ok. I spend a lot of time in toilets. But these days, all I do is generally correct people's grammar.
Timothy: It's much less conventional than cruising. Why did you change your bathroom habits?
Homocult: It started when I noticed a really offensive slogan that was misspelt. I found it hilarious. The message was rendered useless and I felt maybe I should bring it to their attention. If you

are going to put some vile hatred out there, you have to spell it right. The dick wrote something like "Faggots piss off" but with one 'g' missing. I imagined the writer to be a frustrated young man. It's fascinating. I find it homoerotic that people spend so much time writing about cocks and may know little about it.
Timothy: You call yourself Homocult?
Homocult: Yeah, I use a moniker called Homocult. I like the idea that the people who write the homophobic messages treat gay guys as all the same. It's the mentality that all gays do is to recruit other guys. I want to fuck with that a bit and make these dudes think that there's a gang of fags out

016   017

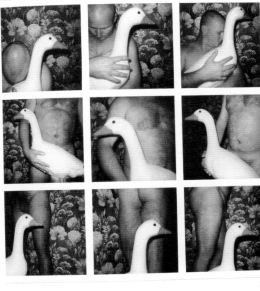

050   054

INDEX

(T)HERE
WWW.T-HERE.COM/UNITED STATES/PUBLISHER: LAURENT GIRARD, JASON MAKOWSKI/
EDITOR IN CHIEF: JASON MAKOWSKI/CREATIVE DIRECTOR: JASON MAKOWSKI,
CHRISTOPHER WIELICZKO/ISSUE YEAR: 2004/ISSUE #: 7/LOCAL COVER PRICE: $10/

032C
WWW.032C.COM/GERMANY/PUBLISHER: 032C WORKSHOP/EDITOR IN CHIEF: NA/
CREATIVE DIRECTOR: JOERG KOCH/ISSUE YEAR: 2000/ISSUE #: 1/
LOCAL COVER PRICE: €4/

A

A
WWW.VEENMANPUBLISHERS.COM/NETHERLANDS/PUBLISHER: ARTIMO/
EDITOR IN CHIEF: NA/CREATIVE DIRECTOR: PAUL BOUDERS/ISSUE YEAR: 2001/
ISSUE #: 1/LOCAL COVER PRICE: €13/

A BIT SPECIAL
WWW.ABITSPECIALMAG.CO.UK/UNITED KINGDOM/PUBLISHER: MARC TAYLOR/
EDITOR IN CHIEF: NA/CREATIVE DIRECTOR: MARC TAYLOR/ISSUE YEAR: 2005/
ISSUE #: 4/LOCAL COVER PRICE: £4/

A/4
WWW.A4MAG.COM/POLAND/PUBLISHER: IWONA CZEMPINSKA/
EDITOR IN CHIEF: MIKOLAJ KOMAR/CREATIVE DIRECTOR: JAKUB JEZIERSKI-PIONTY/
ISSUE YEAR: 2003/ISSUE #: 1/LOCAL COVER PRICE: 7.50 Zł/

ACHTUNG
WWW.ACHTUNG-MODE.COM/GERMANY/PUBLISHER: MARKUS EBNER/
EDITOR IN CHIEF: MARKUS EBNER/CREATIVE DIRECTOR: MARKUS EBNER/
ISSUE YEAR: 2003/ISSUE #: 1/LOCAL COVER PRICE: €8/

AD!DICT
WWW.ADDICTLAB.COM/BELGIUM/PUBLISHER: AD!DICT INSPIRATION BOOKS/
EDITOR IN CHIEF: ANJA SAMSON/CREATIVE DIRECTOR: JAN VAN MOL/
ISSUE YEAR: 2005/ISSUE #: 24/LOCAL COVER PRICE: €12/

AE
WWW.AE-MAGAZINE.COM/FRANCE/PUBLISHER: AE MAGAZINE/
EDITOR IN CHIEF: DON DUNCAN/CREATIVE DIRECTOR: DON DUNCAN/
ISSUE YEAR: 2005/ISSUE #: 1/LOCAL COVER PRICE: €5/

AMERICA
WWW.AMERICAMAG.US/UNITED STATES/PUBLISHER: SMOKEY D. FONTAINE/
EDITOR IN CHIEF: SMOKEY D. FONTAINE/CREATIVE DIRECTOR: GRAHAM ROUNTHWAITE/
ISSUE YEAR: 2004/ISSUE #: 1/LOCAL COVER PRICE: $8/

ANATHEMA
WWW.ANATHEMAMAGAZINE.COM/UNITED STATES/PUBLISHER: KEN MILLER/
EDITOR IN CHIEF: KEN MILLER/CREATIVE DIRECTOR: DMITRI SIEGEL/ISSUE YEAR: 2005/
ISSUE #: 1/LOCAL COVER PRICE: $6/COVER PHOTO: SUSANNAH SAYLER; SPREAD
PHOTO: SIMONE SHUBUK/

ANNA SANDERS
WWW.ANNASANDERSFILMS.COM/FRANCE/PUBLISHER: PIERRE HUYGHE,
PHILIPPE PARRENO/EDITOR IN CHIEF: NA/CREATIVE DIRECTOR: LILI FLEURY/
ISSUE YEAR: 1997/ISSUE #: 1/LOCAL COVER PRICE: FREE/

ANOTHER MAGAZINE
WWW.ANOTHERMAG.COM/UNITED KINGDOM/PUBLISHER: JEFFERSON HACK, RANKIN
WADDELL/EDITOR IN CHIEF: JEFFERSON HACK/ CREATIVE DIRECTOR: ALEX WIEDERIN/
ISSUE YEAR: 2001/ISSUE #: 1/LOCAL COVER PRICE: NA/

ARKITIP
WWW.ARKITIP.COM/UNITED STATES/PUBLISHER: ARKITIP/EDITOR IN CHIEF: NA/
CREATIVE DIRECTOR: SCOTT ANDREW SNYDER/ISSUE YEAR: NA/ISSUE #: 31/
LOCAL COVER PRICE: $30/

ASIAN PUNK BOY
WWW.ASIANPUNKBOY.COM/UNITED STATES/PUBLISHER: KOHBUNNY BOOKS/
EDITOR IN CHIEF: TERRENCE KOH/CREATIVE DIRECTOR: TERRENCE KOH/
ISSUE YEAR: 2001/ISSUE #: NA/LOCAL COVER PRICE: $80/

B

BABY BABY BABY
WWW.CELESTE.COM.MX/MEXICO/PUBLISHER: ALDO CHAPARRO, VANESA FERNANDEZ,
JORGE VERGARA/EDITOR IN CHIEF: JOSÉ GARCÍA TORRES/
CREATIVE DIRECTOR: ALDO CHAPARRO, VANESA FERNANDEZ, JORGE VERGARA/ISSUE
YEAR: 2004/ISSUE #: 1/LOCAL COVER PRICE: N$40/

BEOPLE
WWW.BEOPLE.BE/BELGIUM/PUBLISHER: SCOUMONT/EDITOR IN CHIEF: HILDE BOUCHEZ/
CREATIVE DIRECTOR: BASE/ISSUE YEAR: 2001/ISSUE #: 1/LOCAL COVER PRICE: €9/

BERLINER
WWW.BERLINERMAGAZINE.COM/GERMANY/PUBLISHER: BORIS MOSHKOVITS/
EDITOR IN CHIEF: BORIS MOSHKOVITS/CREATIVE DIRECTOR: THEOS DOHM,
PHILIPP VON ROHDEN/ISSUE YEAR: 2002/ISSUE #: 1/LOCAL COVER PRICE: €11.50/

BIDOUN
WWW.BIDOUN.COM/UNITED STATES/PUBLISHER: BIDOUN MAGAZINE/
EDITOR IN CHIEF: LISA FARJAM/CREATIVE DIRECTOR: KETUTA ALEXI-MESKHISHVILI/
ISSUE YEAR: 2004/ISSUE #: 1/LOCAL COVER PRICE: $10/

BIG
WWW.BIGMAGAZINE.COM/UNITED STATES/PUBLISHER: BIG COMMUNICATIONS/
EDITOR IN CHIEF: MARCELO JÜNEMANN/CREATIVE DIRECTOR: MARCELO JÜNEMANN/
ISSUE YEAR: NA/ISSUE #: 26/LOCAL COVER PRICE: $15/

BILBOK
WWW.BILBOK.COM/FRANCE/PUBLISHER: BILBOK/EDITOR IN CHIEF: PHILIPPE BLONDEZ/
CREATIVE DIRECTOR: PHILIPPE BLONDEZ/ISSUE YEAR: 2003/ISSUE #: 21/
LOCAL COVER PRICE: €7/

BLAG
WWW.BLAGMAGAZINE.COM/UNITED KINGDOM/PUBLISHER: BLAG UK LIMITED/EDITOR
IN CHIEF: MAGDALENA FLORES PEÑAFIEL/CREATIVE DIRECTOR: SALLY A EDWARDS,
SARAH J EDWARDS/ISSUE YEAR: 2000/ISSUE #: NA/LOCAL COVER PRICE: £24.99/

BLANK
WWW.BLANKMGZ.COM/SPAIN/PUBLISHER: DOS CLICK S.L./
EDITOR IN CHIEF: ARMANDO VEGA-GIL RUEDA/CREATIVE DIRECTOR: SALVADOR
CUENCA FRÓMESTA/ISSUE YEAR: 2004/ISSUE #: 4/LOCAL COVER PRICE: €9/

BRANSCH
WWW.BRANSCHMAGAZINE.COM/GERMANY/PUBLISHER: BRANSCH/
EDITOR IN CHIEF: SUSANNE BRANSCH/CREATIVE DIRECTOR: ADELINE MORLON/
ISSUE YEAR: 2002/ISSUE #: 1/LOCAL COVER PRICE: €12/COVER PHOTO: OLAF BLECKER;
SPREAD PHOTO: MAGNUS WINTER/

BULGARIA
WWW.BULGARIAMAGAZINE.COM/FINLAND/PUBLISHER: BULGARIA DESIGN/
EDITOR IN CHIEF: NA/CREATIVE DIRECTOR: JESPER BANGE, JUHA MURREMÄKI,
JARNO LUOTONEN, SAMPO HÄNNINEN/ISSUE YEAR: 2001/ISSUE #: 2/
LOCAL COVER PRICE: FREE/

BUTT
WWW.BUTTMAGAZINE.COM/NETHERLANDS/PUBLISHER: BUTT MAGAZINE/
EDITOR IN CHIEF: JOP VAN BENNEKOM, GERT JONKERS/CREATIVE DIRECTOR:
JOP VAN BENNEKOM, GERT JONKERS/ISSUE YEAR: 2001/ISSUE #: 1/
LOCAL COVER PRICE: NLG 10/

C

CAPRICIOUS
WWW.BECAPRICIOUS.COM/NETHERLANDS/PUBLISHER: SOPHIE MÖRNER/
EDITOR IN CHIEF: SOPHIE MÖRNER/CREATIVE DIRECTOR: SOPHIE MÖRNER/
ISSUE YEAR: 2004/ISSUE #: 1/LOCAL COVER PRICE: €12.50/

CARLOS
WWW.FIFTY-ONE.CO.UK/UNITED KINGDOM/PUBLISHER: FIFTY-ONE/
EDITOR IN CHIEF: MICHAEL JACOVIDES/CREATIVE DIRECTOR: WARREN JACKSON,
MICHAEL JACOVIDES/ISSUE YEAR: 2004/ISSUE #: 6/LOCAL COVER PRICE: £3/

CARL'S CARS
WWW.CARLS-CARS.COM/NORWAY/PUBLISHER: KARL EIRIK HAUG/
EDITOR IN CHIEF: KARL EIRIK HAUG/CREATIVE DIRECTOR: STÉPHANIE DUMONT/
ISSUE YEAR: 2001/ISSUE #: 1/LOCAL COVER PRICE: KR 59/

CELESTE
WWW.CELESTE.COM.MX/MEXICO/PUBLISHER: ALDO CHAPARRO, VANESA FERNANDEZ,
JORGE VERGARA/EDITOR IN CHIEF: JOSÉ GARCÍA TORRES, GRETA SOMORROSTRO/
CREATIVE DIRECTOR: ALDO CHAPARRO, VANESA FERNANDEZ, JORGE VERGARA/
ISSUE YEAR: 2001/ISSUE #: 15/LOCAL COVER PRICE: N$55/

CHARLEY
WWW.DESTE.GR/UNITED STATES/PUBLISHER: LES PRESSES DU RÉEL/
EDITOR IN CHIEF: MAURIZO CATELLAN, BELLA FUNCKE, MASSIMILIANO GIONI,
ALI SUBOTNICK/CREATIVE DIRECTOR: MAURIZO CATELLAN, MASSIMILIANO GIONI,
ALI SUBOTNICK/ISSUE YEAR: 2000/ISSUE #: 1/LOCAL COVER PRICE: $10/

CLAM
WWW.CLAMMAG.COM/FRANCE/PUBLISHER: CLAM TOTAL FASHION BUREAU, LTD./
EDITOR IN CHIEF: VANESSA COQUET/CREATIVE DIRECTOR: ANDY AMADI OKOROAFOR/
ISSUE YEAR: NA/ISSUE #: 4/LOCAL COVER PRICE: NA/

COLORS
WWW.COLORSMAGAZINE.COM/ITALY/PUBLISHER: UNITED COLORS OF BENNETON/
EDITOR IN CHIEF: OLIVIERO TOSCANI/CREATIVE DIRECTOR: EMILY OBERMAN/
ISSUE YEAR: 1991/ISSUE #: 1/LOCAL COVER PRICE: FREE/COVER PHOTO: TOSCANI;
1ST SPREAD PHOTOS: BLAIR CLARK, DAVID HAMSLEY; 2ND SPREAD PHOTOS: AP,
PETER JORDON, BILL DAVILA, T. LOUSOUET/

COMMONS & SENSE
WWW.COMMONS-SENSE.NET/JAPAN/PUBLISHER: KAORU SASAKI/
EDITOR IN CHIEF: KAORU SASAKI/CREATIVE DIRECTOR: KAORU SASAKI/
ISSUE YEAR: 1997/ISSUE #: 11/LOCAL COVER PRICE: ¥448/

COMMONS&SENSE MAN
WWW.COMMONS-SENSE.NET/JAPAN/PUBLISHER: KAORU SASAKI/
EDITOR IN CHIEF: KAORU SASAKI/CREATIVE DIRECTOR: KAORU SASAKI/
ISSUE YEAR: 2006/ISSUE #: 1/LOCAL COVER PRICE: ¥667/

CONTINUOUS PROJECT
WWW.CONTINUOUSPROJECT.COM/UNITED STATES/PUBLISHER: CONTINUOUS PROJECT/
EDITOR IN CHIEF: BETTINA FUNCKE, WADE GUYTON, JOSEPH LOGAN, SETH PRICE/
CREATIVE DIRECTOR: CONTINUOUS PROJECT/ISSUE YEAR: 2003/ISSUE #: 7/
LOCAL COVER PRICE: $2/

CRÈME
PATRICE@ITSROUGE.COM/LUXEMBOURG/PUBLISHER: M. EDITIONS/
EDITOR IN CHIEF: M. MECHERI/CREATIVE DIRECTOR: KARINE CHANE YIN, S110/
ISSUE YEAR: 1999/ISSUE #: 1/LOCAL COVER PRICE: NA/ COVER PHOTO:
EMMANUEL GIMENO; SPREAD PHOTO: GARTH MEYER/

CRITIC EYE
WWW.CRITICEYE.COM/UNITED STATES/PUBLISHER: JESSICA BESHIR, DAVID RENARD/
EDITOR IN CHIEF: NA/CREATIVE DIRECTOR: NA/ISSUE YEAR: 2000/ISSUE #: 1/
LOCAL COVER PRICE: $3/

D

D(X)I
WWW.DXIMAGAZINE.COM/SPAIN/PUBLISHER: EQUIPO D(X)I /
EDITOR IN CHIEF: ALEJANDRO BENAVENT GONZALEZ/CREATIVE DIRECTOR:
ALEJANDRO BENAVENT GONZALEZ/ISSUE YEAR: 2000/ISSUE #: 16/
LOCAL COVER PRICE: FREE/

DANIEL BATTAMS FAN CLUB
WWW.DANIELBATTAMSFANCLUB.COM/UNITED KINGDOM/
PUBLISHER: MADE UP STUDIOS, LTD/EDITOR IN CHIEF: DANIEL BATTAMS/
CREATIVE DIRECTOR: DANIEL BATTAMS/ISSUE YEAR: 2003/ISSUE #: 5/
LOCAL COVER PRICE: $2.50/

DANSK
WWW.DANSKMAGAZINE.COM/DENMARK/
PUBLISHER: UFFE BUCHARD, KIM GRENAA/EDITOR IN
CHIEF: UFFE BUCHARD, KIM GRENAA/CREATIVE
DIRECTOR: LARS DYHR, PETER HAGEN/ISSUE YEAR:
2002/ISSUE #: 1/LOCAL COVER PRICE: KR 200/COVER
PHOTO: DEREK HENDERSEN; 1ST SPREAD PHOTO:
KLAUS THYMANN; 2ND, 3RD SPREAD PHOTOS:
MORTEN BJARNHOF; 4TH, 5TH SPREAD PHOTOS:
BRYAN ADAMS/

DE AVONTUUR BEVAT
WWW.GEBR-GENK.NL/NETHERLANDS/PUBLISHER:
GEBR. GENK, UITGEVERS/
EDITOR IN CHIEF: NA/CREATIVE DIRECTOR: GERLACH
EN KOOP/ISSUE YEAR: 2003/ISSUE #: 1/LOCAL COVER
PRICE: FREE/

DEDICATE
WWW.DEDICATEMAGAZINE.COM/FRANCE/
PUBLISHER: OLIVIER BOUCHÉ/
EDITOR IN CHIEF: OLIVIER BOUCHÉ, GUILLAUME
BESSE, ERIC REDDAD-JORDY/CREATIVE DIRECTOR:
DEDICATE TEAM/ISSUE YEAR: 2001/ISSUE #: 1/
LOCAL COVER PRICE: €12/

DELICIAE VITAE
WWW.TCGSERVER.CO.UK/DV/MAIN.HTML/ITALY/PUBLISHER: DV EDITIONS, LTD/
EDITOR IN CHIEF: KINDER AGGUGINI/CREATIVE DIRECTOR: CRAIG TILFORD/
ISSUE YEAR: 2001/ISSUE #: 1/LOCAL COVER PRICE: NA/COVER PHOTO:
VINCENT PETERS; 1ST SPREAD PHOTO: ROBIN DERRICK; 2ND SPREAD PHOTO:
JASPER GOODALL; 3RD SPREAD PHOTO: ELLEN VON UNWORTH;
4TH SPREAD PHOTO: MATTHIAS VRIENS; 5TH SPREAD PHOTO: BETTINA RHEIMS;
6TH SPREAD PHOTOS: PHIL BYNTER/

DIGMEOUT
WWW.DIGMEOUT.NET/JAPAN/PUBLISHER: PETIT GRAND PUBLISHING/
EDITOR IN CHIEF: YOSHIHIRO TANIGUCHI/CREATIVE DIRECTOR: YOSHIHIRO TANIGUCHI/
ISSUE YEAR: 2005/ISSUE #: 5/LOCAL COVER PRICE: ¥2,000/

DOINGBIRD
WWW.DOINGBIRD.COM/AUSTRALIA/PUBLISHER: BIRD PRESS/
EDITOR IN CHIEF: MAX DOYLE/CREATIVE DIRECTOR: MALCOLM WATT/ISSUE YEAR:
2001/ISSUE #: 1/LOCAL COVER PRICE: $11.95/ COVER PHOTO: PETER ROBINSON/

DOT DOT DOT
WWW.DOT-DOT-DOT.NL/NETHERLANDS/PUBLISHER: DOT DOT DOT, VOF./
EDITOR IN CHIEF: JÜRGEN X. ALBRECHT, STUART BAILEY, PETER BILAK, TOM UNVERAZGT/
CREATIVE DIRECTOR: STUART BAILEY, PETER BILAK/ISSUE YEAR: 2000/ISSUE #: 1/LOCAL
COVER PRICE: €10/

E

ENCENS
WWW.ENCENSREVUE.COM/FRANCE/PUBLISHER: SAMUEL DRIRA, SYBILLE WALTER/
EDITOR IN CHIEF: NA/CREATIVE DIRECTOR: SAMUEL DRIRA, SYBILLE WALTER/
ISSUE YEAR: 2004/ISSUE #: 12/LOCAL COVER PRICE: €5/

EXES
WWW.EXXEXX.COM/ITALY/PUBLISHER: MARINO PARISOTTO/
EDITOR IN CHIEF: GIAMPIERO MUGHINI/CREATIVE DIRECTOR: MANUEL GRIMALDI/
ISSUE YEAR: 2003/ISSUE #: 1/LOCAL COVER PRICE: $170/

EXIT
WWW.EXITMAGAZINE.CO.UK/UNITED KINGDOM/PUBLISHER: STEPHEN TONER/
EDITOR IN CHIEF: STEPHEN TONER/CREATIVE DIRECTOR: MARK CONSTANTINE/
ISSUE YEAR: 2000/ISSUE #: 1/LOCAL COVER PRICE: £12/

F

FAB
WWW.FABRICA.IT/ITALY/PUBLISHER: NA/EDITOR IN CHIEF: SARA BELTRAME/
CREATIVE DIRECTOR: FREDERICO DUARTE, JAVIN MO, JOHANNA NOCK, MAIK BLUHM/
ISSUE YEAR: 2005/ISSUE #: NA/LOCAL COVER PRICE: FREE/COVER PHOTO: REBEKKA
EHLERS; 1ST SPREAD DESIGN: FRANCESCA GRANATO; 2ND SPREAD DESIGN:
JONATHAN HARRIS/

FAD
WWW.FADWEBSITE.COM/UNITED KINGDOM/PUBLISHER: DAN SUMPTION,
MARK WESTALL/EDITOR IN CHIEF: DAN SUMPTION/CREATIVE DIRECTOR: JOHN
CRUMPTON, MARK WESTALL/ISSUE YEAR: 2002/ISSUE #: 2/LOCAL COVER PRICE: £4/

FAESTHETIC
WWW.FAESTHETIC.COM/UNITED STATES/PUBLISHER: DUSTIN HOSTETLER/
EDITOR IN CHIEF: DUSTIN HOSTETLER/CREATIVE DIRECTOR: DUSTIN HOSTETLER/
ISSUE YEAR: 2000/ISSUE #: 4/LOCAL COVER PRICE: $5/

FAIRY TALE
WWW.FAIRYTALE-MAGAZINE.COM/FRANCE/PUBLISHER: VIER 5/
EDITOR IN CHIEF: ACHIM REICHERT, MARCO FIEDLER/CREATIVE DIRECTOR: VIER 5/ISSUE
YEAR: 2005/ISSUE #: 6/LOCAL COVER PRICE: €11/

FANTASTIC MAN
WWW.FANTASTICMANMAGAZINE.COM/NETHERLANDS/PUBLISHER: TOP PUBLISHERS/
EDITOR IN CHIEF: JOP VAN BENNEKOM, GERT JONKERS/
CREATIVE DIRECTOR: JOP VAN BENNEKOM, GERT JONKERS/ISSUE YEAR: 2005/
ISSUE #: 1/LOCAL COVER PRICE: €8.95/

FANZINE 137
WWW.FANZINE137.COM/SPAIN/PUBLISHER: LUIS VENEGAS/
EDITOR IN CHIEF: LUIS VENEGAS/CREATIVE DIRECTOR: LUIS VENEGAS/
ISSUE YEAR: 2004/ISSUE #: 1/LOCAL COVER PRICE: €17/

FIDGET
WWW.FIDGETMAGAZINE.COM/UNITED STATES/PUBLISHER: RUSSELL MILLER/
EDITOR IN CHIEF: NA/CREATIVE DIRECTOR: RUSSELL MILLER/ISSUE YEAR: 2000/
ISSUE #: 2/LOCAL COVER PRICE: $8/COVER PHOTO: ALEXANDRE DE CADANET; 1ST
SPREAD PHOTO: REGGIE CASAGRANDE; 2ND SPREAD PHOTO: JENNIFER TZAR/

FOUND
WWW.FOUNDMAGAZINE.COM/UNITED STATES/PUBLISHER: FOUND MAGAZINE/
EDITOR IN CHIEF: DAVY ROTHBART, JASON BITNER/
CREATIVE DIRECTOR: DAVY ROTHBART, JASON BITNER/ISSUE YEAR: 2001/
ISSUE #: 1/LOCAL COVER PRICE: $5/

285
L

G

GUM
WWW.GUMWEB.COM/UNITED STATES/PUBLISHER: COLIN METCALF, KEVIN GRADY/
EDITOR IN CHIEF: COLIN METCALF, KEVIN GRADY/
CREATIVE DIRECTOR: COLIN METCALF, KEVIN GRADY/ISSUE YEAR: 2002/
ISSUE #: 1/LOCAL COVER PRICE: $20/

H

HAPPENING
HAPPENING@WANADOO.NL/TAIWAN/PUBLISHER: SARINA YEH/
EDITOR IN CHIEF: SARINA YEH/CREATIVE DIRECTOR: JEFF HARGROVE/
ISSUE YEAR: 2003/ISSUE #: 1/LOCAL COVER PRICE: $380/
HÉLÈNE
WWW.PURPLE.FR/FRANCE/PUBLISHER: ELEIN FLEISS/EDITOR IN CHIEF: ELEIN FLEISS/
CREATIVE DIRECTOR: CHRISTOPHE BRUNNQUELL/ISSUE YEAR: 2003/
ISSUE #: 1/LOCAL COVER PRICE: €3.60/
HERE AND THERE
WWW.NAKAKOBOOKS.COM/JAPAN/PUBLISHER: NAKAKO HAYASHI/EDITOR IN CHIEF:
NAKAKO HAYASHI/CREATIVE DIRECTOR: KAZUNARI HATTORI, NAKAKO HAYASHI/ISSUE
YEAR: 2002/ISSUE #: 1/LOCAL COVER PRICE: ¥1,700/

I

I DON'T UNDERSTAND
WWW.TRENDYPOP.COM/FRANCE/PUBLISHER: TRENDY POP/
EDITOR IN CHIEF: MATTEO VIANELLO/CREATIVE DIRECTOR: ALESSIO KRAUSS,
MATTEO VIANELLO, TOMMASO NICOLAO/ISSUE YEAR: 2005/ISSUE #: 1/
LOCAL COVER PRICE: €15/
INFLUENCE
WWW.ISSUEMAGAZINE.COM/UNITED STATES/PUBLISHER: MAR PUBLISHING/
EDITOR IN CHIEF: JAN-WILLEN DIKKERS/CREATIVE DIRECTOR: RAUL MARTINEZ/
ISSUE YEAR: 2003/ISSUE #: 1/LOCAL COVER PRICE: $10/
IS NOT
WWW.ISNOTMAGAZINE.ORG/AUSTRALIA/PUBLISHER: MEL CAMPBELL, STUART GEDDES,
NATASHA LUDOWYK, PENNY MODRA, JEREMY WORTSMAN/EDITOR IN CHIEF:
MEL CAMPBELL, STUART GEDDES, NATASHA LUDOWYK, PENNY MODRA,
JEREMY WORTSMAN/CREATIVE DIRECTOR: MEL CAMPBELL, STUART GEDDES,
NATASHA LUDOWYK, PENNY MODRA, JEREMY WORTSMAN/ISSUE YEAR: 2005/
ISSUE #: 1/LOCAL COVER PRICE: FREE/PHOTO: SHANNON PAWSEY
ISSUE
WWW.ISSUEMAGAZINE.COM/UNITED STATES/PUBLISHER: ISSUE INC./
EDITOR IN CHIEF: JAN-WILLEM DIKKERS, MARTYNKA WAWRYZNIAK/
CREATIVE DIRECTOR: JAN-WILLEM DIKKERS/ISSUE YEAR: 2003/ISSUE #: 7/
LOCAL COVER PRICE: $10/
ITS ROUGE
WWW.ITSROUGE.COM/FRANCE/PUBLISHER: KARINE CHANE YIN/
EDITOR IN CHIEF: KARINE CHANE YIN, PATRICE FUMA COURTIS/
CREATIVE DIRECTOR: KARINE CHANE YIN, PATRICE FUMA COURTIS/
ISSUE YEAR: 2003/ISSUE #: 1/LOCAL COVER PRICE: €19/

J

JE T'AIME TANT
WWW.JETAIMETANT.COM/FRANCE/PUBLISHER: BENOIT VIAL/
EDITOR IN CHIEF: BETTINA/CREATIVE DIRECTOR: BENOIT VIAL/ISSUE YEAR: 2005/
ISSUE #: 1/LOCAL COVER PRICE: €15/

K

K&K
WWW.STUDIOVONBIRKEN.COM/MAG/UNITED STATES/PUBLISHER: STUDIO VON BIRKEN
& STARSTYLING/EDITOR IN CHIEF: N/A/CREATIVE DIRECTOR: KATIA KUETHE,
PHILIPP MÜSSIGMANN/ISSUE YEAR: 2005/ISSUE #: 1/LOCAL COVER PRICE: $10/
K48
WWW.K48RULES.COM/UNITED STATES/PUBLISHER: SCOTT HUG/
EDITOR IN CHIEF: SCOTT HUG/CREATIVE DIRECTOR: SCOTT HUG/
ISSUE YEAR: 2000/ISSUE #: 1/LOCAL COVER PRICE: $19.95/
KILIMANJARO
WWW.KILIMAG.COM/UNITED KINGDOM/PUBLISHER: MICHAEL OLU ODUKOYA/
EDITOR IN CHIEF: MICHAEL OLU ODUKOYA/CREATIVE DIRECTOR: MICHAEL OLU
ODUKOYA, JASON JULES, JAMES GREENHOW/ISSUE YEAR: 2003/ISSUE #: 1/
LOCAL COVER PRICE: £6.50/

LA CINCA I.A.
WWW.LACINCA.COM/NETHERLANDS/PUBLISHER: MIKLÓS BEYER, THOMAS BUXÓ/
EDITOR IN CHIEF: NA/CREATIVE DIRECTOR: NA/ISSUE YEAR: 1998/
ISSUE #: NA/LOCAL COVER PRICE: NA/
LA RAMPA
WWW.LA-RAMPA.COM/CANADA/PUBLISHER: GETHIN JAMES/
EDITOR IN CHIEF: CHANTAL JAMES/CREATIVE DIRECTOR: CHANTAL JAMES/
ISSUE YEAR: 2004/ISSUE #: 2/LOCAL COVER PRICE: $20/
LOOK LOOK
WWW.LOOK-LOOKMAGAZINE.COM/UNITED STATES/PUBLISHER: DEEDEE GORDON,
SHARON LEE/EDITOR IN CHIEF: CAT DORAN/CREATIVE DIRECTOR: LISA EISNER, ROMAN
ALONSO/ISSUE YEAR: 2003/ISSUE #: 1/LOCAL COVER PRICE: $5.95/

M

M PUBLICATION
WWW.M-PUBLICATION.COM/GERMANY/PUBLISHER: KIMBERLY LLOYD/EDITOR IN
CHIEF: PIERO BORSELLINO, KIMBERLY LLOYD/CREATIVE DIRECTOR: KIMBERLY LLOYD/
ISSUE YEAR: 2003/ISSUE #: 3/LOCAL COVER PRICE: €17/
MADE
WWW.MADEMAG.COM/CANADA/PUBLISHER: MADE MEDIA/
EDITOR IN CHIEF: RAIF ADELBERG, MARK GAINOR, CATHEE SCRIVANO,
MICHELLE EVERS/CREATIVE DIRECTOR: RAIF ADELBERG, MARK GAINOR/
ISSUE YEAR: 2001/ISSUE #: 20/LOCAL COVER PRICE: $35/
MARK
WWW.MARKMAGAZINE.COM/AUSTRALIA/PUBLISHER: MARK VASSALLO/
EDITOR IN CHIEF: MARK VASSALLO/CREATIVE DIRECTOR: NA/ISSUE YEAR: 2005/
ISSUE #: 3/LOCAL COVER PRICE: NA/
MARK - ANOTHER ARCHITECTURE
WWW.MARK-MAGAZINE.COM/THE NETHERLANDS/PUBLISHER: MARK PUBLISHERS/
EDITOR IN CHIEF: NA/CREATIVE DIRECTOR: ROBERT THIEMANN/ISSUE YEAR: 2005/
ISSUE #: 1/LOCAL COVER PRICE: €35/
MARMALADE
WWW.MARMALADEMAG.COM/UNITED KINGDOM/PUBLISHER: MARMALADE
MAGAZINE/EDITOR IN CHIEF: KIRSTY ROBINSON, SACHA SPENCER TRACE/
CREATIVE DIRECTOR: SACHA SPENCER TRACE/ISSUE YEAR: 2003/ISSUE #: 0/
LOCAL COVER PRICE: £4.50/
MCSWEENEY'S
WWW.MCSWEENEYS.NET/UNITED STATES/PUBLISHER: MCSWEENEY'S/
EDITOR IN CHIEF: DAVE EGGERS/CREATIVE DIRECTOR: DAVE EGGERS, ELI HOROWITZ/
ISSUE YEAR: 2005/ISSUE #: 16/LOCAL COVER PRICE: $24/
ME
WWW.MEMAGAZINENYC.COM/UNITED STATES/PUBLISHER: CLAUDIA WU/
EDITOR IN CHIEF: ANGEL CHANG, CLAUDIA WU/CREATIVE DIRECTOR: CLAUDIA WU/
ISSUE YEAR: 2004/ISSUE #: 1/LOCAL COVER PRICE: $5/
MEGAWORDS
WWW.MEGAWORDSMAGAZINE.COM/UNITED STATES/PUBLISHER: ANTHONY SMYRSKI,
DAN MURPHY/EDITOR IN CHIEF: ANTHONY SMYRSKI, DAN MURPHY/
CREATIVE DIRECTOR: ANTHONY SMYRSKI, DAN MURPHY/ISSUE YEAR: 2005/
ISSUE #: NA/LOCAL COVER PRICE: FREE/
MINED
WWW.TANKMAGAZINE.COM/UNITED KINGDOM/PUBLISHER: TANK PUBLICATIONS, LTD./
EDITOR IN CHIEF: MASOUD GOLSORKHI, ANDREAS LAEUFER, EKOW ESHUN/
CREATIVE DIRECTOR: MASOUD GOLSORKHI/ISSUE YEAR: 2001/ISSUE #: 2/
LOCAL COVER PRICE: £20/1ST SPREAD PHOTO: JONATHAN FOSTER WILLIAMS;
2ND SPREAD ART: MANUEL DUQUE; 3RD SPREAD PHOTO: MYRTLE;
4TH SPREAD ART: JOHN STRUTTON; 5TH SPREAD ART: ROGER ANDERSSON/
MODA E CONTEXTO
ROSAS.HELIO@GMAIL.COM/BRAZIL/PUBLISHER: EDITORA BOOKMARK/
EDITOR IN CHIEF: JOÃO CARRASCOSA, FLAVIA LAFER, ROBERTO CIPOLLA,
HELIO ROSAS/CREATIVE DIRECTOR: JOÃO CARRASCOSA, FLAVIA LAFER/
ISSUE YEAR: 2001/ISSUE #: 0/LOCAL COVER PRICE: R$15/
MODERN TOSS
WWW.MODERNTOSS.COM/UNITED KINGDOM/PUBLISHER: JON LINK, MICK BUNNAGE/
EDITOR IN CHIEF: JON LINK, MICK BUNNAGE/CREATIVE DIRECTOR: JON LINK,
MICK BUNNAGE/ISSUE YEAR: 2004/ISSUE #: 1/LOCAL COVER PRICE: £4.99/

N

NEXT LEVEL
WWW.NEXTLEVELUK.COM/UNITED KINGDOM/PUBLISHER: BLUESMODERNIST, LTD./
EDITOR IN CHIEF: JIMO TOYIN SALAKO, SHEYI ANTONY BANKS/
CREATIVE DIRECTOR: SHEYI ANTONY BANKS/ISSUE YEAR: 2002/ISSUE #: 1/
LOCAL COVER PRICE: £15/

NICE MAGAZINE
BMC@FLYMAIL.FM/UNITED KINGDOM/PUBLISHER: BRENDAN MICHAEL CAREY/
EDITOR IN CHIEF: NA/CREATIVE DIRECTOR: BRENDAN MICHAEL CAREY/
ISSUE YEAR: 2003/ISSUE #: 1 FASHION VICTIM/LOCAL COVER PRICE: £21/

NORTH DRIVE PRESS
WWW.NORTHDRIVEPRESS.COM/UNITED STATES/PUBLISHER: MATT KEEGAN/
EDITOR IN CHIEF: MATT KEEGAN/CREATIVE DIRECTOR: SARA GREENBERGER,
SUSAN BARBER/ISSUE YEAR: 2004/ISSUE #: 2/LOCAL COVER PRICE: $30/

O

OJODEPEZ
WWW.OJODEPEZ.ORG/SPAIN/PUBLISHER: FRANK KALERO/
EDITOR IN CHIEF: DAVID MÁRQUEZ/CREATIVE DIRECTOR: ALEX CARRASCO/
ISSUE YEAR: 2003/ISSUE #: 1/LOCAL COVER PRICE: €10/

ONE ONE NINE
WWW.ONEONENINE.ORG/UNITED STATES/PUBLISHER: ONE ONE NINE/
EDITOR IN CHIEF: STEVE GREEN, JUSTIN KAY/CREATIVE DIRECTOR: STEVE GREEN,
JUSTIN KAY/ISSUE YEAR: 2005/ISSUE #: 1/LOCAL COVER PRICE: $10/

OUR MAGAZINE
WWW.OUR-MAGAZINE.CH/SWITZERLAND/PUBLISHER: OUR MAGAZINE/
EDITOR IN CHIEF: LINUS BILL, MELANIE HOFMANN, URS LEHNI, NICK WIDMER/
CREATIVE DIRECTOR: URS LEHNI/ISSUE YEAR: 2003/ISSUE #: 1/LOCAL COVER PRICE: NA/

OZONE ROCKS
WWW.OZONEROCKS.COM/JAPAN/PUBLISHER: OZONE COMMUNITY/
EDITOR IN CHIEF: FUMIHIRO HAYASHI/CREATIVE DIRECTOR: KATZUZO YAMAGUCHI/
ISSUE YEAR: 2003/ISSUE #: 1 ROSARION/LOCAL COVER PRICE: ¥3,000/

P

PABLO INTERNATIONAL
WWW.CELESTE.COM.MX/MEXICO/UK/PUBLISHER: JOSE GARCIA TORRES/
EDITOR IN CHIEF: PABLO LEÓN DE LA BARRA/CREATIVE DIRECTOR: PABLO LEÓN
DE LA BARRA/ISSUE YEAR: 2005/ISSUE #: 0/LOCAL COVER PRICE: N$50/

PERMANENT FOOD
WWW.MAURIZIOCATTELAN.ORG/UNITED STATES/ITALY/PUBLISHER: PRESS DU REEL /
EDITOR IN CHIEF: MAURIZIO CATTELAN, DOMINIQUE GONZALEZ-FOERSTER/
CREATIVE DIRECTOR: PAOLA MANFRIN, MAURIZIO CATTELAN/ISSUE YEAR: 1997/
ISSUE #: 1/LOCAL COVER PRICE: FREE/

PETITGLAM
WWW.PETIT.ORG/JAPAN/PUBLISHER: PETIT GRAND PUBLISHING, INC./
EDITOR IN CHIEF: CO ITO/CREATIVE DIRECTOR: TAKAYA GOTO/ISSUE YEAR: 1999/
ISSUE #: 4/LOCAL COVER PRICE: ¥1,429/

PICNIC
WWW.PICNIC-MAG.COM/MEXICO/PUBLISHER: VÉRONIQUE RICARDONI,
VÍCTOR MANUEL RODRÍGUEZ/EDITOR IN CHIEF: LUIGI AMARA, MARÍA VIRGINIA JAUA/
CREATIVE DIRECTOR: VÉRONIQUE RICARDONI/ISSUE YEAR: 2005/ISSUE #: 6/
LOCAL COVER PRICE: N$55/

PLASTIC RHINO
WWW.PLASTICRHINO.COM/UNITED KINGDOM/PUBLISHER: PEPPERED SPROUT, LTD./
EDITOR IN CHIEF: CHRIS MORRIS/CREATIVE DIRECTOR: PETER KELLETT/ISSUE YEAR: 2004/
ISSUE #: 1/LOCAL COVER PRICE: £3.50/

POLISHED T
WWW.POLISHEDT.COM/UNITED KINGDOM/PUBLISHER: PEPPERED SPROUT, LTD./
EDITOR IN CHIEF: NA/CREATIVE DIRECTOR: PETER KELLETT/ISSUE YEAR: NA/ISSUE #: 1/
LOCAL COVER PRICE: £3.50/

PROPHECY
WWW.PROPHECYMAGAZINE.NET/UNITED STATES/PUBLISHER: PROPHECY MAGAZINE,
INC./EDITOR IN CHIEF: ED WEINBERG/CREATIVE DIRECTOR: KEVIN SUTAVEE/
ISSUE YEAR: 2001/ISSUE #: 1/LOCAL COVER PRICE: $4.95/

PURPLE
WWW.PURPLE.FR/FRANCE/PUBLISHER: ELEIN FLEISS, OLIVIER ZAHM/
EDITOR IN CHIEF: ELEIN FLEISS, OLIVIER ZAHM/CREATIVE DIRECTOR: CHRISTOPHE
BRUNNQUELL/ISSUE YEAR: 1999/ISSUE #: 4/LOCAL COVER PRICE: €11/COVER PHOTO:
MASAFUMI SANAI/

PURPLE SEXE
WWW.PURPLE.FR/FRANCE/PUBLISHER: OLIVIER ZAHM/EDITOR IN CHIEF: OLIVIER ZAHM/
CREATIVE DIRECTOR: CHRISTOPHE BRUNNQUELL/ISSUE YEAR: 1999/ISSUE #: 4/
LOCAL COVER PRICE: €9/COVER PHOTO: VIVIANE SASSEN; SPREAD PHOTOS:
RICHARD KERN/

PUTA
WWW.PUTAMAG.COM/UNITED STATES/PUBLISHER: TRUANT MEDIA/EDITOR IN CHIEF:
JAHIM ASSA, TODD C. ROBERTS/CREATIVE DIRECTOR: THOMAS MASTORAKOS/
ISSUE YEAR: 2003/ISSUE #: 1/LOCAL COVER PRICE: $9/COVER PHOTO:
ERIK IAN SCHAETZKE; 1ST SPREAD DESIGN: NEASDEN CONTROL CENTER;
2ND SPREAD PHOTOS: MATTY LIBATIQUE/

Q

QUADRAFOIL
WWW.QUADRAFOIL.COM/UNITED STATES/PUBLISHER: WALID GHANEM/
EDITOR IN CHIEF: WALID GHANEM/CREATIVE DIRECTOR: WALID GHANEM/
ISSUE YEAR: 2004/ISSUE #: 1/LOCAL COVER PRICE: $8/

R

RANK
WWW.CONFUSED.CO.UK/UNITED KINGDOM/PUBLISHER: RANKIN/
EDITOR IN CHIEF: RANKIN/CREATIVE DIRECTOR: RANKIN, WAI HUNG YOUNG/
ISSUE YEAR: 2000/ISSUE #: 0/LOCAL COVER PRICE: £7.95/

RE-
WWW.RE-MAGAZINE.COM/NETHERLANDS/PUBLISHER: ARTIMO/
EDITOR IN CHIEF: JOP VAN BENNEKOM/CREATIVE DIRECTOR: JOP VAN BENNEKOM/
ISSUE YEAR: 1997/ISSUE #: 6/LOCAL COVER PRICE: €8/

REFILL
WWW.REFILLMAG.COM/AUSTRALIA/PUBLISHER: KEEPLEFT STUDIO/
EDITOR IN CHIEF: MATTY BURTON/CREATIVE DIRECTOR: LUCA LONESCU,
MICHELLE HENDRIKS/ISSUE YEAR: 2003/ISSUE #: 1/LOCAL COVER PRICE: $39/

RICHARDSON
WWW.RICHARDSONMAG.COM/UNITED STATES/PUBLISHER: BEATRIX, LITTLE MORE, LTD./
EDITOR IN CHIEF: ANDREW RICHARDSON/CREATIVE DIRECTOR: ANDREW RICHARDSON/
ISSUE YEAR: 1998/ISSUE #: 1/LOCAL COVER PRICE: $25/

ROJO
WWW.REVISTA-ROJO.COM/SPAIN/PUBLISHER: SINTONISON, S.L./
EDITOR IN CHIEF: DAVID QUILES GUILLÓ/CREATIVE DIRECTOR: NA/ISSUE YEAR: 2005/
ISSUE #: 19/LOCAL COVER PRICE: NA/

ROSEBUD
WWW.ROSEBUDMAGAZINE.COM/AUSTRIA/PUBLISHER: RALF HERMS/
EDITOR IN CHIEF: RALF HERMS, FRITZ T. MAGISTRIS, KONSTANZE WAGENHOFER/CREATIVE
DIRECTOR: RALF HERMS, FRITZ MAFISTRIS, KATJA FOESSEL/ISSUE YEAR: 1998/ISSUE #: 3/
LOCAL COVER PRICE: €30/

S

S MAGAZINE
WWW.SPUBLICATION.COM/DENMARK/PUBLISHER: JENS STOLTZE/
EDITOR IN CHIEF: JENS STOLTZE/CREATIVE DIRECTOR: MARTIN T. CHRISTOPHERSEN/ISSUE
YEAR: 2005/ISSUE #: 1/LOCAL COVER PRICE: €12/

S/N°
WWW.SEMNUMERO.COM.BR/BRAZIL/PUBLISHER: BOB WOLFENSON, HELIO HARA/
EDITOR IN CHIEF: BOB WOLFENSON, ROBERTO CIPOLLA, HÉLIO ROSAS/
CREATIVE DIRECTOR: ROBERTO CIPOLLA, HÉLIO ROSAS/ISSUE YEAR: 2002/ISSUE #: 1/
LOCAL COVER PRICE: R$15/

SELF SERVICE
WWW.SELFSERVICEMAGAZINE.COM/FRANCE/PUBLISHER: SELF SERVICE/
EDITOR IN CHIEF: EZRA PETRONIO/CREATIVE DIRECTOR: WORK IN PROGRESS/
ISSUE YEAR: 1995/ISSUE #: 23/LOCAL COVER PRICE: €15/

SEPP
WWW.SEPP-MAGAZINE.COM/UNITED STATES / GERMANY/PUBLISHER: MARKUS EBNER/
EDITOR IN CHIEF: MARKUS EBNER/CREATIVE DIRECTOR: MARKUS EBNER/
ISSUE YEAR: 2002/ISSUE #: 1/LOCAL COVER PRICE: $10/

SHERBERT
WWW.SHERBERTMAGAZINE.COM/UNITED STATES/PUBLISHER: DANIEL WEISE/
EDITOR IN CHIEF: JENNA WILSON/CREATIVE DIRECTOR: DANIEL WEISE/ISSUE YEAR:
2002/ISSUE #: 1/LOCAL COVER PRICE: $3/

SHERMAN
WWW.SHERMANMAGAZINE.COM/UNITED STATES/PUBLISHER: TANK DESIGN INC./
EDITOR IN CHIEF: BEN SEGAL, SETH ZUCKER/CREATIVE DIRECTOR: BEN SEGAL,
SETH ZUCKER/ISSUE YEAR: 2002/ISSUE #: 1/LOCAL COVER PRICE: $9.95/

SODA
WWW.SODA.CH/SWITZERLAND/PUBLISHER: MARTIN LÖTSCHER, IRIS RUPRECHT/
EDITOR IN CHIEF: MICHÈLE BINSWANGER, SUSANNE VON LEDEBUR/
CREATIVE DIRECTOR: MARTIN LÖTSCHER/ISSUE YEAR: 2002/ISSUE #: 18/
LOCAL COVER PRICE: CFH 28/COVER ILLUSTRATION: FLAG (BASTIEN AUBRY
AND DIMITRI BROQUARD); 1ST, 2ND SPREAD DESIGN: MARC KAPPELER; 1ST SPREAD
ILLUSTRATION: MARC KAPPELER; 2ND SPREAD ILLUSTRATION: BENJAMIN GÜDEL/

SPECTOR CUT + PASTE
WWW.SPECTORMAG.NET/GERMANY/PUBLISHER: SPECTORMAG GBR/
EDITOR IN CHIEF: MARKUS DRESSEN, TOBIAS HULSWITT, ANNE KONIG, TILO SCHULZ, JAN
WENZEL/CREATIVE DIRECTOR: MARKUS DRESSEN/ISSUE YEAR: 2001/ISSUE #: 1/LOCAL
COVER PRICE: €4.60/

SPROUT
WWW.SPROUTMAG.COM/JAPAN/PUBLISHER: SPROUT JAPAN, INC./
EDITOR IN CHIEF: YOSHIKAZU SHIGA/CREATIVE DIRECTOR: YOSHIKAZU SHIGA/
ISSUE YEAR: 2002/ISSUE #: 1/LOCAL COVER PRICE: ¥1,200/

STARE
WWW.STAREINC.COM/UNITED STATES/PUBLISHER: JAN-WILLEM DIKKERS,
DAVID RENARD/EDITOR IN CHIEF: JAN-WILLEM DIKKERS, DAVID RENARD/
CREATIVE DIRECTOR: JAN-WILLEM DIKKERS/ISSUE YEAR: 1999/ISSUE #: 1/
LOCAL COVER PRICE: $6/

STEREO
WWW.STEREOPUBLICATION.COM/NETHERLANDS/PUBLISHER: BURO DUPLEX/
EDITOR IN CHIEF: JORIS VAN BALLEGOOIJEN, INGRID DE LUGT, DUNYA STEYNS,
CHRISTEL VAN BEZOUW/CREATIVE DIRECTOR: NA/ISSUE YEAR: NA/ISSUE #: 1/
LOCAL COVER PRICE: €5/POSTCARD PHOTO: D. STEYNS; XEROX PHOTO: A.
GOEDHART; SCREENPRINT: A. DE JONG/

SUGO
WWW.SUGOMAGAZINE.COM/ITALY/PUBLISHER: STUDIO CAMUFFO/
EDITOR IN CHIEF: GIORGIO CAMUFFO/CREATIVE DIRECTOR: SEBASTIANO GIRARDI/
ISSUE YEAR: 2002/ISSUE #: 2/LOCAL COVER PRICE: €22/

T

TANK
WWW.TANKMAGAZINE.COM/UNITED KINGDOM/PUBLISHER: TANK PUBLICATIONS, LTD./
EDITOR IN CHIEF: MASOUD GOLSORKHI, ANDREAS LAEUFER/
CREATIVE DIRECTOR: MASOUD GOLSORKHI/ISSUE YEAR: 1999/ISSUE #: 7/
LOCAL COVER PRICE: £8/COVER PHOTO: JUSTINE/

TERRITORY
WWW.BIGBROSWORKSHOP.COM/MALAYSIA/PUBLISHER: ABDUL NASSER/
EDITOR IN CHIEF: ESTAN/CREATIVE DIRECTOR: SIJUAN/ISSUE YEAR: 2005/ISSUE #: 3/
LOCAL COVER PRICE: $18/

TEXTFIELD
WWW.TEXTFIELD.ORG/UNITED STATES/PUBLISHER: TEXTFIELD PRESS/
EDITOR IN CHIEF: JONATHAN MAGHEN/CREATIVE DIRECTOR: JONATHAN MAGHEN/
ISSUE YEAR: 2003/ISSUE #: 1/LOCAL COVER PRICE: $10/

THE BLOW UP
WWW.THEBLOWUP.COM/UNITED STATES/PUBLISHER: SETH HODES/
EDITOR IN CHIEF: KATE SENNERT/CREATIVE DIRECTOR: SETH HODES/ISSUE YEAR: 2003/
ISSUE #: 1/LOCAL COVER PRICE: $7/

THE COLONIAL
WWW.THECOLONIAL.INFO/UNITED STATES/PUBLISHER: CW WINTER/
EDITOR IN CHIEF: CW WINTER/CREATIVE DIRECTOR: CW WINTER, LUCAS QUIGLEY/
ISSUE YEAR: 2005/ISSUE #: 1/LOCAL COVER PRICE: $8/

THE CURVE
WWW.BIGFRANKMEDIA.COM/UNITED KINGDOM/PUBLISHER: BIGFRANK MEDIA/
EDITOR IN CHIEF: MARK GRAHAM/CREATIVE DIRECTOR: FARHAN BAIG/
ISSUE YEAR: 2002/ISSUE #: 1/LOCAL COVER PRICE: £10/

THE ILLUSTRATED APE
WWW.THEILLUSTRATEDAPE.COM/UNITED KINGDOM/PUBLISHER: CHRISTIAN PATTISON,
MICHAEL SIMS/EDITOR IN CHIEF: CHRISTIAN PATTISON, MICHAEL SIMS/
CREATIVE DIRECTOR: DAREN ELLIS/ISSUE YEAR: NA/ISSUE #: 19/LOCAL COVER PRICE: £5/

THE INTERNATIONAL
THEDEEP@CLUB-INTERNET.FR/JAPAN/PUBLISHER: FICTION INC. TOKYO/
EDITOR IN CHIEF: MAKOTO OHRUI/CREATIVE DIRECTOR: MAKOTO OHRUI/ISSUE YEAR:
2000/ISSUE #: 1/LOCAL COVER PRICE: ¥1,600/

THE PHOTO ISSUE
THEPHOTOISSUE@GMAIL.COM/UNITED STATES/PUBLISHER: OMAR JUDE LAURENT/
EDITOR IN CHIEF: JODIE ABRAMS/CREATIVE DIRECTOR: SARA FIELD/
ISSUE YEAR: 2005/ISSUE #: 1/LOCAL COVER PRICE: NA/COVER PHOTO:
GIULIETTA VERDON-ROE; SPREAD PHOTOS: NEIL HARRIS, DITTE OSTERGAARD,
MARCO MALESPIN/

THE PURPLE JOURNAL
WWW.PURPLE.FR/FRANCE/PUBLISHER: ELEIN FLEISS/EDITOR IN CHIEF: ELEIN FLEISS,
SEBASTIEN JAMAIN/CREATIVE DIRECTOR: LAETITIA BENAT, DORA HERZOG/
ISSUE YEAR: 2004/ISSUE #: 1/LOCAL COVER PRICE: €7.50/

THEY SHOOT HOMOS DON'T THEY?
WWW.THEYSHOOTHOMOSDONTHEY.COM/AUSTRALIA/
PUBLISHER: SHANNON MICHAEL CANE/EDITOR IN CHIEF: SHANNON MICHAEL CANE/
CREATIVE DIRECTOR: NIK DIMOPOULOS/ISSUE YEAR: 2005/ISSUE #: 1/
LOCAL COVER PRICE: $12.50/

TRUCE
WWW.TRUCE-ONLINE.COM/SWITZERLAND/PUBLISHER: TRUCE MEDIA GROUP/
EDITOR IN CHIEF: CARL J. WIGET/CREATIVE DIRECTOR: STEFAN JERMANN/
ISSUE YEAR: 2005/ISSUE #: 1/LOCAL COVER PRICE: CFH 22/

U

UN PAQUET DE SCHISMES
DECLERCQALAIN@HOTMAIL.FR/FRANCE/PUBLISHER: ASSOCIATION "COMME CHACUN
DE NOUS ÉTAIT PLUSIEURS, ÇA FAISIT DÉJA BEAUCOUP DE MONDE."/
EDITOR IN CHIEF: SYLVIE ASTIÉ, ALAIN DECLERCQ, GWÉNAËLLE PETIT PIERRE/
CREATIVE DIRECTOR: ALAIN DECLERCQ/ISSUE YEAR: 2000/ISSUE #: 1/
LOCAL COVER PRICE: NA/

UOVO
WWW.UOVO.TV/ITALY/PUBLISHER: THE BOOKMAKERS ED./
EDITOR IN CHIEF: LUCA ANDRIOLO, JEAN-MICHEL LOPEZ, VITO MORANO,
SILVIA SELLA/CREATIVE DIRECTOR: CHIARA FIGONE, FRANCK VEYRIERES/
ISSUE YEAR: 2004/ISSUE #: 9/LOCAL COVER PRICE: €10/

V

V
WWW.VMAGAZINE.COM/UNITED STATES/PUBLISHER: VISIONAIRE PUBLISHING/
EDITOR IN CHIEF: STEPHEN GAN/CREATIVE DIRECTOR: STEPHEN GAN/
ISSUE YEAR: 1999/ISSUE #: 1/LOCAL COVER PRICE: $5/COVER PHOTO: MARIO TESTINO/

VOLUME
WWW.ARCHIS.ORG/NETHERLANDS/PUBLISHER: ARCHIS FOUNDATION/
EDITOR IN CHIEF: OLE BOURMAN/CREATIVE DIRECTOR: OLE BOURMAN/
ISSUE YEAR: 2005/ISSUE #: 1/LOCAL COVER PRICE: €13.75/

VORN
WWW.VORNMAGAZINE.COM/GERMANY/PUBLISHER: JOACHIM BALDAUF,
AGNES FECKL/EDITOR IN CHIEF: MARK ALEXANDER HOLTZ/
CREATIVE DIRECTOR: JOACHIM BALDAUF/ISSUE YEAR: 2004/ISSUE #: 1/
LOCAL COVER PRICE: €18/

W

WERK
WWW.WORKWERK.COM/SINGAPORE/PUBLISHER: WERK/
EDITOR IN CHIEF: THESEUS CHAN/CREATIVE DIRECTOR: THESEUS CHAN/
ISSUE YEAR: 2000/ISSUE #: 12/LOCAL COVER PRICE: SGD 15/

WISH U WERE HERE XXX
WWW.WISHUWEREHEREXXX.COM/UNITED STATES/PUBLISHER: AMANDA HUNT,
GLENN HUNT/EDITOR IN CHIEF: AMANDA HUNT, GLENN HUNT/
CREATIVE DIRECTOR: GLENN HUNT/ISSUE YEAR: 2000/ISSUE #: 1/
LOCAL COVER PRICE: $14/

Y

YUMMY
WWW.EAT-FAST.NET/FRANCE/PUBLISHER: ALEXANDRA JEAN, PASCAL MONFORT/
EDITOR IN CHIEF: PASCAL MONFORT/CREATIVE DIRECTOR: ALEXANDRA JEAN/
ISSUE YEAR: 2005/ISSUE #: 1/LOCAL COVER PRICE: €30/

Z

ZEMBLA
WWW.ZEMBLAMAGAZINE.COM/UNITED KINGDOM/PUBLISHER: SIMON FINCH/
EDITOR IN CHIEF: DAN CROWE/CREATIVE DIRECTOR: VINCE FROST/ISSUE YEAR: 2003/
ISSUE #: 1/LOCAL COVER PRICE: £4.95/

ZING
WWW.ZINGMAGAZINE.COM/UNITED STATES/PUBLISHER: ZING LLC/
EDITOR IN CHIEF: DEVON DIKEOU/CREATIVE DIRECTOR: CHETAN MANGAT/
ISSUE YEAR: 2005/ISSUE #: 20/LOCAL COVER PRICE: $25/

ZOO
WWW.ZOOMAGAZINE.DE/GERMANY/PUBLISHER: BRYAN ADAMS/
EDITOR IN CHIEF: SANDOR LUBBE, CLAUDIA RIEDEL/
CREATIVE DIRECTOR: JOSE KLAP, SANDOR LUBBE/ISSUE YEAR: 2004/ISSUE #: 4/
LOCAL COVER PRICE: €5/